INFLATION UNDER CONTROL?

Free prices and wages are the heart of our economic system. I do not intend to impose wage and price controls . . . .

Richard M. Nixon

The foolish and the dead alone never change their opinions.

James Russell Lowell

INFLATION UNDER CONTROL?

HC
110
W24
P64

Jerry E. Pohlman

Senior Economist
Data Resources, Inc.

RESTON PUBLISHING COMPANY, INC., *Reston, Virginia*
A Prentice-Hall Company
Reston, Virginia

Library of Congress Cataloging in Publication Data

Pohlman, Jerry E
    Inflation under control?

    Bibliography: p. 233
    1. Wage-price policy—United States. 2. Inflation (Finance)—United States. 3. United States—Economics conditions—1961–   4. Unemployed—United States.
I. Title.
HC110.W24P64   339.5'0973   75-34271
ISBN 0-87909-355-2
ISBN 0-87909-354-4 pbk.

To

Mary Greer

© 1976 by
RESTON PUBLISHING COMPANY, INC.
A Prentice-Hall Company
Reston, Virginia 22090

All rights reserved. No part of this book may be reproduced in any way, or by any means, without permission in writing from the publisher.

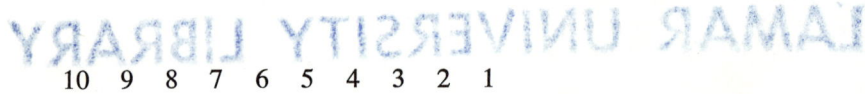

10 9 8 7 6 5 4 3 2 1

Printed in the United States of America

CONTENTS

	PREFACE	vii
	INTRODUCTION	ix
	FOREWORD	xi
Chapter 1	**THE FRAMEWORK**	1

Summer, 1971, 2
The Bias Against Controls, 3
The Policy In Perspective, 4
The Inflation-Prone Economy?, 6
An Overview, 7

Chapter 2	**THE RATIONALE FOR FREE MARKETS**	13

The Ideology, 13
The Mechanics of the System, 15
The Assumptions, 16
Making the System Go, 16
Some Deficiencies, 23
Conclusion, 29
Appendix 2–1. A Brief Aside on the Role of Theory in Economic Analysis, 30

Chapter 3	**UNEMPLOYMENT AND INFLATION: AN OVERVIEW**	35

Unemployment, 36
Inflation, 47
Appendix 3–1. Unemployment, Poverty, and Welfare, 56

Chapter 4	**A CLOSER LOOK AT UNEMPLOYMENT: THEORIES AND REMEDIES**	61

Aggregate Demand, Employment, and Unemployment, 61

Classical versus Keynesian Economics, 63
The Structural Thesis, 70

Chapter 5 **THE ATTEMPT TO REACH NON-INFLATIONARY FULL EMPLOYMENT** 81

The Trade-Off Between Unemployment and Inflation, 90

Chapter 6 **THE EXTENT OF MARKET POWER** 101

The Market Power of Business Firms, 102
The Market Power of Labor Unions, 109

Chapter 7 **THE WORSENING TRADE-OFF** 131

Chapter 8 **ARGUMENTS SURROUNDING CONTROLS** 145

Chapter 9 **FURTHER QUESTIONS CONCERNING THE NATURE OF CONTROLS** 161

Chapter 10 **CAN CONTROLS WORK? EXAMINING THE EVIDENCE** 177

World War II, 178
The Guideposts, 180
European Experience with Incomes Policies, 187

Chapter 11 **THE ECONOMIC STABILIZATION PROGRAM: PHASES I THROUGH IV** 203

The Inauguration of the New Economic Program—August 1971, 204
The Mechanics of the Control System, 205
Examining the Rules, 209
Phases III and IV, 215

Chapter 12 **FURTHER ASSESSMENTS, FURTHER CONSIDERATIONS** 221

Costs and Benefits, 226
An Ongoing Assessment: Lessons from the Seventies, 227

BIBLIOGRAPHY 233

INDEX 242

PREFACE

The field of economics has taken many twists, turns, and detours within the past five years. Moving from a position of high eminence as society's soothsayers and medicine men, the profession has, of late, fallen upon ill times. The exhuberant days when economic engineers were credited with being able to fine tune the economy have given way to less glamorous times of unfulfilled promises, faulty predictions, and misleading forecasts. In a few short years the economy has moved from what was proudly hailed as the longest continuous upswing in history to a baffling combination of inflation, stagflation, recession, and unemployment.

Much of the present illness, of course, cannot rightly be attributed to the economic prognosticators in charge. Misguided policies were often adopted for political purposes while economists issued futile warnings of the probable consequences. The public, however, was not prone to make such distinctions. And, as the nation's economic fortunes turned from good to bad to alarming, the economic lieutenants aboard the political ship could hardly be spared by an unforgiving public.

At the same time, the profession was scarcely free of guilt. Having spoken eloquently and persuasively of automatic stabilizers, permanent full employment, and a new era free from cyclical swings, lost jobs, and hard times, economists were not likely to be excused by an irate public when these promises fell far short of the fact.

Caught up in the rising tide of economic optimism during the heady years of the 1960s, economists of every ilk were prone to view their profession with unblemished satisfaction and not a small degree of exaggerated smugness. Today, the tide of events has largely washed away such beliefs. In their place is a general feeling that the monetarists and Keynesians, as well as those in between, are increasingly unable to understand, explain, or predict the course of the economy. There exists a gnawing apprehension that those in charge of the course of the economic ship are unable to decipher and understand these tides, much less steer a steady course through them.

In large part, the waves upon which the economic ship is foundering consists of two opposing and deadly currents: unemployment and inflation. It was long believed that either of these social maladies could be cured but only at the expense of the other. Later, in the happier days of economic euphoria, many optimists even believed that both evils could be controlled simultaneously. Today, there is a pervading gloom throughout the kingdom that, perhaps, neither problem can be adequately dealt with.

The purpose of this book is to discuss and analyze the dual problems of unemployment and inflation. These related problems, and the policies adopted to deal with them, form what is perhaps the most crucial economic problem facing the United States—if not the entire Western world—during the final quarter of the twentieth century. In particular, this book deals with one of the most current of the various policies designed to deal with the unemployment/inflation dilemma—namely, direct controls on wages and prices. However, the discussion and analysis go beyond the narrow purview of market controls and into the nature of the problems that gave rise to this policy. Only by examining the nature of the problem can one adequately analyze proposed remedies.

Most control programs go from initial periods of popularity to later periods of disillusionment: certainly the last effort, the Phase-I-through-IV experiment of 1971 to 1974, was no exception. At the same time, the unrelenting forces of inflation and unemployment, and the seeming inability of public policies to deal with them, suggest that some sort of controls program will remain in use as an economic stabilization tool.

Thus, regardless of one's ideological disposition toward controls, economic realities suggest that it may not be long before we see the revival of a peacetime incomes policy. Within this context, this book deals with the inflation/unemployment dilemma and those policies designed to deal with it. For, in spite of gyrating public policies, the rocky outcrops of inflation and unemployment seem as treacherous as ever. And, in spite of a general feeling of resigned disillusionment with all policies and policymakers, these acute social problems cannot be solved by a determined effort not to think about them. The search for more effective economic stabilization policies will surely continue, in this country and elsewhere. This book, then, deals with the considerations that must go into this search.

J. POHLMAN

INTRODUCTION

There can be little doubt today that inflation has become the central problem of economic policy throughout the industrialized world. This has not been an oversight development. The problem began to get recognition with the advent of full employment during World War II. Thereafter the emphasis everywhere has been upon preserving full employment during peacetime. For a quarter century this goal has been attained, except for minor deviations here and there. The goal itself, of course, has now become a political necessity, to be met at almost any cost.

But, to use Professor Boulding's phrase, a snake long since has been found lurking in this Keynesian Garden of Eden—the viper of inflation. Is permanent inflation the inevitable price of pursuing full employment? Is inflation itself susceptible of "management," as with total demand itself? If so, how can it be managed effectively? The answers to both questions, it may be suggested, depend upon one's view of the inflationary process itself.

In the United States, some implicit and quite possibly tentative answers have been dramatically supplied by President Nixon's "New Economic Policy" of August 15, 1971, and Phases I and II of that policy. Behind NEP lies a long period of experimentation to cope with inflation: price and wage controls during World War II and the Korean War, exhortations for responsible behavior during President Eisenhower's administrations; the guideposts of Presidents Kennedy and Johnson; the initial policy of indirect monetary and fiscal restraint of President Nixon; and finally the direct intervention provided by NEP itself.

Why this seismic shift in the economic policy of a Republican President? Are we to conclude that inflation cannot be checked except by some form of direct controls? Will such controls spread inevitably until we find ourselves in a centrally regulated economy? Is there a trade-off of a calculable and inverse type between the rate of unemployment and the rate of inflation; even more, is this presumed trade-off subject to a worsening trend? Can the NEP system be expected to work? Should we consider it as temporary, or is it likely to remain in force for decades to come?

And, looking at matters in a little different way, can we maintain our traditional policy of organizational *laissez-faire* toward management and the unions as regards wage-setting and most price-making? Or do we conclude that something has upset the balance between the two groups, such that power is no longer nicely countervailing, as Galbraith once thought, that permanent state intervention is now required if we are to combine successfully full employment with price stability.

Professor Pohlman has addressed himself both boldly and thoroughly to all these questions, and others as well. In undertaking the task, he has surveyed broadly the ample literature of the field. For those who wish to understand the issues surrounding both inflation and efforts to control it, here is a book that provides a readable and well-sustained analysis of these very difficult and deeply disturbing questions.

George H. Hildebrand

Maxwell M. Upson   Professor of
Economics and Industrial Relations
Cornell University

FOREWORD

The United States has suffered from a decade of unprecedented peacetime inflation. Many generally accepted causes have been cited for the inflation that started in 1965 after a half-decade of remarkable price stability. But as 1975 comes to a close there is no evidence whatsoever that the United States is on the threshold of reasonable price stability, nor that the dangers of worsening inflation are behind us. In fact, there is widespread concern that recovery may be associated with a rising rate of inflation. The solution to the inflation problem, however, remains elusive. There continues to be disagreement concerning this persistent, corrosive and divisive problem.

The planned recession from which the United States barely began to recover in mid-1975 has been the longest and the most costly since the 1930s. It was a programmed recession designed as the major if not sole weapon in the fight against inflation. That was also true of the 1969–70 recession. Both were dismal failures in restoring stable prices. The pace of inflation did slow somewhat from previous peaks, but recession neither brought us closer to price stability nor provided us with any basis for confidence that further and sustained progress in slowing the pace of inflation was in prospect, short of a depression.

The rate of inflation worsened in mid- and late 1975 as the economy entered the early stages of a modest recovery. For nearly two years after the economy suffered from a slower than normal growth and a substantial decline in output and employment, prices continued to rise until practically the end of 1974. Wholesale prices dropped for four successive months from December 1974 to March 1975, but in the seven months since March wholesale prices have risen at an annual rate in excess of 10 percent. Consumer prices in the six months after March 1975 have risen at an annual rate of about 7.5 percent. The pace of inflation appears to be accelerating rather than abating. The issue is undermining our economic lives and is dominating our basic economic policies. Administration fiscal and monetary problems are overwhelmingly couched in terms that relate more to inflation than to recovery.

The assumptions in President Ford's budget for fiscal year 1975 as well as the Mid-Session Budget Review released in May 1975 point to a very slow and gradual reduction in unemployment along with abnormal rates of inflation throughout the balance of the 1970s. Consumer prices are expected to increase by more than 4 percent per year up to 1979 and unemployment is not projected to be as low as 5 percent even by 1980. Clearly the "soft economy" approach is the only solution being offered by the Administration toward solving the problem of inflation. It is costly and is not succeeding.

The important issue of controls as one of the means of fighting inflation is Jerry Pohlman's main focus. Controls under Phase I and Phase II from August 1971 to January 1973 were substantially successful; but Phases III and IV were dismal failures. Serious efforts were not made after January 1973 to restrain inflation through controls. Many officials concerned with the controls program under President Nixon did not believe in that program and it was largely ignored after Phase II was abandoned. Now, those responsible for that program refer to their failure as proof that controls will not work.

Perhaps the recent introduction of price and wage controls in Canada will be interesting to observe, especially if those in charge in Canada truly believe that something can be done about inflation and that fair and firm controls can break the inflation spiral.

Almost no one argues that we need widespread freezes of wages and prices or strong controls across-the-board. However, some economists, including myself, are convinced that some governmental intervention is needed to break the spiral so that we can get back to both full employment and reasonable price stability. It will require varied actions but some controls will be central to that effort.

Jerry Pohlman has had much experience in this critical field. He writes lucidly and he stimulates thought, although many will not fully agree with all of his diagnoses and prescriptions. It is important that this book be read widely, especially by those who are seriously concerned with solving the problems of inflation and who are not concerned with achieving price stabilization through widespread unemployment and low utilization of resources.

Robert R. Nathan
Economic Advisor
Robert R. Nathan Associates, Inc.
Washington, D.C.

THE FRAMEWORK 1

> The country is not in good condition.
> Calvin Coolidge

"Silent Cal's" remark is as sadly relevant in the 1970s as it was when he made it over forty-five years ago. In spite of a fourteen fold increase in the nation's output and a resulting and undeniable leap in the living standard of most Americans, economic conditions remain distressingly grim.

Indeed, today's economic problems seem, to many, to be nearly as intractable as they did almost a half-century ago during the Great Depression. At that time, the overwhelming problem was the enforced idleness of over a quarter of the nation's labor force. Today the problem is also an unacceptably high level of unemployment—although not at Depression levels—but combined with the curse of inflation. As we enter the final quarter of the twentieth century the coexistence of these two social evils raises serious and unresolved questions concerning the mixed capitalistic system.

It now seems clear that both the economy and public opinion concerning it have shifted markedly during the past decade. As a result, we are now in largely uncharted territory with respect to both the inflation/unemployment dilemma and the policies being considered in response to this dilemma.

Consider the 1970s: Early in 1971, then President Richard M. Nixon stated that "free prices and wages are at the heart of our economic system; we should not stop them from working even to cure an inflationary fever. I do not intend to impose wage and price controls . . ." (21, p. 7). But reality has a strange and unrelenting way of altering even the strongest of convictions. And reality was soon to catch up with Mr. Nixon. Six months later, in August, the President, an avowed laissez-faire, free-market enthusiast, announced the imposition of a ninety-day freeze on wages and prices to be followed by an indefinite period of governmental regulation. In this important and abrupt move, the President ushered in an area of controls to supplement "market forces" as a regulator of the economy, declaring his program to be "the most comprehensive new economic policy to be undertaken by this country in four decades."

SUMMER, 1971

As in the 1930s, there existed in the summer of 1971 the nagging problems of reality. Americans (generally an impatient lot to begin with) were unwilling to accept pronouncements that prosperity lurked around the next corner—"1971 will be a good year and 1972 a very good year." And, as with the conventional economic theory of the 1930's, there was one rather serious drawback to the Nixon Administration's economic policies—they were not working. Appeals for more patience were falling on the deaf ears of workers who continued to view with alarm the steady erosion of the real wages. Nor was patience a luxury the administration could afford. Acutely aware of the upcoming elections, the President knew he could be tossed out of office by an irate public if his optimistic forecasts failed to materialize. These political instincts for the probable consequences of failure of the economic scene caused him to make an historical shift in economic policy that remains, even after its demise, the subject of continuing controversy and debate.

In terms of philosophical outlook, the policy change reflected a shift not seen since Franklin Roosevelt pledged himself to give the nation a New Deal. "It is common sense to take a method and try it," exhorted Roosevelt in an address to Oglethorpe University on May 22, 1932. "If it fails, admit it and try something else. But above all, try something." In the fall of 1971 Richard Nixon seemed ready to accept this advice. What followed were four and one half "phases" of a New Economic Policy, spanning the Phase I of 1971 to the Phase Out of 1974, none of which did much to settle the arguments over the appropriateness of market controls. Meeting with enthusiastic approval in 1971 and 1972, the program was generally discredited by 1974 with few observers mourning its demise in April of that year.

The problems, however, remain. The need for effective stabilization policies has never seemed more acute than during the last half of the

1970s. Indeed, the economic gyrations of the mid-1970s make 1971 appear mild in comparison.

What kind of economic events and problems necessitate a search for new stabilization policies? In particular, what is the economic impact of wage and price controls in light of these problems? Regardless of one's immediate attitude toward controls, their use, in one form or another, is likely to continue as a part of the economic landscape well into the foreseeable future.

What were the economic circumstances that led to this drastic turnabout by a previously reluctant president? Briefly, although administration economists continued to find hopeful signs in the economy before the first freeze was imposed, things continued to be less than encouraging. Consumer spending was down and displayed no immediate indication of bounding upward. Economic growth continued to be nonexistent, while unemployment hovered around 6 percent of the work force. At the same time, in spite of record high interest rates, wholesale prices continued to climb at an annual rate of 5 percent in the six months preceding the freeze. The immediate prospects for improvement in any of these factors appeared dim. In addition, the international balance of payments problem was approaching crisis proportions and eventually proved to be the dog-wagging tail. The imposition of the freeze, it was hoped, would appease domestic critics who were becoming increasingly vocal in their demands for action. At the same time the new policy, it was reasoned, would convince our trading partners around the world of the seriousness of our intent.

THE BIAS AGAINST CONTROLS

Americans have long been suspicious of governmental interference in the marketplace. This penchant for little or no regulation of economic matters was reinforced by traditional economic pedagogy. Teaching that a "free" and "competitive" market would naturally tend toward a "full employment equilibrium," few economists subscribed to the need for governmental manipulation of the economy. Indeed, elaborate models demonstrated that competitive markets, if left alone, would tend toward maximum output, full employment, an equitable (if not equal) distribution of income, and an optimum growth rate. With such theoretical justification, it is small wonder that most Americans accepted the notion that uncontrolled markets were the best markets. The American dream, along with the accepted economic theories, had little truck with "muckrakers" and "fuzzy-minded intellectuals" who tended to throw a cloud of doubt over the virtues of the free-market system.

Beliefs, however, tend to become difficult to hold onto in the face of a conflicting and unrelenting reality. With a quarter of the nation's work force unemployed during the Great Depression and millions more living in squalor and misery, pronouncements that prosperity was "just around the corner" held little appeal. The public was aware that the economy was sick and showed few signs of improving. Catching up with the public, economists at last responded with the "new economics" of John Maynard Keynes. Since then, and especially since the enactment of the Employment Act of 1946, Americans have expected their government to further the twin goals of full employment and price stability. No longer is the economy regarded as capable of responding automatically to deficiencies and maladjustments.

Keynesian ideas were not, of course, immediately accepted.[1] An ideology as powerful as that forged during America's formative years is not easily altered. Thus, even while there is now a general acceptance by most economists of the broad outlines of Keynesian policy, there are still vehement disagreements concerning specific policy prescriptions. And, although most economists now favor the implementation of the broad Keynesian concepts of compensatory monetary and fiscal policy, many are still prone to view with horror governmental attempts to interfere directly in the marketplace. It is one thing to entrust the government with a responsibility for controlling broad, aggregate movements within the economy; it is quite another to extend to it a responsibility and authority to meddle with specific, individual markets.

This deep suspicion on the part of many observers toward market interference comes not only from an ideological and theoretical bias against regulation but also from a healthy respect for the myriad problems such controls raise. The track record of price and wage controls in this country as well as others is not a particularly encouraging one, and skeptics have strong historical as well as theoretical support for their arguments.

THE POLICY IN PERSPECTIVE

The economic problems that led to the creation of the now-defunct Pay Board and Price Commission are neither new nor unique. These problems consist of a fundamental dilemma that has plagued most Western nations since World War II and even before: How can an economy that places a premium on free markets achieve both full employment and stable prices at the same time? Indeed, many observers

---

[1] A discussion of "Keynesian" as opposed to "classical" economics is included in Chapter 3.

believe that this dilemma poses one of the most serious challenges to the economies of the free world for the remainder of the twentieth century.

The dilemma arises because, living in an imperfect world, policies designed to attack one aspect of this problem are likely to exacerbate the other. The President's Council of Economic Advisors neatly summarized the problem in 1971:

> The goals for the performance of the economy in 1971 are clear. Our objectives should be to move along a path through 1971 that will bring the unemployment rate in 1972 down to the zone of reasonably full employment, and at the same time to get the rate of inflation down to the 3 percent range. The general nature of the policies that would help to achieve each of these goals is also clear. We can reduce unemployment, at least in the short run, by expansive economic policies which would make the demand for output rise rapidly and so raise employment. We can reduce the rate of inflation by restrictive economic policies which would repress the demand for output, increase unemployment and unutilized capacity, and thereby encourage business and labor to settle for smaller advances in prices and wages. While these "solutions" are clear, the problem is also clear. We cannot do as much as would be possible in one direction without injurious results in the other (21, p. 75).

Such a situation is not new here or abroad. It has prompted governments throughout the world to search for "incomes policies" that will enable a better "trade-off" between full employment and price stability to be reached. Thus far, such policies have had only scattered success, and it is by no means clear that such policies can ever have a lasting degree of success.

Just what is an "incomes policy"? Basically, it is an attempt on the part of the central government to hold prices and wages below the levels they could (and do) attain in the absence of government interference. As such, the policy can range from a mild form of "jawboning" and "moral suasion" to the imposition of an absolute freeze such as that of 1971. In between are such efforts as the wage and price "guidelines" of the Kennedy-Johnson years as well as the more recent Price Commission and Pay Board formulations. Regardless of the arrangement, the purpose of the various incomes policies are the same: to hold down prices and wages in order to keep unemployment to a minimum and, at the same time, to preserve relatively free markets.

If the dilemma between stable prices and full employment has, like the poor, always been with us, one might reasonably ask why there is such an increasing amount of attention given to the problem today. The answer lies in the increasing severity of the dilemma itself. Since World War II, during each business cycle, the level of unemployment associated with stable prices has creeped ever higher. The problem was first seriously observed in the middle and late 1950s as unemployment became more intractable while prices continued to climb. Assertions started up to the effect that the economy was becoming "inflation prone" and, in particular, that powerful unions and corporations were able to push up wages and prices even in the face of high unemployment and low-capacity utilization rates.

Throughout the early 1960s the same observations were made. Although prices were stable during this period, unemployment remained high and many economists warned that attempts to stimulate the economy by increasing aggregate demand would be thwarted by inflationary pressures. The guidelines and guideposts were formulated in an effort to stave off such pressures. By the late 1960s the fears of the soothsayers were borne out: Unemployment was lowered through massive deficit spending but inflation became increasingly severe and, indeed, showed signs of becoming even more tenacious. Thus, the economic transmission was thrown into reverse and a "planned recession" was engineered in an effort to halt the inflationary spiral. The outcome, however, proved to be disappointing and, indeed, alarming. The economy responded by slowing down but the price indexes refused to follow suit, continuing instead on their upward course. After two and one-half years of on-and-off direct controls, the situation hardly improved. Inflation reached record levels in 1974 while unemployment did the same during 1975 in the recession that followed.

AN INFLATION-PRONE ECONOMY?

Many observers believe that the economy is becoming more prone to inflation or to unemployment as we move beyond the post-war era. At the same time, strong arguments are advanced to the effect that things are not getting worse in terms of the economy itself but, rather, that the present problems represent bungling by the government (in particular, with respect to the financing of the Viet Nam War) and that our current troubles are the price we must pay to rectify these past mistakes. In this view, once the price has been paid the economy can return to a more "normal" state, and the apparent worsening of the unemployment/inflation dilemma will disappear.

While accepting as fact governmental mismanagement, a thesis of this book is that the economy is, for a number of reasons, becoming more inflation prone. This is not to say that the price system no longer works —such a conclusion is hardly warranted. Such a harsh prognosis ruled out, however, a more suitable conclusion might be that the price system, if left alone, is no longer capable of performing within socially accepted limits. Neither the public nor its elected representatives will accept the amount of inflation necessary to bring about full employment. Nor will they accept the unemployment necessary to ensure stable prices. As a result, action must be taken to reduce both evils simultaneously. There is no assurance, of course, that such action will always or necessarily be successful. It is quite certain, however, that such action will be taken.

AN OVERVIEW

In an attempt to understand the deep bias that most Americans have against controls, one must first understand the power of the free-market system. Thus, Chapter 2 focuses on the workings of the unfettered market. The theory of perfect competition is developed since it provides the rationale for nonintervention. Indeed, in the perfectly competitive economy, many of the problems that lead to intervention in private markets are nonexistent. Only by appreciating the logical power and explanatory value of this system of free markets, can one understand the very strong bias against controls. In addition, the persuasive power of this theory should not be underestimated, for it represents a monumental intellectual achievement. Nor should the ability of economic doctrines to influence the minds and actions of even those persons who profess a disposition against "theory" be underestimated. As Lord Keynes noted in a famous passage, "practical men, who believe themselves to be quite exempt from any intellectual influences, are usually the slaves of some defunct economist . . ." (49, p. 383).

Chapter 3 presents an overview of the vexatious problems of unemployment and inflation. Since the rationale for controls on wages and prices arises out of this dual problem, it is necessary to examine the nature of these problems in terms of their impact and their seriousness —in a sense, examining the patient before speaking of cures. A thesis of this book is that both unemployment and inflation are extremely serious deficiencies within the "mixed" economy.

For one thing, the impact of unemployment on the people directly affected, as well as the resultant loss of output for the rest of the economy, is an urgent problem deserving immediate and protracted attention. And the problems are not only economic. The entire social structure is shaken by prolonged and high unemployment as crime increases, cities strangle for a lack of funds, frustrations mount, and disillusionment with "the system" becomes endemic.

The evils of inflation are also myriad. As fixed incomes are continuously eroded, more and more of the population—especially the aged—

are pushed into lives of squalor and poverty. Frugality becomes stupidity as speculation becomes responsibility. Again the social fabric wears thin as inflation breeds increasing discontentment and the stable elements of society become increasingly threatened by forces beyond their control or apprehension.

Market controls, designed to deal with these evils, cannot be analyzed adequately without first examining the *causes* of inflation and unemployment. Unfortunately, these areas of significant disagreement among economists account, in large part, for the differences in professional opinion concerning the propitiousness of market controls. If there is disagreement about the causes of inflation (or unemployment), one could hardly expect unanimity with respect to remedial measures. It is of paramount importance, then, to discuss the economic theories that underlie the dilemma between full employment and inflation—the subject of Chapter 4.

A full examination of unemployment and inflation requires also the recognition of market imperfections. Having looked first at the nature of perfect markets and then at the extent of the problems, we next examine the reasons why markets do not operate as we would like them to. To a large degree, viewpoints concerning controls differ because views differ about how closely the economy behaves in the manner depicted by the perfectly competitive model. If an observer holds that the economy is characterized by a good deal of competition (in the classical sense) and that the competitive model continues to constitute a fairly close approximation of reality, he regards controls as doing little good—in fact, as doing substantial harm. If, on the other hand, one believes that the economy no longer resembles, with any degree of accuracy, the competitive model and, furthermore, that it is moving *increasingly farther* from this ideal, then controls may make sense.

The argument in Chapters 5 and 6 is that the latter of these two possibilities is the more accurate: that is, the economy is continually drifting farther from the textbook model of perfect competition and, as a result, is becoming increasingly inflation prone. Or, to put the proposition in policy terms, measures to promote full employment will run into an inflationary threshold at increasingly higher rates of unemployment. Conversely, policies aimed at price stability will necessitate increasingly higher levels of unemployment.

Such a viewpoint rests upon what are believed to be dual tendencies of the past thirty years, both of which operate to push the economy farther from the competitive model. The first involves structural changes within the economy, which many observers believe are evolving with increased rapidity. The second is the continued growth of "power" factors within the economy, a growth that further hampers the self-corrective mechanisms of the market.

It is a well documented and accepted fact that "power" forces operate within the economy in labor as well as in product markets. Unions have the power to extract large pay increases while also being able to prevent wages from moving downward at times when demand is falling. At the same time, large corporations have the power to set prices, within limits, rather than simply taking a price as determined by the market. There is, however, considerable disagreement as to the *degree* of this power and the extent to which it makes possible the distortion of the market mechanism.

This question lies at the heart of the debate concerning the appropriateness of controls. If there is little market power and if this power is not increasing, controls will do little good. Indeed, in this view, the promotion of an incomes policy to restrain wages and prices serves only as a smokescreen to hide the real cause of inflation—inept governmental policy. An incomes policy, in this analysis, becomes an attempt to place the responsibility for unemployment and/or inflation on unions and companies while diverting attention from the real source—the monetary authorities.

Rejecting this view are those who believe the monopoly power possessed by unions and business firms to be significant. Indeed, the only justification for market interference (an incomes policy) is, in the final analysis, the existence of cost-push inflation, along with structural bottlenecks and imbalances. And this type of inflation rests upon the premise that the economy contains structural elements that do not conform to the competitive model. The extent of these nonconformities is examined in Chapter 6.

The existence of market power alone, however, will not resolve the arguments concerning the efficacy of controls. A demonstration of *increased* market power, it may be contended, is required to make the case for controls. This is a difficult proposition to confirm. Powerful unions and large corporations have existed for some time and, without evidence that they are growing *more* powerful, one is hard pressed to explain why they are just now exerting sufficient market influence to worsen the inflation/unemployment dilemma. Chapter 7 addresses itself to this question.

Few economists seriously dispute the contention that the extremely tenacious inflation experienced through the mid-1970s began as a classical case of demand-pull in the late 1960s. There were, however, few signs of demand-pull elements remaining in 1970 as unemployment reached and exceeded 6 percent and the price level continued its unrelenting upward path. Cost-push elements clearly seemed to be taking over the momentum. Unions and corporations seemingly found it within their power to continue wage and price increases even in the face of falling demand: that is, even though they did not seem to possess (or use) the power to *start* the inflationary spiral, powerful corporations and unions did seem to be able to keep it going. Similarly, by 1975 when unemployment had reached a post-war peak of over 9 percent, it became increasingly difficult to explain the continuing inflation in terms of excess demand.

One explanatory viewpoint, that power increases during times of inflation, produces a middle ground position concerning the appropriateness of an incomes policy. Under this view, controls are necessary only until the inflationary spiral is stopped and the "inflationary psychology" broken. After this, the argument goes, we can once again revert to free markets as unions and managements put down their weapons, relax somewhat, and stop beating the public over the head. Maybe so. But given today's militancy in all quarters, smoldering frustrations, and structural imbalances within the economy, it may be a long time indeed before everyone relaxes. To expect such changes to reverse themselves in the near future and thereby enable a return to less tension-filled times may coincide nicely with the current revival of nostalgia, but it has little basis in reality. "I hope it—but I doubt it," wrote Mark Twain.

There are many deficiencies in a market system that are often forcefully—and rightly—brought to light. The one positive area, however, that produces the most agreement is the efficiency of the price system in allocating resources. Indeed, resource-allocation benefits of the price system has made grudging admirers out of the free market's most severe critics. When one contemplates the hundreds of thousands of allocative decisions made daily through the interaction of market forces, the efficiency of this system becomes increasingly apparent. Market controls, however, tend to limit the efficiency of this mechanism by thwarting the signals given through price changes. If prices (including wages) are unable to respond to market pressures, they will be unable to induce a movement of resources—physical as well as human—into more productive areas. And, to the extent that the controls are effective, this reduced efficiency will become apparent. (If the controls are ineffective it makes no sense to have them in the first place.) These allocative considerations must, then, be taken into account when assessing the overall effectiveness and desirability of market controls. These and other questions concerning the imposition of controls are discussed in Chapters 8 and 9.

If we are to have some sort of on-again/off-again market controls—an incomes policy—in the future, what are some of the prospects for their success or failure? In an attempt to assess this, we turn, in Chapter 10, to previous experiences for a guide. A relevant experience in the United States to draw upon is that of the guidelines and guideposts of the Kennedy-Johnson era. These were our first peace-time experiences with market intervention and had all the shortcomings of a first effort. They were not, however, as is frequently asserted, an unmitigated failure. True, as inflationary pressures waxed stronger in the late 1960s, voluntary controls were apparently no longer restraining wage and price settlements; but it does not follow that they failed to serve their intended function. It was always admitted by the most vocal proponents of the guideposts that they could only be expected to be effective within a relatively narrow band in the spectrum between loose markets and excess aggregate demand. No one really expected guideposts to be able to contain a serious case of demand-pull inflation, and their failure to do so in the late 1960s cannot be considered as overwhelming evidence of the policy's failure. This is not to say, of course, that there were not serious deficiencies associated with the guideposts. There were, and any fair assessment of the success or failure of this policy cannot overlook them.

The United States is not the only country to experiment with an incomes policy in an attempt to reduce the unemployment/inflation tradeoff. Various European countries have brushed elbows with the policy, and again the picture of success has been a cloudy one. Certainly no one would argue that these attempts have spelled a clear record of solid achievement with respect to solving the stable-price/full-employment dilemma. However, there are scattered instances of effectiveness, and one should examine the conditions surrounding these successes as well as the conditions that led to failure. These experiences are discussed in Chapter 10.

Chapters 11 and 12 cover the most recent experience, the Phase I through Phase IV program of 1971 to 1974. This program remains highly controversial, moving from a high point of public acceptance and professional approval at its inception to disillusionment and frustration at the end. The experience, however, marks the first official peacetime incomes policy for the U.S., and as such the program and its relative effectiveness deserve a close look.

Whether the direct market intervention of the 1970s represents another largely irreversible turn in trek down the economic road remains to be seen. One thing, however, appears certain: Regardless of the future path of the social economy, the point at which the consideration of controls is no longer a part of our economic life lies a long way off. And it appears equally certain that this road will present many unforeseen curves, bumps, and detours. The journey will be, at the very least, a challenging one.

THE RATIONALE FOR FREE MARKETS

2

> The ideas of economists and political philosophers, both when they are right and when they are wrong, are more powerful than is commonly understood. Indeed, the world is ruled by little else.
>
> John Maynard Keynes

THE IDEOLOGY

Americans have long disdained the imposition of governmental controls on their lives whether in the legal, social, or economic sphere. This attitude is, perhaps, the most pronounced in response to governmental decrees in the marketplace. The right to strike a mutually agreeable bargain is a right long cherished in the United States, and the parties to such a bargain are prone to view with hostility any edicts requiring prior approval of the deal. Indeed, it has traditionally been only in wartime periods of severe national emergency that American society has granted its government the power to impose such controls. In such times the American people, along with the peoples of most countries, have conceded to the state powers vigorously denied in times of lesser national stress.

The mood is somewhat different today. Market controls were in effect from 1971 to 1974 with no clear sign of a national emergency. Whether such controls *can* work is an open question that is still hotly contested. At the same time, a good deal of the populace, along with many eminent economists, are now willing to accept peacetime controls as a means of reducing the unemployment/inflation dilemma. Does this mean that Americans have suddenly altered their long-held opposition to market controls? Hardly. Does it mean that such fundamental changes have taken place in the American economy that they will demand the periodic adoption of controls? Perhaps. And the acceptance of peacetime controls almost certainly means that they will be considered as a policy option for a long time to come, with or without a national emergency. This latter fact impels a closer examination of the rationale and logic of wage and price controls.

It is, of course, no accident that most Americans abhor controls. Coming to this country in flight from the long history of European despotism and tyranny, early settlers readily accepted the maxim that "that government which governs best governs least." The American ideal became one of an independent spirit coupled with a Puritan work ethic. The good life was seen as consisting of rugged individualism where each man was free to make his own way. There was scant room for an overseeing government in such a framework. Nor did it matter that actual life deviated from this norm. In reality man was interdependent rather than independent, and the advent of the factory system was making him more so all the time. In addition, there was little opportunity for everyone to compete on equal terms—as was the American ideal—when there existed such overwhelming inequalities in the distribution of income, as well as natural endowments. The important thing is that the newly settled American believed in the doctrine of rugged individualism or what has been termed the Horatio Alger Myth.

Hard work, independence, and frugality did produce results. And when an entire nation could see these results, it was difficult to dispute the logic of the dream. "Success," wrote Nietzsche, "has always been a liar." Perhaps. But the success of the American dream in forging a mighty industrial machine that was responsible for providing a decent living for the majority of its citizens is testimony to the power of this ideology—be it a lie or not. And the fact that this belief system, which praises the virtues of a free market and condemns the imposition and futility of controls, persists in the face of twentieth-century skepticism and existentialism is testimony to the strong elements of truth it contains.

The American belief in free markets, stemming from the natural law philosophy of John Locke and Thomas Jefferson, was not without a good deal of intellectual support from economic thinkers. Indeed, Adam Smith himself declared his goal to be that of finding "one great connecting principle" of the social sciences similar to Newton's Law of Gravity which had been accepted as the final, crowning achievement of the physical sciences (101, p. 16). Of course, one rarely announces an intended pursuit of such a goal without at some point delivering on the promise. So it was with Adam Smith. Building upon the work of earlier mercantilists writers and the natural law philosophers, Smith proclaimed that he had discovered the "universal law of social gravitation."

Man, he declared, possesses one immutable characteristic: he is attracted by profits and repelled by losses.

By itself, of course, this contained little that was novel. Many social philosophers (Thomas Hobbes and the Benthams in particular) had already constructed and elaborated upon such "selfish systems" in which man responded to the pain-pleasure principal. What Smith added, however, was of tremendous importance: By following such selfish instincts the individual, working through society, will automatically bring about the best of all possible worlds. "It is not from the benevolence of the butcher, the brewer, or the baker, that we expect our dinner," wrote Smith, "but from their regard to their own interest. We address ourselves, not to their humanity but to their self love, and never talk to them of our own necessities but of their advantages." Furthermore, "it is his own advantage, indeed, and not that of society, which he has in view. But the study of his own advantage naturally, or rather necessarily leads him to prefer that employment which is most advantageous to the society." Explaining how this is to come about, Smith states, in what is undoubtedly his most famous passage:

> He generally, indeed, neither intends to promote the public interest, nor knows how much he is promoting it. . . . By directing that industry in such a manner as its produce may be of the greatest value, he intends only his own gain, and he is in this, as in many other cases, led by an invisible hand to promote an end which was not part of his intention (102, p. 14, 423).

THE MECHANICS OF THE SYSTEM

How was it possible that by following his own "selfish instincts" man could bring about a just and benevolent society? Although it has been refined, altered, and expanded, the system envisioned by Smith is still at the heart of modern price theory and it continues to form the heart of the economic bias against market controls. There have been, of course, innumerable refinements. "Profit maximization" has replaced "selfishness" and "equilibrium" has replaced the "invisible hand." In addition, there has been a tremendous amount of mathematical and theoretical sophistication, but the essence of the system remains intact. To understand the power of this ideology and the economics that underlie it, then, we must examine the underlying mechanics of the free-market system. Without an appreciation of the workings of the unregulated economy, one can scarcely make meaningful judgments concerning regulations. And, without a feeling for the power of laissez-faire market theory and philosophy, one cannot appreciate the negative feelings that most Americans have toward controls.

THE ASSUMPTIONS

Any sound intellectual system is based upon certain assumptions. The capitalist system—or "perfect competition" to use the technical term—is no exception. Basically, only three are necessary. The first assumption is that man is a selfish creature à la Adam Smith.

The second of these assumptions is that every producer and consumer is so small in relation to the total market that he is unable to influence the price of the product he is selling or buying. The classical example is the individual farmer who has no control over the price of the goods he takes to the market. Another example is the typical stock market investor who must take the price of the security as given and is incapable of influencing this price by his actions of buying or selling.

The third assumption is that there is perfect mobility of resources, both physical and human. In other words, if the return to capital is higher in one area than in another, the investor is able to move his capital from the low-paying area to the high-paying one. Similarly, labor is free to migrate from one job or area to another in response to higher wage rates. When this assumption is combined with the first one concerning profit maximization ("utility maximization" with respect to individuals), the result is not just that capital and labor are free to move, but that they do in fact move. Given these three assumptions (some include perfect knowledge on the part of buyers and sellers to make the system complete), competitive price theory is able to explain virtually every economic phenomenon and problem. In fact, as an intellectual system the theory has few rivals. And, while the assumptions may stretch one's credulity, they were accepted by most economists as close enough to reality—at least in the long run—to be useful.[1]

MAKING THE SYSTEM GO

Production

With these assumptions in mind, we can proceed to the actual working of the economic system. Take, first, the question of what is to be produced—a question that every society must face regardless of its political and economic institutions. Within the capitalist system of perfect competition, the consumer is king—or at least he was until the advent of

---

[1] For a brief discussion of the assumptions of the theory as well as economic theory itself, see Appendix 1 of this chapter.

the "managerial revolution," Madison Avenue, and J. K. Galbraith. The consumer, by spending on the objects he desires, directs the production of the economy with no assistance from a centralized government. The capitalist entrepreneur, ever mindful of the profits to be made, listens closely to the call of society and rushes to fill the needs of the consumer. And how does he know where these needs are? By watching for profit-making opportunities.

Suppose, for example, that a low-calorie, 90-proof Scotch is developed. Demand, of course, would be tremendous for such a product. The person (or company) who developed this particular delight would soon find himself in short supply and, as a result, the price of the remaining spirits would be bid up. Higher prices, however, mean larger returns and soon the producer of the low-calorie Scotch would find himself in charge of an extremely profitable business enterprise.

Such a situation would not long escape the watchful eyes of other aspiring capitalists. In an effort to reap some of the profits for themselves, competitors would begin producing low-calorie Scotch. This would increase the supply which, in turn, would force the price down. This process of new entry into the field, along with the increasing output of existing firms, would continue just as long as there were excess (above-normal) profits to be made in the production of the new Scotch. As the price dropped and these profits disappeared, entry into the industry would cease, the selling price would just equal the cost of production (plus a normal rate of return on investment), and the market would be in what economists have called, since the days of Sir Isaac Newton, "equilibrium." The consumer, simply by spending on what he desires, has directed production. The capitalist, by listening to the call of profits, has met the consumer's needs. And the system, by allowing for competitive interplay among producers and consumers, has "decided" upon what to produce.

Allocation

In a like manner, the system determines the allocation of physical and human resources. Consider the allocation of labor. Again, suppose there were an autonomous increase in the demand for a given product induced by a technological breakthrough (the invention of diet Scotch). As demand increases (a shift in the demand curve to the east), the Scotch producing firms will attempt to increase their output (in order to maximize profits) and, as a result, will require additional labor. As the entire industry attempts to increase production they will find it necessary to raise wages in order to attract the new employees. As this occurs, workers are drawn from other industries and firms (perhaps from declining bourbon producers who are now in a slump), and the industry is thereby able to increase the supply of Scotch. Labor (as well as other resources in a similar manner) has been reallocated in accordance with the changing consumer preferences.[2] Again, no coercion was needed, no direction from above, and no conscious effort by anyone to do what was in the "public good." Consumers, by spending their money on what they desire, and producers, by chasing profits, were able to reallocate the resources of society. And in the process both objectives were met.

Exploitation

The pure theory of price competition also ensures that there will be no exploitation of either labor or the consumer by the producer. Such a conclusion again rests upon the assumption of mobility. Take the case of the producer who attempts to charge a price that more than covers his cost (plus a "reasonable" profit). Immediately the ever-watchful competition will observe that large profits are to be made in this market and they will begin to move in. To the dismay of the producer but the delight of the consumer, the price will soon be bid down until once again it only covers costs. At this point there will be no exploitation.

One might object that this is not always possible. Many products are difficult to make and require vast outlays of investment to gear up for production. Few individuals, for example, could compete with a General Motors or a U.S. Steel should they observe larger than normal profits in these areas. Such an objection, however, even though valid in reality, violates the assumption of perfect resource mobility. For if mobility is perfect, there is no way to keep competitors at bay because of size or any other barrier. Also, to the spoilsport who insists that it would indeed be impossible for other firms to readily enter these markets, the theorist will point out that what is needed is simply a little "longer run." In the long run there is competition from new firms as well as from alternative products, i.e., buses compete with trains, and airplanes compete with both. Thus, in the long run, although we still do not have "perfect" competition, we may have "workable" competition. (One is reminded here of Lord Keynes' famous observation that in the long run we're all dead.)

Nor is it easier for the capitalist to exploit labor. Suppose that an employer attempts to pay an employee less than his worth to the firm,

---

[2] How *much* wages will have to be increased depends upon the elasticity of the supply function for labor in this particular industry. If only one firm attempts to hire more labor, it will be able to do so at the existing wage rate since the supply curve it faces is perfectly elastic. On the other hand, the labor supply curve for the entire industry is less elastic and a rise in wages will be necessary to increase output.

i.e., less than his marginal revenue product. Again, competitors will soon be aware of profits to be made by hiring this employee at a wage slightly above what he is now getting (in order to lure him to the new company) but still less than his productivity (in order that a profit might be made by exploiting him). Another competitor, however, will soon see this and pay a still higher wage. Soon the wage will again be bid up to the level of the employee's productivity, and there will be no exploitation of labor. And, since there is perfect mobility, this would take place very rapidly (instantaneously, one supposes) thereby foreclosing the possibility of any exploitation of the work force.

For those who are prone to scoff at this process as unrealistic, it should be emphasized that this outcome depends once more upon the assumption of perfect mobility. Also, the true believer will again answer that even if there is some exploitation in the short run due to imperfect markets, this will be taken care of in the long run where all resources are perfectly mobile. (One may conjecture that to the consumer or employee being exploited in the short run, such talk of equity in the long run smacks more of propaganda than of economic wisdom.)

Unemployment

If the theory of price competition is able to answer all of the previous questions satisfactorily, there remains the problem of special concern to the applicability of market controls—unemployment. And, not surprisingly, the theory also has an answer for this: There can't be any. Of course, there will be some persons temporarily unemployed as they quit one job and move to another ("frictional" unemployment) and there will, in addition, be those persons who do not want to work. But there will never be any serious unemployment due to a malfunction in the economic system.

Consider the two principal causes of unemployment: (1) deficient aggregate demand and (2) structural changes in the economy.[3] According to the classical system, there could be no lack of aggregate demand due to a concept known as "Say's Law" which holds that "supply creates its own demand." And if supply creates its own demand, it would be impossible to ever have an excess of goods (i.e., deficient demand).

The skeptic might wonder how such a notion could possibly be believed. To see this logic, picture a very simple economy in which there are few tasks to be performed and little division of labor is employed in doing them. One man produces what he and his family need and perhaps has something left to barter with for his neighbor's surplus

---

[3] These types of unemployment are discussed in some detail in Chapters 3 and 4.

production. Now, given that work is painful and to be avoided unless some gain can come from it, no one would produce a surplus unless he intended to trade it for something he needed. To produce an excess of anything above what is wanted or needed with no intention of using it to obtain something else would be irrational—and a profit-seeking economic man is anything but irrational. With his excess supply (that above his own needs), he has the wherewithal to bargain with others in a like situation. Thus, his supply has become the demand for someone else's product.

As with the individual, so with the economy—or so it was assumed. Supply would always create its own demand; ergo, no lack of demand. And even if not perfect, the concept of Say's Law held enough validity to enable the classical economists to assume that there could be no serious problem of deficient demand. As discussed in Chapter 4, it became rather difficult to hold to such a theory in the face of ten years of massive unemployment in the 1930s.

Consider now the answer given by classical price theory to the other major cause of unemployment, that of structural changes. At any given time, some sectors of the economy are expanding while others are declining. And, as demand declines in a given sector, employment falls, thereby causing unemployment. Right? Wrong. Two factors are at work here. First, as demand declines the price of the product falls and, in the factor (or labor) market, the wages of labor drop. This decrease in wages combines with the falling product price to mitigate some of the impact of the declining demand. More importantly, as consumers spend less of their income in the declining sectors, they have more to spend elsewhere. As a result, demand increases in these areas along with a concomitant increase in the product and factor (labor) prices. Thus, as the demand shifts into other areas, labor moves from the declining sectors to take advantage of the new employment opportunities. And, while society has now shifted priorities and is receiving more of the new product, the pricing system has, with no outside interference, taken care of the unemployment problem.

Automation

Another form of structural unemployment that has given rise to a great deal of concern is that of technical change or "automation."[4] Suppose that a technological advance is introduced that is labor-saving in nature. (This is usually the case although many innovations are capital

---

[4] Automation is thought by some to produce deficient demand unemployment as well as creating structural problems. For present purposes it will suffice to consider only the structural elements.

saving also.) There are two possibilities: first, the innovation may come in an already existing industry and, second, the innovation may develop an entirely new industry. Taking the latter case first, it can be seen that an innovation that develops a new industry will not, by itself, decrease employment. Indeed, the innovation may produce new employment. The television industry, which grew up during the 1950s, provides an example of this type of employment-generating innovation.

The second case, that of a technological advance in an already existing industry, is somewhat more complex. The effect may be to either increase or decrease the amount of employment depending upon the degree to which prices drop because of the cost-saving techniques (there would be no incentive to introduce the change if costs would not decline as a result) and the responsiveness of the buyers to such a drop. In more technical terms, the employment effects depend upon the price elasticity of demand for the product which is a measure of the responsiveness of quantity changes to price changes. If, for example, a relatively small drop in the price of the product induces a substantial increase in the amount consumers will buy (elastic demand), total employment may increase because of the increased volume *in spite of* the fact that the amount of labor per unit of output has decreased. An example of this would be the auto industry where employment generally increases each year even though rapid technological advances have reduced the man-hour requirements per car. The lower (relative) price of the automobile changed it from a luxury good to a necessity. It is now within the reach of most Americans and, because of these cost reductions, total employment has increased in the industry in spite of the introduction of labor-saving capital improvements. Employment of coal miners, on the other hand, has been quite different. Here technological advances (along with rising wages and rising competition from substitute sources of energy) have had the effect of reducing the total amount of employment.

In either case, the price system, if working properly with the above assumptions, ensures that there will be no unemployment. A technological advance in an industry facing a relatively inelastic demand curve creates the most serious employment problem. But here the analysis is the same as that provided by the above example of the declining industry. As employment shrinks in the industry and costs go down (again, there would be no reason to innovate unless this resulted in a cost reduction), consumers have more money to spend in other areas. This, in turn, increases demand in these areas and provides for a concomitant increase in employment. As a result, the persons put out of work in the area affected by the technological advance are put to work in other sectors of the economy. In the process, the entire output of the society increases and everyone is better off. (Of course, not *everyone* from the declining industry will be quickly re-employed. But this represents an adjustment deficiency in the system and was of limited concern to classical price theorists.)

Inflation

Finally, inflation, the other side of today's economic dilemma, is no problem in the perfectly competitive society. In the classical environment, money played no independent role but merely provided a lubricant that ensured the smooth running of the entire system. Money simply provided a medium of exchange so that bartering with goods and services—a very clumsy way of conducting society's economic affairs—would be unnecessary. There may be temporary increases in prices in various sectors of the economy as demand shifted, but these are offset with simultaneous decreases in other sectors. As a result, the aggregate price level remains constant. Prices in this economy simply reflect the relative abundance or scarcity of various commodities and, since supply always equals demand (Say's Law), the aggregate price level remains unchanged. (Of course, if the monetary authorities injected too much money into the economy, the general price level could rise. But this was viewed as the fault of a meddling government and not a deficiency of the price system itself.)

Further Wonders

Solving such economic problems as these—distribution, allocation, unemployment, and inflation—would seem to be a very admirable feat for any economic system. But the classical price system held even more wonders. It also provided for a maximum amount of economic growth by forcing the ever-watchful entrepreneur to continually innovate (cut costs) in order to remain competitive. The entrepreneur most astute at cost reduction reaps the short-lived profits that can be made before his competitors catch up with him. By then there are no further economic profits to be reaped. The consumer is then the final recipient of the advantages of economic progress.

At this point, the process may seem futile for the entrepreneur. There are no permanent gains and if ever he outdistances his competitors, they soon catch him again. But woe to the capitalist who thinks in this manner, for he is soon left behind and, indeed, forced out of business as his rivals continue to innovate and he is unable to meet their cost reductions. Thus, he has no choice but to innovate and, to come full circle back to Adam Smith, ". . . he intends only his own gain" and is "led by an invisible hand to promote an end which was no part of this intention."

Clearly, the American ideology of independence, coupled with an intellectual system as powerful as that provided by the theory of the capitalist price system (which itself had no small part in forging this ideology), became tremendously biased against any governmental intervention in the market place. Rarely have the beliefs and desires of the common man been so strongly reinforced by the intellectual system of the philosophers. And, while showing its age, this ideology is still intact in the 1970s. In particular, it explains a good deal of the antipathy shown toward the general idea of controls on the economy. While the individual's common sense may tell him that when price increases and unemployment gets out of hand "something must be done," there is still a small voice in the back of his mind insisting that somehow intervention in the markets must be wrong. Indeed, given the American's cultural and political background, coupled with his indoctrination of the values of laissez-faire economics, it would be difficult to understand how he could think otherwise.

SOME DEFICIENCIES

Problems with the Theory

A tremendous advantage of competitive price theory is that it provides a set of logical deductions that exhibit few "intellectual loose ends." By carefully stating the assumptions (or, at times, not so carefully stating them), the theorist is able to arrive at a legion of "optimum" and "maximizing" results. Even as one moves from the comparative ease of perfect competition into the realm of oligopoly and monopoly, the results may not be quite so attractive theoretically—but they are still satisfactory in terms of logical neatness and precision.

However, while the market performs many functions, and performs them well, there are some inherent deficiencies in the system which, because of the enthusiasm for the free market's advantages, are often overlooked. Much of the lack of attention to these problems results from a misunderstanding by many persons of the nature of price theory and, indeed, from a misunderstanding of the nature of theories in general. A good deal of the blame must rest with economists themselves who, in extolling the virtues of competitive price theory, have neglected to display proper respect for its deficiencies and limitations.

One large problem arises when the assumption of profit maximization is relaxed. And this may be precisely the case when a lack of perfect mobility allows the firm to do *other* than maximize profits. That is, if it is difficult for new firms to enter the industry, there is no reason why the existing firms *must* maximize profits. They may do so, but they may not. At this point, the results of many theoretical models become indeterminant since no one can ascertain with certainty how the businessman will respond to various changes.

As a result of these muddy theoretical waters, price theorists have tended to shy away from models other than those based upon profit maximization.[5] Whether intended or not, this penchant for theoretical neatness has resulted in a tremendous amount of intellectual energy being expended upon refining the results of the competitive theory while a strong bias has developed against models of the economy that are not "quantifiable." At times the subject of analysis—the economy—has become lost in the race to further perfect the intellectual trappings of the economic tool.

A more serious deficiency of the theory is the preoccupation with "comparative statics," that is, the notion of comparing one stationary state with another. The method of determining the impact of a given change in one of the parameters (say, a demand shift) is to concentrate on what the price and output equilibrium levels were before the shift and to compare this with the new equilibrium level after the shift. While this may be useful in determining the long-run consequences of a given change, it tends to minimize the problems inherent within the change itself. Which is, of course, another way of saying that the assumption of perfect mobility may be quite inaccurate in the short run and, as a result, serious transitional problems are often overlooked.

For example, Figure 2-1 depicts the factor (labor) market and the product market facing a given industry. (Call it industry X for lack of a more imaginative name.) The supply and demand schedules are represented in the usual manner with demand in both markets being a decreasing function of price and supply an increasing function. The parameter change under consideration is a decline in the demand for the industry's product and the effect of this change on price and quantity in the product market and wages and employment in the labor market. We begin, as is customary with such analyses, with an equilibrium situation in both markets indicated by the intersection of the supply and demand schedules. In the product market this results in a price and quantity of P_1 and Q_1 respectively, and in the labor market a level of wages at W_1 and of employment at E_1.

The drop in demand for the firm's product is indicated by the westward movement in the demand schedule from D_1D_1 to D_2D_2. This shift can be assumed to have occurred for any number of reasons, such as the rise of a competitive industry whose products consumers now prefer. For example, the demand for kerosene lamps declined with the intro-

---

[5] Some theorists, most notably William Baumol, have attempted to insert a greater degree of realism into their models. In this case, Baumol puts forth an alternative theory of behavior based upon sales maximization (with a profit constraint). Although more realistic—and more predictive—than many of the profit maximization models, this variation still depends on "maximizing" behavior on the part of the firm.

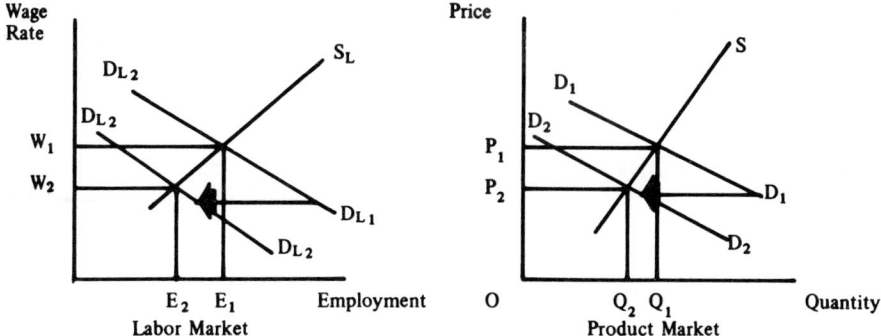

Figure 2–1. Labor and Product Markets Facing Industry X

duction of electricity. By using these simple economic diagrams, we can then trace the effects of this demand shift on both the product and labor markets. At the new equilibrium level in the product market there are now Q_2 units produced, selling for a price of P_2. Both price and quantity thus decrease reflecting the consumer's altered preference. By the same token, demand now decreases in the labor market from $D_{L1} D_{L1}$ to $D_{L2} D_{L2}$ since the demand for labor is derived from that for the product. This has the effect of pushing down the equilibrium wage and employment levels to W_2 and E_2, respectively, and both markets once again are in equilibrium. This same analysis, of course, may be applied in a greatly refined manner to any number of changes in the various parameters of the system.

There is nothing wrong with such an analysis and, in fact, it becomes quite useful when examining various market forces. When used as intended, such theory has been responsible for generating an extraordinary number of insights into the economic mechanism. Unfortunately, however, by analyzing the problem in this manner, one tends to overlook the very real problems that may arise in the process of moving from one equilibrium position to another.

Consider the labor market. It is fine to say that the new equilibrium situation is reached after wages decline to W_2 and employment declines to E_2. But this masks the problems encountered in getting from the former position to the latter one. Of course, if mobility were perfect this would pose no problem, and in the long run (with increased mobility) this may indeed be the new equilibrium position. The problem is that in the short run the persons represented by the decrease in employment from E_1 to E_2 may not readily find new jobs in other sectors of the economy. The theory tells us that as demand decreases in industry X it increases in another industry, thus providing the needed employment opportunities. But the new jobs may be located in California while the old ones may have been in Massachusetts and, especially for older workers, such new opportunities are the same as no opportunities.[6]

By concentrating on the elaboration of such models, economists tended to neglect the short-run problems of adjustment, in spite of the fact that the long run is only an accumulation of short runs. To be sure, theorists admitted that such problems did exist and even spoke at length about the need for improved adjustment mechanisms to make the process of movement less painful. For the most part, however, these pronouncements represented tokens of appeasement handed up to critics who continued to view with alarm the realities of the marketplace. Such tokens soothed the conscience of the theorist as he continued to further elaborate upon ever more esoteric models. And if, as many economists argue, these "structural" problems of adjustment are becoming more acute, the theory that ignores them becomes increasingly divorced from reality and less able to make accurate predictions concerning the condition of the economic patient.

The theoretical structure displayed another disturbing quality—the adoption of emotion-laden and value-packed terms to describe what are essentially technical features of economic models. Phrases such as "perfect competition," "pure competition," "free markets," and "optimum allocation" cannot help but bias one toward acceptance of these models. If a market is "perfect" or "pure," is it possible for one to prefer a market that is "less perfect" or "impure"? And, more to the point, if a "free market" leads to "optimum allocation," such a market must be preferred to one that is "unfree" and provides a less-than-optimum allocation of resources.

Economists, especially the best of them, were careful to note that such terms had technical meanings and were not to be taken as value judgments of the system. Such caveats had little effect. If perfect competition (even if it's only a model) can be shown to maximize everything that's good (employment, growth, allocation) and at the same time minimize everything that's bad (unemployment, misallocation, stagnation), who could question such a concept and not wish to pursue it as a policy goal?

Problems in the Economy

Aside from the inherent difficulties and misleading characteristics of the theory itself, there were disturbing elements within the economy that refused to conform to the competitive model and, indeed, were seen by many to be drifting farther away from the theoretical constructs. A major problem, as the nineteenth century passed by and the economic

---

[6] Such problems are the essence of structural unemployment, a subject discussed in some detail in the next chapter.

machine rumbled into the twentieth, was that of economic power. Economic power, at least for the purposes at hand, can be defined as the ability to influence (or set) prices somewhat independently of market forces. (Prices, in this context, include the price of labor—wages—as well as the price of commodities.) No one, of course, would contend that any business corporation or labor union holds absolute power, that is, the ability to set prices and/or wages with total disregard for market forces. The question is one of degree. If powerful corporations and unions are able to dictate, within certain degrees, the level of prices and wages, the competitive model, to that same degree, becomes inappropriate. Thus, as corporations and unions grow in size and power, to a like degree the significance and accuracy of the competitive model decreases.

Market power acts to nullify the assumptions of the system, namely profit maximization, mobility, and the inability to administer prices. All of these assumptions become less realistic as the size and power of corporations affect the market more and more. And if fixed costs are high, entry into that industry will be extremely difficult. Then, since other firms will not be able to readily enter the market, mobility is, by definition, less than perfect. And in some highly capital-intensive industries where entry costs are extremely prohibitive, mobility may be *much* less than perfect. This, then, gives the corporation in question a measure of economic power since it is able to set prices above that which could be charged in a competitive situation while not fearing the entry of competitors who could undercut the market.

At the same time, it is no longer a necessity for the corporation to maximize profits. (In a purely competitive market, maximizing profits means making only a normal rate of return and failure to maximize profits means going out of business. Hence, there is no choice for the businessman who wishes to avoid becoming an ex-businessman.) Thus, the corporation that possesses a degree of market power may attempt to maximize profits or it may not attempt to maximize profits. One can cite examples of both types of behavior. A theory that bases all behavior on the assumption of profit maximization must, therefore, be less predictive under such circumstances than it would be in an economy characterized by greater competition.[7]

---

[7] It is precisely such a situation that has given rise to a good deal of speculation concerning the degree of "social responsibility" that a corporation should or should not have. No such problem exists in a perfectly competitive economy since any firm which chose to carry out some type of social responsibility rather than to maximize profits would soon be out of business. Only if the businessman uses some discretion as to what to do with the firm's funds does the question of social responsibility arise. And discretion on the part of the firm's behavior is another way of saying that the company has succeeded in isolating itself in some degree from market forces.

Union power as well as corporate power represents a violation of the perfectly competitive economy. To the extent that unions are able to push the wages of their members above that which they could obtain in a strictly competitive market, the result is increased unemployment or decreased wages for the non-union sector of the economy (or some combination of the two).[8] It is now commonly acknowledged even by the staunchest supporters of traditional price theory that both prices and wages (and especially wages) are "sticky" in a downward direction. This is true even in the absence of labor unions, but there is little doubt that union power has increased this phenomenon. Given this state of affairs, a decrease in demand for the product and a concomitant decrease in the firm's demand for labor may not lead to a decrease in wages. Instead, the unemployment generated by the decrease in demand becomes more acute and the problems of reallocating resources through the price mechanism more difficult.[9] The result is again to undermine the crucial assumption of perfect mobility.

Market Power

It could be (and is) frequently argued that there is still enough competition in the economy to make the competitive theory useful and, furthermore, that even where the above assumptions are invalid, the theory is still useful so long as it is able to make accurate predictions.[10] Unfortunately, as the economy moves toward the 1980s, both the explanatory value and the predictive value of the perfectly competitive model appear to be diminishing. Not that such models do not provide a useful starting point for an analysis of price and employment analysis. Unfortunately, they all too often provide both the starting and the stopping point.

It is, of course, nothing new to argue that there are large power blocks within the economy that make the competitive model of questionable value. Beginning in 1932 with Berle and Means' *The Modern*

---

[8] This is true only if unions are imposed on an otherwise perfectly competitive economy. If they gain power in an industry characterized by very large employers who possess monopsony power, they may be able to increase *both* wages and employment. Also, the question of whether unions *are* in fact able to increase the wages of their members is an unsettled one. A discussion in Chapter 6 addresses itself to this question.

[9] It should be noted in passing that this phenomenon of sticky prices and wages will also exacerbate the problem of inflation in an economy characterized by market power. As demand shifts, prices will be bid up in the growing sector but, if they are unable to fall in the declining sector, the result will be an increase in the general price level. This occurrence, known as "demand shift" inflation, is discussed in the following chapter.

[10] For a discussion of this, see Appendix 2-1 following this chapter.

Corporation and Private Property, various authors have spoken of a "managerial revolution" whereby the owner-entrepeneur is replaced by the corporate manager as the real controller of the capitalist machine. Culminating with John Kenneth Galbraith's *New Industrial State,* these observers have continually stressed that to the extent that owners no longer control the corporation, the profit motive may be lessened. At the very least, there is no inherent reason why the managers should be interested solely in increasing the firm's profits when their own income may be more a function of the size of their department or some other variable rather than of overall corporate profits.

Thus, it may be argued that one would have to show that the concentration of power has *increased* in order to argue that the competitive theory has become less relevant. Such may well be the case. The control of large business organizations is increasingly concentrated in fewer hands while the control of financial institutions appears to be even more concentrated.

With respect to the labor market, few would dispute the contention that unions have become more powerful during the twentieth century. Certainly the 1930s brought about a major institutional change in this country with the result being an increased amount of power in the hands of labor unions. The proportion of the nonagricultural labor force belonging to unions has grown appreciably since the 1930s and currently stands at approximately 30 percent. This, however, is only a rough indicator of union power. It may well be that, as management has accepted the fact that unions are here to stay, there is less reluctance to share wage-setting decisions with them—especially when increases can be passed on to the consumer. Also, there is some evidence that union power has been increasing rapidly in the past few years with the greatly expanding union membership among public employees.

There is, therefore, evidence that market power significantly alters the competitive view of the economy.[11]

CONCLUSION

Such, then, is a brief overview of the classical economic price system which has given most Americans—lay persons as well as economists—a strong bias against market controls. There can be no doubt that the theory represented a theoretical and philosophical masterpiece. Unfortunately, the ideal of the theory and the reality of the American economy have diverged to the point that the competitive model can no longer

---

[11] Chapter 6 deals with the question of market power in more detail.

accurately describe or predict economic behavior. While still extremely useful in limited applications, the theory continues to lose favor as a means of viewing the total economy.

Another in a series of critical blows to the free-market theory came on August 15, 1971, when Richard Nixon reversed his long-held faith in the competitive model and instituted the wage and price freeze which was subsequently followed by the Pay Board and the Price Commission. This action can rightly be viewed as a case of an unyielding reality finally catching up with and overtaking an increasingly irrelevant ideology. The fact that Mr. Nixon—an avowed free-market proponent—was the one to take such action should convince nearly everyone of the power of circumstances to alter beliefs.

We now turn our attention from the area of beliefs and ideologies to that of the two unrelenting problems that gave rise to this changed attitude: unemployment and inflation.

APPENDIX 2–1. A BRIEF ASIDE ON THE ROLE OF THEORY IN ECONOMIC ANALYSIS

Questionable Assumptions

The assumptions of classical price theory, it may be argued although few, are highly unrealistic. Recall that these assumptions are: (1) profit maximization on the part of the business firm and utility maximization on the part of the individual; (2) all firms are too small to influence the price of the goods and services they buy and sell, i.e., they are all "price takers"; and (3) all resources, physical and human, are perfectly mobile and thereby able to move into those areas where the returns are highest.

Certainly not everyone attempts to maximize his income nor does every firm consider profit maximization to be the ultimate goal. Also, it is foolish to assume (much less believe) that all businesses are "price takers" and are therefore unable to influence, let alone set, the price at which they sell their wares. Similar objections can be raised concerning the mobility of capital and labor. Once erected, there is little "mobility" to, say, a steel plant; and anyone who has moved his family across town, let alone across the country, will attest to the fact that labor is less than perfectly mobile.

Such objections are not without merit. No one can seriously suggest that the American economy is (or ever was) characterized by "perfect competition" such as depicted in these assumptions. Nor can anyone honestly believe that it would ever be possible to achieve a "perfectly competitive" society. True as they may be, however, these objections, by themselves, invalidate neither the purpose nor the results of classical price theory.

The First Line of Defense

These objections may be answered in one of two ways.

The first concerns the *degree* to which the assumptions are correct. After all, the fact that we do not live in a vacuum hardly negates the law stating that two bodies fall at equal speeds regardless of their weight. Nor does the fact that there is friction in the world render the theory of inertia useless. Even though frictions do exist, the theory is a close enough approximation of reality to explain much of what occurs.

Thus, even though not all companies strive to maximize profits at all times, a theory that considers this as the major motivating force is sufficiently accurate to explain a good deal of the behavior of business firms. Nor does every person necessarily strive to maximize income. It is enough for the theory if, other things being equal, someone would prefer higher wages to lower wages. Such an assumption, even if not completely accurate, certainly explains much of a person's economic behavior.

Similar reasoning applies to the concept of mobility. Although all resources are not completely mobile and, indeed, in the short run very few may exhibit such characteristics, in the long run there is a great deal of movement of physical and human capital from one industry to another as well as from one area of the country to another. Thus, while it may be impossible to move to a steel plant during its lifetime, when the locations of new plants can be and often are changed. And, although it may be difficult for many individual persons to change their work habits and life styles when new opportunities open in emerging industries, new entrants to the labor force will be drawn into these sectors thereby insuring that there will be a large degree of mobility in the long run.

The most serious objections surround the assumption that all firms are price takers and are thus unable to influence the market. To be sure, oligopoly and monopoly have come into the mainstream of economic theory, but their principal value lies in their micro-economic explanations of pricing and output decisions and not in their explanations of macro-economic relationships. In line with the other replies, however, it can be (and many times is) asserted that the economy does exhibit enough competition to make the model based upon this assumption valuable. Oftentimes such concepts as "workable" or "sufficient" competition are put forward as explanations of the "real world." Again, the idea is that even though we don't have perfect competition, what we do have is sufficient—especially in the long run—to make the competitive theory useful.

The Second Line of Defense

The second line of defense for the assumptions of the price system is that the realism of the assumptions really doesn't matter, and, indeed, should be of no concern. This assertion may appear a bit startling until one reflects upon the purpose of price theory—or any theory for that matter. Many defenders of the classical price system argue that the sole purpose of a theory is to enable meaningful predictions to be made, and that, if the theory can do this, it matters little whether or not the assumptions are realistic. Consider, for example, the purpose of a road map, i.e., to enable a course to be charted from one geographical point to another. The lowly map is a totally unrealistic representation of reality, that is, of the terrain one must traverse. Indeed, if the map *were* an accurate reflection of reality (an aerial photograph) it would be useless for its intended purpose. Only because it abstracts from reality is it able to perform its function and, as such, it oversimplifies, distorts, and completely misrepresents what the real world is like.

Using this same logic, there is no reason for economic theory to represent reality (i.e., that the assumptions be accurate). The final test lies in the predictive power of the model. If it can accurately predict economic behavior or patterns of the future, the realism of the assumptions are of little importance. Many proponents of the competitive theory argue that this is precisely the situation that exists. The worth of the competitive model, in this view, can only be gauged by the correctness or lack thereof of the predictions the model makes. Realism is of no concern.

Remaining Doubts

The above lines of defense are unquestionably strong. However, while it is true that the perfectly competitive theory was never an accurate reflection of reality, it also appears to be true that the likeness between the image and the reality have been moving farther apart in the twentieth century. As a result, while the theory may have done an adequate job of explaining (and predicting) the U.S. economy in an earlier period, these explanations are becoming less satisfactory and the predictions less precise. That is, the growth of large concentrations of corporate and labor market power is putting increasing strain on the already tenuous relationship between the competitive theory and the real world. Workable competition is becoming less workable, and sufficient competition is becoming less sufficient. To the extent that this is the case, one might expect that the predictions of the theory would become increasingly inaccurate. A thesis of this book is that this is indeed the case and, as a result, the competitive theory, although of great value for specialized, specific purposes, is growing increasingly irrelevant as an explanation of price and wage movements in the final quarter of the twentieth century.

UNEMPLOYMENT AND INFLATION: AN OVERVIEW

3

> When more and more people are thrown out of work, unemployment results.
>
> Calvin Coolidge

As pointed out in Chapter 1, market controls on the economy are a response to two economic problems of major significance: unemployment and inflation. Indeed, many economists believe that a major economic problem of the rest of the century will be the need to reach high levels of employment while maintaining stable price levels.

These areas of concern are, of course, closely related. If the only concern were to control the price level, there is little doubt that a prolonged period of high unemployment fostered by a deliberate governmental policy of restricting aggregate demand would halt inflation. Unfortunately, the severe recession that such a policy would necessitate is considered by most persons to be unacceptable. On the other hand, a governmental policy of greatly increasing aggregate demand could (as every wartime experience bears out) reduce the unemployment rate to virtually any desired level. This policy, however, carries an unacceptably high price tag in the form of inflation. The problem, then, is to lower the trade-off between the dual evils of unemployment and inflation.

This is where controls on prices and wages come in. By restraining wage and price increases, aggregate demand is able to drive the unemployment rate down instead of igniting inflationary pressures—the essence of incomes policy, which nearly all market economies have had occasion to experiment with since World War II.

An incomes policy, however, also carries a social price tag. This takes the form of restrictions on the behavior of business firms, labor unions, and individuals. Americans are reluctant to relinquish such freedoms and can only be expected to do so in serious situations. Specifically, they must feel that the alternatives are less acceptable than the controls. The only way in which controls can be adequately evaluated, then, is to consider them in relation to their alternative, that is, no controls. In other words, does the American economy need controls at all? In an attempt to answer this, we will look in some detail at the nature of unemployment and inflation as they affect the American economy. Only by understanding the illness can one prescribe the medicine.

UNEMPLOYMENT

The Severity of Unemployment

In mid-1975 there were over 8 million unemployed persons in the United States yielding an unemployment rate of over 9 percent. No one disputes that this is an unacceptably high level. But what, then, constitutes an "acceptable" level? Just how high is a 9 percent or a 6 percent rate and what is the American economy capable of achieving? Furthermore, what does a figure such as this indicate for different sectors within the economy? For different groups? For different occupations? And for different individuals?

Finally, what are the causes of unemployment? Examining this question is much more than an idle academic exercise. If the causes of unemployment cannot be dissected and analyzed, the chances of reducing the level through appropriate public policies are greatly reduced. Unfortunately, this is no easy task. Several different types of unemployment can and do exist at the same time thereby making the job of determining the correct cause extremely difficult. And, as in many facets of economics, appearances can be deceiving.

Concerning the severity of unemployment, there is no doubt that even a 6 percent level is bad by almost any standard. In the twenty-eight years since 1948, only one year (1961) has averaged this poorly, and no year came even close to 1975's average of approximately 9 percent. In terms of international comparisons, the United States continues to do worse than most European countries—a trend that has been increasingly evident in the post–World War II years. But even taken on its own terms, there are a number of reasons for the overriding concern with unemployment and why levels above 4 or 5 percent are alarming.

To begin with, each 1 percent of unemployment represents approximately 1 million persons out of work. Assuming a 4-percent national average rate, in 1975 there were nearly 5 million *additional* unemployed persons. It is well documented that a disproportionate number of these persons have low incomes to begin with, making the problem even more acute for those who lose their job. Also, even with the increased coverage of Unemployment Insurance since 1970, resulting from passage of the Employment Security Amendments to the Social Security Act, almost 12 million employees are still not covered by this insurance. Many of these are in low-paying occupations such as household domestic work and agricultural employment. In addition, even among the workers covered by Unemployment Insurance the benefits are often far from adequate and, in fact, have been decreasing as a percent of earnings. Most persons receiving unemployment insurance receive less than half of their previous wages.

The tragedy of unemployment, however, is not limited to those persons represented by the monthly average, even though this, by itself, constitutes a major source of human suffering. The number of persons who, at some time or another, experience unemployment during the year is estimated by the Department of Labor to be approximately four times the average monthly rate. Thus, if unemployment averages 8 million persons a month, approximately 32 million persons experience *some* unemployment during the year. The reason for this lies in the fact that, to a degree, different persons are counted in each month's survey. The raw unemployment figures therefore understate the extent to which persons are exposed to the insecurities of the labor market, and, as a result, with any given unemployment rate there exists a much larger body of persons living on the margins of employment—oscillating between work and enforced idleness. Obviously, as the unemployment rate moves upward, the number of persons experiencing acute feelings of job insecurity increases much faster.

Even those individuals fortunate enough to escape the ranks of the jobless are not unaffected. As the unemployment rate increases, the total job outlook becomes worse. One result of this is that many persons who would prefer full-time work are able to find only part-time employment. These persons, referred to as "involuntary" part-time employees, were estimated by the Department of Labor to number 3.8 million in early 1975, an increase of over 1.5 million since 1974. Since they are working, however, they are not included in the monthly unemployment statistics.

Nor is the fact that unemployment involves a general down-grading

---

[1] Unless otherwise noted, data are from U.S. Department of Labor sources.

of skills reflected in the monthly rate. As the employment situation becomes worse, many employers discharge first those employees with the least skill in an effort to cut costs while maintaining their skilled labor force. As a result, many of the remaining employees must do work below that for which they are qualified. The taxi driver with a Ph.D. in Physics is an extreme but poignant example of this. Such a situation represents a misallocation of resources and a waste for the nation as well as personal dissatisfaction and hardship for individuals all along the line.

Finally, when unemployment increases, the overall efficiency of the labor markets diminishes. Persons are reluctant to give up existing jobs in order to look for something more in line with their talents and, again, both the nation and the individual suffer the consequences of this decreased efficiency. Conceptually, the welfare of both individual and the economy is greatest when every person is in a job where his productivity is the highest. A smoothly functioning labor market operates to move toward this goal through the twin mechanisms of wage rates and employee mobility. At times of high unemployment, however, mobility is severely restricted since voluntary movement sharply declines. Persons fear leaving their present position to search for better ones. (Unemployment rates and voluntary quit rates are inversely related.) As a result, the labor market mechanism becomes increasingly ineffectual in performing its role of allocating resources and, to the extent that these effects become widespread, the entire economic machine grinds down to a lower level of speed and efficiency.

Unemployment and Poverty

Those persons who are concerned with the suffering brought about by poverty, as well as those persons who are alarmed by ever-increasing welfare costs, should be particularly concerned by unemployment. Most persons living in poverty are able and willing to work. Employment and higher earnings would represent, for these persons, a direct route into the mainstream of American society. If the nation is serious in its commitment to reduce and eliminate poverty, it is absolutely essential that it pursue economic policies aimed at achieving full employment.[2]

The Incidence of Unemployment

Average unemployment rates are just that—averages. As a result, many important distinctions among various groups of the population are

---

[2] Appendix 3–1 at the end of this chapter consists of a discussion of the relationship between unemployment, poverty, and welfare.

hidden when viewing only this raw figure. Table 3-1 provides a breakdown of different selected characteristics of the unemployed for selected periods of the past fifteen years.

As illustrated dramatically in Table 3-1, for any given level of un-

Table 3–1. Selected Unemployment Rates, 1961–1975 [Percent]*

	1961–65 average	1969	Aug. 1971	1973	1974	Aug. 1975
All workers	5.5	3.5	6.1	4.9	5.6	8.2
Sex and age:						
Both sexes 16–19 years	15.9	12.2	17.0	14.5	16.0	20.8
Men 20 years and over	4.4	2.1	4.5	3.2	3.8	6.0
Women 20 years and over	5.4	3.7	5.8	4.8	5.5	8.1
Race:						
White	4.9	3.1	5.6	4.3	5.0	7.5
Black and other minorities	10.4	6.4	9.8	8.9	9.9	13.4
Selected groups:						
White-collar workers	2.8	2.1	3.5	2.9	3.3	4.6
Blue-collar workers	7.1	3.9	7.6	5.3	6.7	11.0
Craftsmen	4.8	2.2	5.5	3.7	4.4	7.0
Operatives	7.3	4.4	8.3	5.7	7.5	13.1
Nonfarm laborers	11.8	6.7	10.5	8.4	10.1	14.3
Private wage and salary workers in nonagricultural industries	5.9	3.5	6.2	4.8	5.7	8.7
Construction	12.8	6.0	10.2	8.8	10.6	15.0
Manufacturing	5.6	3.3	6.9	4.3	5.7	10.5

* Number of unemployed in each group as percent of civilian labor force in that group.
Source: Department of Labor.

employment, different subgroups experience widely different rates. Teenagers, by all measures, experience the worst unemployment, ranging from three to four times that of the total economy. (Also, since participation rates fall as unemployment increases, the data in Table 3-1 understates the actual differential. See Appendix 3-1.)

Of particular interest concerning unemployment is that it is less susceptible to general improvements in the economy than that of other groups. For example, during the 1961-65 period, teenage unemployment stood at 15.9 percent. By 1969 this figure dropped to 12.2 percent, a decline of some 23 percent. During the same period, however, the rate for males over 20 years old went from 4.4 to 2.1, or a decrease of 52 percent. The overall rate dropped approximately 36 percent but this includes, of course, the impact of the relatively small drop among teenagers.

The rate for nonwhite teenagers is particularly distressing. Table 3–2 presents the unemployment rates for white and nonwhite teenagers throughout the 1960s and 1970s through January, 1975, at which time the nonwhite rate stood at an almost unbelievable 41.1 percent!

When one considers that at this high rate the actual figure is probably understated by a considerable amount, the implications are truly disastrous. The improved conditions during the late 1960s did little to improve the situation, and, in fact, teenage unemployment increased again

Table 3–2. Teenage Unemployment Rates

	White	Non-White
1959	13.1	26.1
1960	13.4	24.4
1961	15.3	27.6
1962	13.3	25.1
1963	15.5	30.4
1964	14.8	27.2
1965	13.4	26.2
1966	11.2	25.4
1967	11.0	26.5
1968	11.0	25.0
1969	10.7	24.0
1970	13.5	29.1
1971	15.1	31.7
1972	14.2	33.5
1973	12.6	30.2
1974	14.0	32.9
Jan. 1975	18.4	41.1

Source: Department of Labor.

with the general worsening of conditions in 1974 and 1975. It appears that teenage unemployment grows worse along with the general rate but fails to improve when the overall situation improves. This is part of what many consider to be a worsening "structural" unemployment problem—a subject discussed next.

The relative position of nonwhite teenagers also displays indications of worsening with respect to white teenager unemployment rates. While the nonwhite teenage rates are consistently in the neighborhood of double that of the white rates, this ratio has been increasing somewhat in recent years. This is in contrast to what has been happening with the overall white/nonwhite ratio: While the unemployment rate for blacks of all ages (which make up approximately 92 percent of the "nonwhites" of all ages) has usually been about twice that of whites, this differential decreased slightly in recent years.

Skill Levels

In general, occupations requiring few skills exhibit high unemployment rates. This is historically true and also true of the unemployment situation in the 1970s. Blue collar workers typically have higher rates of unemployment than white collar workers and, along with this, the least skilled of the blue collar workers have significantly higher rates of joblessness than the higher skilled workers. A further examination of Table 3–1 will substantiate this fact.

In part, this is due to the fact that unskilled workers typically have less education than skilled workers and unemployment rates are inversely related to the level of educational attainment. Thus, by achieving a higher education (or skill) level, a person will reduce his chances of joining the ranks of the unemployed (as well as earning higher wages).

Such a conclusion coincides nicely with the general conception of the American Dream. Hard work aimed at improving one's qualifications will pay off in terms of higher wages and lower unemployment. And, for the most part, this dream is borne out by reality. A disturbing exception, however, has recently been suggested by research carried out by Bennett Harrison for the Department of Labor (118, p. 93). Mr. Harrison concludes that while increased education pays off for the white person, it is of questionable economic value for the nonwhite ghetto resident. For nonwhites in these neighborhoods, increases in education do not seem to pay off in terms of either increased earnings or decreased unemployment. Thus, the reluctance of many inner-city youths to continue with formal education cannot be attributed solely to irrational behavior; in part, this reluctance stems from the fact that the economic returns are small.

Distressing as they are, however, such instances can still be considered as exceptions to the general rule. For the most part, as one proceeds up the occupational ladder, employment prospects and earnings increase. At the same time, an acceptance of relatively high rates of unemployment make educational and other self-initiated methods of fighting joblessness increasingly less attractive. Training oneself for a nonexistent job can only lead to further frustration and disillusionment.

Age and Sex

Typically, as one moves from younger to older elements of the population, the unemployment rate decreases. After approximately 45 to 50 years of age, however, the unemployment rate begins to creep slowly upward. Although unemployment is, for the most part, more characteristic of the young population than the old, there are problems faced by the older unemployed persons that are frequently more acute than those faced by the young. Typically, they are unemployed for longer periods than the young and, once a job is lost, another may be very difficult to find. The well-known problems associated with a lack of skills is particularly acute for older persons whom employers are reluctant to retrain. Geographical mobility is also more of a problem for older persons who are frequently hesitant to move to new areas in search of employment.

The fact that unemployment rates have not changed markedly for older persons may be deceiving with respect to their actual situation. The unemployment rate for men over 65 years of age was 4.5 percent in 1959, 3.2 percent in 1970, and 4.4 percent in 1974. However, the participation rate of this group also fell substantially during the 1960s from 34.3 percent in 1959 to 26.7 in 1970. In part, this undoubtedly reflects the fact that many of these persons became discouraged in their search for employment and dropped out of the labor force. To a certain extent, of course, it also represents liberalized social security and retirement benefits. The precise degree of each influence is impossible to isolate, but the lack of any sharp institutional changes during the 1960s would indicate that the "discouraged worker" effect is operating to a degree and that, as a result, the relative employment situation of older persons has deteriorated somewhat.[3]

The unemployment rate for women in the labor force continues to be somewhat higher than that for men, and the differentials remain fairly constant regardless of economic conditions. (See Table 3–1.) Strangely, this does not necessarily reflect the fact that the job situation is worse for women than for men. The reason for this seeming paradox again lies in the behavior of the labor force participation rates. In short, this rate has been increasing very rapidly for women while decreasing somewhat for men, thereby implying that, even if jobs open up more rapidly for women, their unemployment rates could be (and are) still higher than those for men. Such has been the case. The total labor force participation rate for women rose from 33.9 percent in 1950 to 43.3 percent by 1970 and 46 percent by 1974.

Interestingly, the bulk of the increase has been among white, married women who seem to have more freedom to join the labor market than earlier. For nonwhite women the rate has always been high in comparison to whites and continues to move upward. With respect to nonwhite women, the "additional worker" effect seems to be strong: With lower

---

[3] For a further discussion of "discouraged workers" and "labor force participation rates," see Appendix 3–1 following this chapter.

wages and higher unemployment rates for nonwhite *men* than for white men, more black *women* enter the labor force.

The difference between the employment situation for men and women can also be seen by looking at the absolute changes in the civilian labor force. During the two and one-half decades from 1950 to 1974, the male labor force increased by approximately 11 million workers (from 44 million to 55 million) while the number of women increased by nearly 18 million (18 to 36 million). The fact that the differential in unemployment rates increased only slightly during this period reflects the fact that jobs were being created faster for women than for men. It must be added, however, that many more of these jobs are part-time than is true for males, and also that many more of them are in low-paying occupations with little upward mobility. Thus, the unemployment experience, even with the inclusion of participation rate data, still omits a good deal of the employment story for women.

Sectors and Occupations

Unemployment affects different industry sectors and occupational groups very unevenly. Unemployment rates in manufacturing are typically much higher than those in the service industries, even though employment has been increasing rapidly for the latter group and only slowly for the former. (This long-term trend reversed in the middle to late 1960s but this appears to have been a temporary turnabout due to the Viet Nam War buildup with its emphasis on manufacturing. By the 1970s the pattern was again back to its earlier growth path.)

In large part, these industry shifts also reflect the differential employment and unemployment patterns among different occupational groups. That is, the unemployment rate is consistently higher for blue collar workers than white collar workers. In part, this is because the structure of American industry is shifting toward sectors such as finance and trade which employ a large proportion of white collar workers.

Within the different occupational classifications (blue collar, white collar, etc.), those persons with the least skills and/or education display consistently higher unemployment rates than the more skilled workers. A glance at Table 3–1 bears this out. This is occurring in response to the rapid shift of employment from unskilled to skilled occupations. From 1958 to 1970 there was a *decrease* in the total number of unskilled workers (farm and non-farm laborers) while, during this same period, the labor force increased by over 15 million persons! These data lend a good deal of credulity to the assertion that the quickest way to become unemployed in today's (and tomorrow's) economy is to remain unskilled. The trends are clearly moving in the other direction.

Structural changes such as these have, to be sure, continuously occurred within this and every other growing economy. And, while these sectoral changes have long been recognized as a source of unemployment, it is asserted by many economists that these structural changes are now occurring with greater speed than before, thereby making the adjustment process more difficult. To the extent that this is true (a subject discussed next), the "normal" rate of unemployment will move upward in the economy. And, to the extent that this happens, it will be increasingly difficult to reduce the unemployment level without triggering an upward movement in the price level. Thus, the distribution of unemployment among the different sectors and groups within the economy is very important from the standpoint of attempting to reduce the overall level which, of course, is simply the aggregate of these various components. Whether the economy is more "inflation prone" (or "unemployment prone") than during earlier periods remains to be seen. The issue is, however, extremely important concerning the necessary or lack thereof for an active incomes policy.

Types of Unemployment

While it is valuable to look at the unemployment problems in terms of the persons, occupations and sectors that are affected, this tells us relatively little about the *causes* of the unemployment. It is to these different causes that we now turn our attention. Unfortunately, as will become apparent, it is easier to classify the reasons for unemployment conceptually than to determine how much of each type exists at any given time. Indeed, the problem of identification lies at the center of a lively controversy among professional economists. Nor is this controversy a mere intellectual exercise. It is a debate in which the whole nation has a stake since it involves important policy questions which, in the end, will determine whether we are able to solve the unemployment/inflation dilemma. These questions concerning the types of unemployment also lie at the heart of one's viewpoint concerning direct controls on prices and wages. After discussing the conceptual differences in types of unemployment, then, we will examine this heated controversy.

Although there are several different classification schemes for subdividing unemployment, it will serve our purpose to consider only four broad categories and only two of these in detail. These types are: (1) frictional, (2) seasonal, (3) deficient demand, and (4) structural.

1. Frictional Unemployment

Frictional unemployment is often referred to as the minimum amount of joblessness that can be reached in a free society. It is that type of unemployment that arises as persons quit one job in search of a better one, are laid off because of a relatively small change in the demand for labor, or are entering the labor force for the first time and have not yet found employment. Frictional unemployment is, in large part, what the term implies. It arises because of "frictions" in the labor market that impede instant adjustments. In short, it consists of the movement between jobs and, as such, could be eliminated by prohibiting this movement—a price most free societies are unwilling to pay. This does not mean that frictional unemployment cannot be lowered through public policies. Programs aimed at increasing the efficiency of the labor market make it easier for persons to move from one area to another (both occupationally and geographically), thereby reducing the average time between jobs (duration of unemployment).

Also, it is interesting that the *voluntary* portion of unemployment (quits) moves *inversely* with the general overall unemployment rate. As labor markets tighten (unemployment decreases), the voluntary quit rate *increases* as more persons attempt to switch jobs. With high unemployment the opposite occurs as employees become reluctant to quit one job in search of a better one. (The *duration* of the unemployment, however, varies *directly* with the general unemployment rate.) Frictional unemployment, then, is less serious than the other major types.

2. Seasonal Unemployment

Seasonal unemployment is exactly what the term implies: unemployment because of seasonal fluctuations in demand. This can be due to the weather or to an artificial season, such as the introduction of model changes in the auto industry. It is a serious cause of unemployment and one that is rightly the subject of public concern. Many of the persons affected by it, such as migrant workers, are at the low end of the income scale to begin with, and further unemployment for these persons causes serious hardships.

On the other hand, this type of joblessness is predictable and therefore more "insurable." Also, in many occupations, wage rates reflect the fact that the work is seasonal and therefore compensate the worker with increased income during the period when he is employed. High wages in the construction industry are often explained, at least partially, in these terms.

3. Deficient Demand Unemployment

Only spending creates job. The more spending, the more jobs. The essence of deficient demand unemployment is that not enough spending is taking place in the economy to produce that number of jobs necessary to bring unemployment down to acceptable levels. If there is a deficiency of aggregate demand (too little spending), there will be insufficient jobs to produce full employment. And, at overall unemployment rates of 5 to 6 percent or more, there is general agreement that the crucial problem *is* a lack of demand. The identification problem arises when the unemployment rate falls to around 4 or 5 percent. At this point the nature of the remaining unemployment becomes unclear. Is it then due to a lack of demand or to a structural mismatch between available people and available jobs? The answer is unclear but very important since, in large part, the type of policies to be undertaken to reduce unemployment depends upon the cause of the unemployment.

Deficient demand unemployment is also referred to as "cyclical" unemployment caused by swings in the business cycle. Until recently it was thought that this type of unemployment was largely under control with the use of macroeconomic demand management policies. Political-economic events of the past five years have increasingly led to a questioning of this belief. This is discussed more fully next.

4. *Structural Unemployment*

As noted, structural unemployment involves a mismatch between available people and available jobs. It arises because of the dynamic nature of a changing economy where certain industries are growing while others are declining and, at the same time, technological changes are altering the skill requirements of jobs. The coal miner in Appalachia who loses his job because of the introduction of new machines is structurally unemployed. So is the New England textile worker who is part of a declining industry and unable to acquire the skills necessary to become a part of the growing electronics industry that is replacing textiles as a major employer in this area. (The electronics industry around Boston, it might be noted, later suffered from its own structural problems.)

In large part, structural problems are the result of the failure of labor markets to function in the smooth manner depicted in the perfectly competitive model. If workers were able to adjust instantaneously to shifts in demand, there would be no structural unemployment. Or, if persons could readily gain the necessary skills for new jobs, there would be no long-term unemployment due to lack of these skills. Unfortunately, the labor market is oftentimes unable to make changes this rapidly and, although the necessary adjustments occur in the long run, structural changes can and do create large amounts of unemployment and hardship in the short run.

There are similarities between structural and frictional unemployment since both deal with labor market frictions. A principal difference between the two is in terms of severity. Structural unemployment is the more severe of the two. It lasts longer, is less voluntary in nature, and affects far larger numbers of persons.

INFLATION

The Recent Record

(If unemployment were the only economic evil to contend with, the policy prescription would be relatively simple: spend freely and create jobs. Unfortunately, as the past few years have amply demonstrated, such a policy contains a lethal side effect—inflation. If we refer to inflation as simply an increase in prices (regardless of the cause) there are "tolerable" as well as "intolerable" levels. From 1961 to 1965 the consumer price index rose by slightly more than 1 percent per year while the wholesale index remained virtually constant. Such increases provided no cause for alarm. By late 1965, however, the wholesale index began to move more rapidly, increasing an average of 2 percent during the year and another 3.3 percent in 1966. Consumer prices soon followed. This latter index increased 2.9 percent in both 1966 and 1967, then by 4.2 percent in 1968, and 5.4 and 5.9 percent respectively in 1969 and 1970.)

During 1971, just prior to the first wage-price freeze, the indexes showed little sign of easing their upward climb. In the first six months of the year the average rate of increase in consumer prices was 4.6 percent (on an annual basis), while from July to August of 1971, this index rose at an annual rate of 4.8 points and the wholesale index rose by an annual average of 3.6 points. The relative slowdown in the overall wholesale index was misleading, however, since agricultural prices fell substantially at this time. Considering only the price of industrial commodities, the wholesale index rose by a very rapid (for that period) annual rate of 7.2 percent from July to August of 1971. The inflationary pressures of the late 1960s and early 1970s were not abating in the summer of 1971.

Of course, the experiences of 1973 to 1975 made these rates appear quite moderate by comparison. Following an increase of 4.6 percent in 1972, the wholesale price index soared by 13.1 percent in 1973 and then by a staggering 18.9 percent in 1974. The consumer price index increased by 3.3, 6.2, and 11 percent during the same three years.

When inflation reaches this level, it can no longer be ignored. Just what rate must be reached before inflation becomes a matter of concern is unclear, but there is little doubt that the 5- and 6-percent averages early in the new decade were serious. This concern, of course, heightened as the pace of the inflation increased. As a result, public concern turned increasingly to inflation and the problems it was creating.

The Trade-Off

Since inflation is often viewed as a necessary cost of reducing unemployment, the two can be viewed, roughly, as alternatives. That is, we know that if unemployment is increased high enough and for long enough, prices will no longer continue to increase. But this policy brings us back to all of the problems associated with high unemployment. On the other hand, by spending freely unemployment can be pulled down. But this means inflation and this is deemed by many persons as too high a price to pay for full employment. For this reason, there is often considered to exist a trade-off between the level of unemployment and the level of inflation. Before looking at the possible causes and cures of inflation, then, we must briefly consider why it is considered to be so bad and, in addition, the probable consequences of continued price hikes.

Consequences of Inflation

As prices continue to rise and as the *rate* of increase accelerates, it becomes increasingly difficult for rational spending and investment decisions to be made. Ideally, an investment should reflect the probable returns (plus a risk factor) of the opportunity. With unstable prices, however, it becomes very difficult to judge just what these returns may be since much of the outcome depends upon what happens to the price level and not solely upon the merits of the investment. Investments that have a relatively low rate of return are thus shunned since the return, even if safe, may not cover the rise in prices. At the same time, a premium is placed on speculative ventures since only in these areas will the return be sufficient to cover the risk along with possible price increases. As a result, speculators are rewarded while those who desire only to invest in a productive enterprise are punished. As Arthur Okun, former chairman of the Council of Economic Advisors, so aptly put it, inflation creates "sharpies" and "suckers," with the former being the speculators who attempt to beat the inflation and the latter being the more cautious saver who is looking only for a nominal return on his money (78, p. 20). The effect is also cumulative; as inflation becomes worse, fewer of society's resources are channeled into productive pursuits and, instead, are increasingly diverted into speculative pursuits. (There is, of course, a constructive role to be played by speculators. Again, however, what is true for the parts is not true for the whole. Although some speculation provides a useful service, when everyone engages in it, its usefulness declines. At that point the winners are offset by the losers with no net gain.)

While inflation misallocates the funds of investors, it also misappropriates the expenditures of consumers. Saving for a rainy day is no longer prudent since the interest to be earned on savings provides a poor hedge against price increases. Thus, consumers also turn to speculative methods of holding their hard-won savings and are often badly burned in the process. As an alternative, they can continue to hold their assets in more liquid form and watch the hungry appetite of inflation continue to dwindle their resources. Whichever route if followed, it leads to mounting frustrations on the part of middle class wage earners who become increasingly cynical toward the supposed virtues of thrift.

The traditional link between effort and reward is severed as inflation makes a mockery out of the dual ethic of hard work and frugality. Seeing his efforts thwarted by the unstable atmosphere of rapidly increasing prices, the working man senses that something is deeply wrong with the social and economic fabric. And, out of this intense frustration with events beyond his control, comes the desperate feeling that something must be done, however drastic, in an effort to restore stability. In this manner, a severe inflation can tear at the very heart of society by radicalizing the stable middle classes.

Serious inflation is not only an economic phenomenon of rising prices. It is also a social phenomenon signaling the destruction of the social contract itself. And its destructive elements are aimed at the most stable segment of society—the middle class. By making this class increasingly insecure and apprehensive, unchecked inflation can trigger a reactionary mood that will eventually stop at nothing in an attempt to restore order and stability. Such is the power of a runaway inflation.

What is the point at which "creeping" inflation can develop into "runaway" or "galloping" inflation? Some economists believe that one must necessarily lead to the other although most observers no longer see such a close relationship. For example, even though between 1952 and 1965 the consumer price index went up every year (except 1955), it failed to attain a rate of increase of 2 percent. There was no clear danger during this period that the "creeping" prices would begin "galloping." When does this danger become a reality? Although no precise figure can be given (just as there is no precise figure for "full employment" or "acceptable unemployment"), conceptually the danger begins when price changes must be taken into account when investment and expenditure decisions are made. (See Okun, 78, pp. 4–5.) Surely the past several years have seen the threshold crossed whereby nearly everyone must consider the effects of inflation on his decisions.

When consumers feel that they should spend now to avoid future price hikes, inflation is playing a role in their decisions. What is the effect of this? One major consequence is that by so doing, they will bring about the very effect that they fear—higher prices. That is, the expectation of inflation becomes a self-fulfilling prophecy. The same applies to the company that speeds up its capital equipment purchases to avoid paying higher prices in the future. The increased spending acts to push up the prices, thereby helping to fulfill the expectations. It is also at this point that inflation diverts the consumption, saving, and investment paths into more speculative areas and away from where their productive rates of return are highest. While no exact figure denotes when inflation is taken into account, historical experience suggests that somewhere in the neighborhood of 3 to 4 percent is a close approximation. To this point, there is not enough of an increase in prices to warrant concern by consumers, investors, and savers. But somewhere near here inflation does become a relevant decision criterion, and this fact alone helps to raise the price level even further.[4]

In addition to the obvious fact that the purchasing power of the dollar is decreasing, inflation gives rise to other economic problems of immediate concern. As was so well illustrated in the late 1960s, domestic inflation led to serious balance of payments problems as the surplus of imports over exports continued to climb. This, in turn, put increasing pressure on the dollar as foreign governments grew reluctant to hold them in ever-growing numbers. The convertibility of these dollars into gold had been a fiction for some time, since the value of the entire U.S. gold supply was insufficient to cover potential foreign demands. Thus, when President Nixon announced that the U.S. was "temporarily" suspending gold payments in return for dollars (thereby allowing the dollar to float in world markets), the action was little more than a case of

---

[4] With lower levels of inflation, there is also the possibility that real prices are increasing very little or not at all. This is because the consumer price index is unable to measure accurately all of the quality changes and, hence, may overstate the amount of price increases. There are other factors (such as the failure to take adequate account of discounting) that also give the index an upward bias. Although some factors give the measure a downward bias (such as accepting manufacturer's claims of quality improvements), the net bias of the index is probably to *overstate* the price rises. Also, some items, especially services and government, are very difficult to measure, thereby providing ample room for error in the indexes. For example, does the fact that more first class mail now travels by air offset the increase in postage rates? Such unanswerable questions put a margin of error in any price index no matter how carefully constructed.

Many economists believe that, on balance, the quality improvements not accounted for amount to 1 to 1½ percent per year and, therefore, an index moving upward by this amount would reflect stable prices. Whatever the margin of error, however, it becomes of small concern when prices are moving upward at 5 to 6 percent or more a year. Even with a degree of error this level represents a real and substantial decrease in purchasing power and is a proper area for concern.

policy catching up with reality. Indeed, it is undoubtedly true that it was the immediacy of the international situation, fostered in part by domestic inflation, that triggered the wage-price freeze in 1971. Because the worldwide inflation severely distorted the fixed exchange rate mechanism, this system was to be replaced in 1973 with a system of floating rates. Under this system, differential inflation rates are reflected (along with other aspects of a country's economic situation) by continually adjusting currencies in the form of "appreciation" and "depreciation," rather than through formal "revaluation" and "devaluation."

The Impact of Inflation

The redistribution effects of inflation are well known. Persons on fixed incomes (mainly, retired persons on pensions) are penalized, often to the point of poverty. Creditors lose while debtors are able to pay off in cheaper dollars. And, while it may be true that everyone is hurt by inflation, this is "more true" for some than for others. Although everyone may suffer from a *runaway* price level, some groups clearly suffer disproportionately at lower levels of inflation. In terms of who pays the bill, it is much the same as unemployment: At high levels the entire economy pays; at low levels, selected groups pay.

To a degree, the groups who feel the greatest impact are the same for inflation as with unemployment. There are, however, some important differences. Inflation hurts older persons more than younger ones while the opposite is true for unemployment. Also, within limits, the business community is more apt to become alarmed at the disruptive effects of price increases than with the more personalized problems of unemployment which, indeed, they may view as mitigating recruitment difficulties.

At the same time, the groups that are hurt the most by unemployment *or* inflation tend to be those groups that can least afford it. This is not really surprising. As one might expect, the well-to-do are able to protect themselves from the cold and brutal winds of the market place whether they be blowing in the direction of decreasing employment or increasing prices. Such protection options are not available to the poor.

Finally, as with the structure of unemployment, the impact of inflation is felt differently in different sectors of the economy. For instance, in 1970 when the total consumer price index increased 5.9 percent, the index for consumer commodities rose by 4.7 percent while the index for services jumped 8.1 percent. The five-year period from 1965 to 1970 illustrates this same trend: commodity prices increased by approximately 19 percentage points while the service index rose by over 29 points. On the other hand, the commodity based inflation of 1973–74 reversed this trend: The commodities component of the CPI increased by 7.4 percent in 1973 and 12.0 percent in 1974, while the services component increased by 4.4 and 9.3 percent. The services, however, are continuing to catch up as commodity prices are passed through the system.

Rapid inflation also produces severe disruptions in the signals provided by the market system. This was evident in late 1973 and 1974 as market signals—especially with respect to the level of profits—caused businesses to react in ways that exacerbated the recession. Thus, the distorting effects of rapid price increases help to sow the seeds of the recessions that invariably follow inflationary periods.

The uneven pace of rising prices in various sectors of the economy suggests, as does the uneven impact of unemployment, that aggregate measures that affect overall total level of demand are unable to achieve overall stability. Turning aggregate faucets on and off in an effort to fine-tune the economy has appeal from an overall viewpoint in that such exercises are most attractive than dealing with the grubby details of the economic machine itself. Unfortunately, however, it is impossible to tune the economy to peak efficiency without getting one's hands dirty. The structure of the U.S. economy is too complex to give uniform responses in all sectors to the same policies.

Types of Inflation

Just as there is no single cause of unemployment, there is no single cause of inflation. If, in either case, a single causal factor were responsible, the problem of choosing appropriate policy tools would not be nearly as vexing as it is. And, just as the conceptual differences in unemployment are easier to grasp than the identification of the different types, so it is with inflation. The purpose of this section is to briefly set out the major factors that are responsible for rising price levels. These causal types will be referred to in somewhat greater detail in the ensuing discussion since it is largely with respect to different types of inflation that different policies make sense. Here we only discuss the conceptual classifications. The formidable task of *identifying* the types when many causes may be contributing to the price rise will be addressed later.

Demand-Pull Inflation

In the classical view of economics, there was one and only one cause of inflation—demand pull. This is inflation caused by "too much money chasing too few goods" with the result being that prices are "pulled up." Consider the analogy of an auction where there is a set amount of goods to be sold. Suppose that everyone at the auction is determined to spend all of the money he has with him. Now, if some generous soul were to come along and give everyone an additional sum of money, say $5.00, which also had to be spent, the result would be an increase in the average price of the goods of exactly $5.00. Such is the situation the economy faces at full employment. By definition it is impossible (or nearly so) to increase output in the short run when operating at full capacity. If, at this point, spending suddenly increases, the only possible result is an increase in the average price level, i.e., inflation.

In 1968 the economy was approaching full employment. The unemployment rate had been below 4 percent for the preceding two years and was continuing to move downward. The consumer price index was already moving upward and showed signs of increasing momentum. In short, the economy was operating at near-capacity levels, and output could be increased only slightly in the short run. But the government in 1968 was attempting to finance an unpopular war without increasing taxes and, as a result, engaged in deficit spending to the tune of some 25 billion dollars. The result was a reallocation of resources into government stockpiles and, at the same time, a further upward pull on the price level. This was a classic case of demand-pull inflation and it set the stage for increased and price hikes in 1969, 1970, and 1971.

Cost-Push Inflation

Not all inflation can be so easily defined as the result of excessive demands as in the above case. In the middle to late 1950s, both the wholesale and consumer price indexes began to creep upward, while unemployment rates were well above 4 percent and capacity utilization rates were somewhat lower than they had been earlier in the decade. Thus, there did not appear to be any signs of excessive aggregate demand.

This presented a disturbing situation. According to traditional economic pedagogy, prices and wages should not begin moving upward until labor markets become tight and utilization rates become high. Yet, without either of these conditions, this is exactly what was happening in the late 1950s. The reason that such a situation could exist is that markets are not perfect and, therefore, do not react in the manner one would expect from perfect markets. Instead of everyone being a price taker as in the competitive model, some institutions were price settlers; that is, they possessed a degree of market power. Market power, a phenomenon that economic theory has never been able to deal with adequately, is a principal reason, along with structural mismatches, for the failure of the economy to behave in accord with competitive predictions.[5]

---

[5] Several innovative attempts have been made to introduce the concept of market power into the mainstream of the theory of the firm. The most successful of these include Chamberlain and Robinson's theory of monopolistic competition and imperfect competition, Sweezy's kinked demand

If a union possesses market power, it will be able to resist wage decreases and, indeed, insist upon increases during times of less than full employment. Similarly, the corporation with market power is able to maintain prices and, perhaps, push them still higher even without a general shortage of the goods in question. On the other hand, when prices decline for the individual farmer, it does him no good to restrict output by himself in an attempt to drive the price back up. As an individual he has no influence on the price. Instead, he may even produce *more* in an attempt to keep his income from falling along with prices. Such is not the case when demand slackens for a large producer of, say, steel. Here the reaction of the producer is to cut back production and hold prices up. Indeed, if demand for steel decreases *enough,* the reaction may be to *increase* prices in an effort to bolster sagging profits. (Chances are this action would be accompanied by the flexing of political power on the part of the industry in an attempt to persuade the government to put increased restrictions on the entry of foreign steel. Such imports have a strongly competitive effect—something many large producers in this country find to be exceedingly un-American.)

Cost-push inflation, then, is produced when large market powers—both union and corporate—are able to push costs (wages) and prices up *without* the existence of excess demand. It follows that the more market power the union or firm has, the greater will be the potential for this type of inflation. Also, if the degree of monopoly power possessed by unions and firms is *increasing,* it follows that cost-push inflation will be more prevalent—especially when coupled with the increased militancy that seems to pervade most institutions of society. Possible reasons for this apparent increase in market power are discussed in Chapter 6.

One of the reasons for the lack of agreement about the type of inflation present at any given time is the lack of a precise method of identifying the different types. As Professors Samuelson and Solow have demonstrated (92), it will not help to look at which went up first, prices or wages, in an attempt to see whether wages pushed up prices or prices

---

curve for oligopoly (which does not explain how prices are set, only why they don't move), and Baumol's sales maximization hypothesis. All are useful and realistic attempts to deal with observed market power. However, they still suffer from the theoretical deficiency that there is no reason the firm *has* to act in the prescribed manner if it chooses not to. In the perfectly competitive model the firm has no choice but to act in the predicted manner. This constitutes a decided advantage in terms of theoretical elegance. Marxism remains the most serious attempt to introduce power into capitalist economic theory but this has never been fashionable within American economic thought. And Thorstein Veblin, the most astute American thinker to introduce power concepts into economic thinking, suffered a fate of professional ostracism and indifference for his efforts.

pulled up wages. First, the base period chosen as the starting point is completely arbitrary and, as a result, everyone's actions can rightly be seen as catching up with everyone else's. No one is the leader in the perpetual chase. Also, suppose that the seller of the product has a degree of market power (that is, the power to set prices within limits) and that he sets his prices at a certain level above costs. Suppose also that the labor market is competitive and wages respond only to market forces. Into this situation inject an increase in demand for the firm's product. The first reaction of the firm is an attempt to increase output. To do this more labor must be hired and, as the industry seeks to expand, wages are bid up. As a result of this increase in costs, the firm now raises prices in order to maintain profits. As Samuelson and Solow point out, such a sequence *appears,* from the standpoint of timing, to be a case of cost-push inflation when, in fact, it has been pure demand pull. As so often is the case, appearances are deceiving and common sense turns out to be more common than sense.

Demand-Shift Inflation[6]

This common type of inflationary movement is a special variety of the cost-push species. It occurs because of market power on the part of the two principal economic actors, unions and business firms. In this case they do not necessarily have the power to push wages and prices up, but they still possess the power to keep them from moving down. As demand shifts from one sector of the economy to another—as it is always doing in a dynamic, growing society—prices and wages tend to rise in the new sectors in an effort to lure resources into these markets. According to the competitive model, such increases are offset by decreases in the prices and wages of the declining sector. This, however, is seldom the case, especially with respect to wages. As a result, the average level of wages and prices, instead of remaining constant, continually creeps upward. The result: a cost-push inflationary bias in the economy.

Implications of Cost Push

Essentially, cost-push inflation is the result of power forces operating within the marketplace and prohibiting the free movement of wages and prices as depicted in the competitive model. And, regardless of the internal consistency and elegance of the perfectly competitive model, such market power is a fact of life. As a result, policies implied by the

---

[6] This term was coined by Brookings Institution economist Charles L. Schultze.

competitive model are inadequate to deal with this type of inflation. Thus, policymakers may be forced by unpleasant realities to move beyond the mechanical manipulation of aggregate demand and into the messy field of direct market intervention. The fact that such intervention is unpleasant does not imply that it is unnecessary. However, a fuller discussion of these implications must await a consideration of the structural changes taking place in the economy. After considering the theoretical nature and concomitant policy implications of unemployment in somewhat greater detail, we will be in a position to combine unemployment and inflation and consider their combined policy implications.

There should be no doubt about the seriousness of either unemployment or inflation as national problems requiring top priority. Although they are somewhat different with respect to the incidence of their effects, both evils hit particularly hard at those groups least able to defend themselves. Resulting from imperfections in the market mechanism, both of these social diseases bring hardship and suffering on their victims as well as insecurity, apprehension, and instability on the entire populace. Their simultaneous reduction is, and should be, a subject of immediate and serious public concern. The rest of this book deals with the advances economists have made toward this goal, as well as the many formidable problem areas remaining. The fact that there is currently no solution to the dilemma of inflation and unemployment should not be taken to imply that serious advances are not possible. Instead, this should be taken as an indication that in this area of public policy, like so many others, total solutions are Utopian dreams. Perhaps the best we can hope for is a movement in the right direction—and this alone has proven to be no easy feat.

APPENDIX 3–1. UNEMPLOYMENT, POVERTY, AND WELFARE

The relationship between unemployment, poverty, and welfare is so important, and so often misunderstood, that it requires a separate, albeit brief, discussion. It is frequently asserted that people should work rather than accept welfare. "Workfare instead of welfare." At the same time, others insist that most welfare recipients are unable to work for one reason or another. What is the truth?

Briefly put, the *poverty* problem is overwhelmingly one of unemployment and low pay (along with the concomitant labor market inefficiencies produced by the lack of jobs), while much of the *welfare* problem lies beyond market cures. The misconception arises by confusing the *welfare population* with the *poverty population* when actually the latter is much larger than the former. This can be seen by comparing the

UNEMPLOYMENT AND INFLATION: AN OVERVIEW

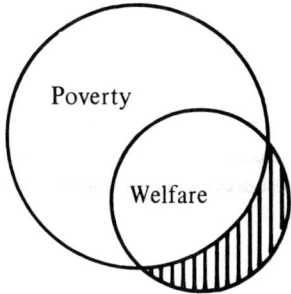

Figure 3–1.

relevant areas in Figure 3–1. Welfare is represented as a subset of poverty, thereby indicating that a relatively small portion (estimated at ¼ to ⅓) of the poverty population actually receives welfare assistance.

Since the welfare and poverty populations consist, to a degree, of different persons, it is reasonable to expect that different characteristics would apply to the two groups and, indeed such is the case. Most of the persons currently receiving welfare are unable to work because they are too young, too old, disabled, or sick. This is not true of the poverty population, however, and, as a result, this group is quite responsive to labor market improvements. This is a fact of great importance concerning the role of an improved employment situation as a means of alleviating poverty.

Note that the welfare subset is depicted as falling outside of the poverty population to the extent of the shaded area in Figure 3–1. This area represents the persons receiving welfare who are not, in fact, living in poverty. While no one can be sure of the exact extent of this "cheating," it is known to be quite small in relation to the number of legitimate welfare recipients. Unfortunately, the existence of even this small group has done much to incite reactionary demands from the general population to "do something" about the welfare situation. Reducing this area would do much to gain acceptance by the public for improvements in the welfare system.

In 1968 the Department of Labor conducted a special study of the relationship between unemployment and poverty (91). It found that an entire third of the men who headed families living in poverty had worked fulltime (over 35 hours per week) during the year. The problem of inadequate wage rates is all too apparent in such cases. Another one-third of these men worked part-time during the year and the remaining one-third did no work. Thus, a full two-thirds of the male heads of poverty families were *directly* connected with the labor force and would have seen their economic situation improved had the employment (and wage) situation improved.

But even this understates the case. Of the one-third who did *not* work during the year, many were *unemployed*. This means that they had an attachment to the labor force since, to be included in the unemployment statistics, one must be actively seeking a job. Furthermore, the unemployment rates are invariably higher in poverty areas than in other parts of the economy indicating that a significant portion of the nonworkers were looking for jobs.

The connection between unemployment and poverty appears even stronger when one considers the behavior of the "labor force participation rates" in relation to the unemployment rates. These rates reflect the extent to which the population, or some subgroup thereof, is "participating" in the labor force, either by working or looking for a job. That is, the *participation rate* for any group of persons consists of the percentage of the group which is either working (employed) or seeking work (unemployed). An important question, then, becomes the extent to which the participation rate in itself is related to the unemployment rate.

Two hypotheses have been put forward: that of the "discouraged worker" and the "additional worker." The "discouraged worker hypothesis" states that as the unemployment rate of a given group of persons increases, the labor force participation rate of that group will *decrease* as members of the group become discouraged in their search for employment and stop looking, i.e., drop out of the labor force. The "additional worker hypothesis" states that as one member of the family (say the man) loses his job as the unemployment rate increases, other members of the family (say his wife) will begin looking for work in an effort to supplement family income. In this case, the labor force participation rate has *increased* along with (and because of) the increasing unemployment rates.

Which view is correct? In fact, they both are. The relevant question is which effect outweighs the other and what is the *net* result of the participation rate movement? Several studies have been undertaken in an attempt to determine this and, although there are differences with respect to the size of the effect, the overwhelming evidence is that, on balance, the *discouraged* worker effect is the stronger of the two.

This is a matter of importance. Among those persons in poverty who are not working, many become discouraged because of high unemployment rates and therefore drop out of the labor force. As a result of this, the unemployment rate understates the percentage of these persons who would in fact be amenable to improvements in the employment picture and would, should this picture improve, take jobs. Thus, if we add to the number of unemployed persons those who are not counted as unemployed since they have severed their connection with the labor force, the proportion of the one-third of the male family heads who could work, referred to above, is even greater.[7]

Concerning the question of poverty, the Labor Department has estimated that if the labor force participation rates in the poverty sections of the nation's urban areas (53.7 percent) were the same as the rest of the nation, there would have been an additional 350,000 workers in the labor force in 1968. More recently, the Bureau of Labor Statistics estimated that, in 1971, the *total* number of "discouraged workers" (poverty as well as nonpoverty groups) was approximately 700,000.

Since the level of joblessness of the most disadvantaged workers is consistently understated, serious implications arise concerning efforts to mitigate poverty. Even more than the unemployment figures indicate, the miseries of poverty can be alleviated through increased employment. Thus, when speaking of the *poverty* population as opposed to the *welfare* population, work and welfare *are* substitutes. The unmistakable implication of this is that if the nation is serious in its desire to reduce poverty, the most advantageous route lies through increased job opportunities and improved labor markets. Attempting to eliminate poverty through transfer payments alone would be extremely inefficient as well as futile. (It would also be inflationary to the extent that such payments result eventually in increased expenditures without increased output; whereas employment of the same persons increases total output of the economy thereby mitigating price level pressures.)

With burgeoning welfare costs placing increasing burdens on state and local governments, there is increasing pressure for the federal government to assume the costs of welfare. Many proposals in this area are variants of a "negative income tax" plan. Although this idea has been relatively dormant for the past few years, its inclusion on a very limited scale in the 1975 tax reduction may revive interest in the concept. The enactment of a form of a negative income tax plan would make the only criterion for welfare eligibility the lack of income (coupled, in some proposals, with the acceptance of available work). The effect of this would be to enlarge the welfare area of Figure 3–1 until it coincided with

---

[7] The discouraged worker effect is important from another aspect. Since people drop out of the labor market when the unemployment rate increases, it follows that those groups experiencing the highest rates of unemployment have the largest number of "drop outs." Thus, as one moves from the low unemployment groups to the high unemployment groups, the figures become increasingly inaccurate, and the error is on the side of *understating* actual unemployment. In other words, the difference in the unemployment experience of different subgroups within the population is even greater than the figures indicate. This should be kept in mind when considering the unemployment rates for different sectors of the population.

the poverty area. That is, everyone living in poverty would "automatically" be eligible for public assistance. This would make employment (or the reduction of unemployment) *even more* important for the success of the welfare program since without large reductions in joblessness the costs of public assistance would soon become prohibitive. In addition, high unemployment severely restricts tax revenues (a fact that accounts for much of the current financial plight of Federal and state governments), thereby decreasing the means with which to pay for these increased costs.

The effect of a decreased unemployment rate on poverty can be seen by looking at the results of poverty reduction during the 1960s. In 1959 the unemployment rate stood at 5.5 percent (having just moved down from 6.8 percent in 1958). At the same time, approximately 35.5 million family members (22.4 percent of all family members) were living in poverty. In 1969 the average unemployment rate was 3.5 percent and the number of family members living below the poverty line had been reduced to 24.3 million (12.2 percent). Thus there was a reduction of some 38 percent in the number of family members living in poverty during the 1960s.

To be sure, not all of this can be attributed to the decrease in unemployment during the decade. There was a significant upgrading in the welfare and manpower programs as the Great Society program was initiated. Also, the *relative* level of the poverty line decreased. Most of the decrease in poverty during the 1960s, however, was not due to massive transfer programs. Instead, the prosperity of the 1960s (the longest continuous upswing in history) with its concomitant growth in output and employment was largely responsible. The evils associated with unemployment were reversed as a marked increase in the efficiency of the labor markets became apparent. This was strongly felt in the decrease in poverty throughout the decade.

This consideration, however, again brings us back to the central point: as the unemployment rate is lowered, inflationary pressures increase and the cost of further reductions becomes prohibitive from this standpoint. This pressure began to become evident in the consumer price index in the late 1960s and continued to make itself felt with increasing severity throughout the remainder of the decade and well into the 1970s.

Given the seriousness of the unemployment problem along with its many implications, methods aimed at a reduction in this inflationary threshold deserve careful consideration. Direct controls on prices and wages are one of the possible methods of achieving this.

A CLOSER LOOK AT UNEMPLOYMENT: THEORIES AND REMEDIES

4

> I have known people to stop and buy an apple on the corner and then walk away as if they had solved the whole unemployment problem.
>
> Heywood Broun

Before discussing the efficacy of market controls as a means of reducing the trade-off between unemployment and inflation, it is first necessary to further examine the nature of the two major causes of unemployment: deficient aggregate demand and structural imbalances. These two causes, as well as the controversy surrounding them, hold important implications concerning the appropriateness of different stabilization policies.

AGGREGATE DEMAND, EMPLOYMENT, AND UNEMPLOYMENT

Deficient demand unemployment, or cyclical unemployment, is caused by swings in the business cycle that operate in ways that prevent the economy from growing at a steady rate. As the experience of the 1970s demonstrates, these cyclical swings can still be severe and, as a result, are extremely important.

The record levels of inflation and unemployment reached in the first half of the 1970s severely undercut the success of macroeconomic policies in smoothing out the business cycle. Most economists would still agree, however, that the level of sophistication in this area is now to the point where extremely wide patterns of cyclical behavior can be avoided;

a good deal of the economic woes of the past few years are the result of political decisions that overrode economic considerations.

There is little doubt that macro-economic tools of monetary and fiscal policies can be powerful agents of economic stabilization. Such policies, however, and the theoretical constructs upon which they are based, did not develop in the absence of real problems. They are the outgrowth of attempts to explain ten years of serious depression in the face of a prevailing economic doctrine that held that prolonged unemployment was impossible.

As in the 1970s, economic realities in the 1930s were failing to conform to the accepted theories. And, since in both instances the realities displayed precious few signs of altering their course to fit the prevailing theory, policymakers were forced to look for new theories to fit the reality.

To put the abrupt policy turnabouts of the 1970s into perspective, it is instructive to first look at the Keynesian Revolution of the 1930s. It is largely from this revolution that our aggregate economic policies are still forged and, as a result, we are still prone to think in terms of the problems of the 1930s when facing the problems of the 1970s.

It is not that present problems are so different as to make Keynesian policy irrelevant. Quite the contrary. Keynesian doctrine is still highly regarded and much of our present dilemma stems from failing to carry this doctrine to its logical conclusion. Being born of the experience of the 1930s, Keynesian theory was principally concerned with alleviating unemployment. The inflationary side of the coin was not the problem. Today, when attempting to alleviate unemployment by the same mechanism—increasing aggregate demand—we are confronted with the barrier of intolerable inflation.

Controls, in large part, are a response to this. While Keynesian policy constructs a floor under which the economy is not allowed to fall, there are inadequate provisions for a lid to prevent inflationary upward movements.

Furthermore, the Keynesian Revolution was extremely important in convincing policymakers (as well as economists) that the economy was not automatic and did not necessarily and inexorably move toward a full employment equilibrium. This being the case, the economy, it was reasoned, would require deliberate intervention by the government in order to bring about full employment. Policy considerations, of course, become much more complex and trying when the burden of achieving an "acceptable" unemployment level is placed upon mortal men instead of upon an automatic, free-market mechanism which tends toward this level without outside intervention. This form of "existentialism in the marketplace" was not an easy faith to live with in the 1930s any more than it is in the 1970s. As a result, the lesson must again be learned as economists struggle with imperfect, pragmatic stabilization tools instead of relying only upon impersonal market forces (even if directed by discretionary monetary and fiscal policy) to maintain stable price levels.

CLASSICAL VERSUS KEYNESIAN ECONOMICS

The market mechanism provides for an optimum allocation of resources under conditions of perfect competition. At the same time, this system ensures that the economy would, if left alone, work toward full employment of all resources—including labor. Should anything upset these delicate equilibrium conditions, forces automatically come into play that right the situation. Briefly, the classical system of full employment works along the following lines:

Purchasing Power

First, "Say's Law" guarantees that there is no general lack of aggregate demand. Supply creates its own demand and, as a result, there can be no interruption in the circular flow of commodities moving in one direction and labor services in the other. Total spending equals total production, and there is no general lack of purchasing power. Should production (supply) increase, demand automatically increases by a like amount since this new supply, by itself, represents new purchasing power for those who own it.

Should there ever be a *temporary* decline in demand due to someone's miscalculation and a consequent production of goods that society does not want, a back-up mechanism comes into play that ensures, even in this situation, that unemployment will not result. This mechanism consists of flexible wages and prices. If too much of a commodity is produced (the market is misjudged), the result will be a decline in price until the market is cleared. Since the physical volume of production (sales) does not decrease, there is the same number of employees needed to produce it but, of course, the wage rate falls. As this happens, then, both capital and labor seek more profitable markets and, by so doing, resources are reallocated into areas more to the consumer's liking. And all without any unemployment.

Saving and Investment

Consumers, however, do not spend all of their income; they save a part of it. Other things being equal, this means a "leak" in the expenditure stream and a consequent decline in aggregate demand to a point representing less than full employment. Other things, however, seldom remain equal and such was the case within the classical system. Just as consumers do not wish to spend all of their income on the products produced by businessmen, neither do businessmen desire to use all of their productive resources for satisfying consumer demand. Instead, a certain proportion of output is siphoned off for investment purposes; that is, the production of capital goods for use in creating future output. Now, so long as the leakage in the expenditure stream (saving) just equals that in the production stream (investment), aggregate demand remains equal to aggregate supply and there is no unemployment due to a deficiency in demand. Somehow, then, saving must equal investment.[1]

The mechanism to ensure that savings equal investment is the interest rate. The classical school viewed both investment and saving as a function of the interest rate, with the former inversely related to it and the latter directly related.

Why they reasoned, would anyone agree to forego present consumption for future consumption? Since present pleasures are preferred by most persons to future pleasures, an individual would have to be paid if he is to refrain from current consumption. Such payment is in the form of an interest rate and, indeed, forms the primary explanation for the existence of interest. As with any supply function, the more that is paid (the higher the interest rate), the more will be supplied. Therefore, the amount of saving was seen as varying directly with the rate of interest.

Interest, on the other hand, represents a cost to the firm that wishes to invest. Thus, in deciding how much to invest, the rational businessman will calculate the probable return of a projected investment (including a risk factor) and compare this with the cost of the funds. (This will be an "opportunity cost" if he uses his own funds, but still a cost.) Since some investment opportunities naturally possess a higher probable return than others, the wise businessman can be expected to undertake the most profitable ones first. The amount of new investment opportunities undertaken, under these circumstances, depends on the interest rate. As the interest rate is lowered, more investment opportunities become profitable. Hence, more are undertaken. Thus, the demand for money slopes downward to the east with larger amounts being desired with lower interest rates.

With both savings and investment seen as functionally related to the rate of interest, they can be plotted on the same graph and intersect at an equilibrium level—the same as any supply and demand schedule. Now, if there is any exogenous change in one of the parameters (a shift

---

[1] In modern analysis of national income accounts, these amounts equal each other by definition since involuntary accumulation is considered investment. Such was not the case in the classical system, however, where they would equal each other because of market forces.

in the saving or investment schedule), the market will automatically bring about a new equilibrium level. For example, suppose that a new invention occurs and several business firms wish to invest in it. This would shift the demand curve outward, thereby representing the fact that, at any given rate of interest, more money may be desired. At the old interest rate, however, businessmen are unable to attract the desired amounts of capital, and they begin to bid the rates upward as they compete for the scarce funds. This induces consumers to save more and, finally, a new equilibrium level is reached with higher interest rates and more saving and investment. Of course, the reverse would happen should the demand for money fall, and similar analyses can be made for autonomous changes in the desires of consumers to save. In any case, the result is an equilibrium situation in the money markets where saving equals investment. And, at this point, there are equal "leakages" in the expenditure and production streams, no lack of aggregate demand, and no unemployment. All, again, without any interference from a meddling and clumsy government.

Into this highly simplified economic model we can now introduce the role of government with respect to its taxing and spending decisions. Consumers not only have their expenditures cut by saving, but also through taxes. At the same time, the government uses this money to purchase goods and services from the business sector, that is, it reallocates resources. As long as the funds the government takes from the one stream (taxes) equals the amount it takes from the other stream (production), aggregate supply and demand remain equal. This, of course, implies that the government must operate with a balanced budget and this, in turn, became a hallmark of the classical school.

Unemployment

Finally, should any part of this mechanism fail to operate properly (a short-run possibility), the flexible wage-price mechanism ensures that there is no increase in unemployment—at least "involuntary" unemployment. If the demand for labor drops in a given sector, wages and employment both drop (an upward sloping supply curve for labor) but again come into equilibrium where supply intersects demand. At this point, everyone who desired employment at the going wage is employed; hence, there is no unemployment. (The number of persons working would be less in this situation, but only because some do not accept employment at the going wage rate, that is, their portion of the supply curve lies above this rate. The fact that they are no longer employed, then, is their "choice" rather than an indication of a flaw in the economic mechanism.) Such, in a highly simplified form, is the classical macro-economic model of full employment equilibrium. Concluding, as it did, that no serious unemployment can develop, it conveniently rationalized the belief that the economic machine automatically operated at full throttle and, therefore, at full employment.

The Keynesian Response[2]

Keynes attacked this theoretical structure principally on two grounds: First, he disputed the contention that the interest rate mechanism brings about an equilibrium between savings and investment. Second, he argued that wages and prices are not flexible, especially in a downward direction, and, more importantly, that *even if they were* they do not ensure sufficient aggregate demand.

With respect to the savings decisions of individuals, it is not clear even on *a priori* logical grounds that increased interest rates call forth increased savings. Some people save with a definite purpose in mind, such as college for the kids, a new house, or retirement. To the extent that this is true, and the goal of saving is to acquire a fixed sum of money at some future point in time, the amount of saving is *inversely* related to the interest rate. As the interest rate goes up, it becomes necessary to save less to reach a given goal. Thus, on strictly logical grounds, it cannot be asserted with a high degree of certainty that higher interest rates call forth increased saving.

More importantly, Keynes argued that saving is simply what is left over after consumption and, therefore, only indirectly related to the interest rate. If consumption, as he argued, is a function of income, then saving must also be a function of income and related to the interest rate only directly through the influence of the interest rate on total (aggregate) income. (It may be true, as the heavy advertising that is done by banks would indicate, that the rate of interest strongly influences *where* saving is done. This, however, is quite different than asserting that the interest rate determines *how much* saving is done by the individual.)

What about investment? Other things being equal, Keynes and his followers did believe that the rate of interest determines through the marginal efficiency of capital, the amount of investment undertaken. Again, however, the *a priori* assumption in this respect is very questionable. In particular, Keynes believed the *expectations* of businessmen to be extremely important in determining how much they are willing to invest at any given rate of interest. As expectations of the future business

---

[2] The homogeneity of economic thought was never so complete as implied when speaking of the classical school or the Keynesian School. There were—and are—wide ranges of thought within each as well as many economists who would subscribe to neither school. For the purpose of presenting a general summary, however, it will suffice to paint the picture with a wide brush.

A CLOSER LOOK AT UNEMPLOYMENT: THEORIES AND REMEDIES 67

climate improves, new investments are undertaken. On the other hand, if businessmen view the future outlook as dim, investment will not be forthcoming *regardless* of the rate of interest. Indeed, argued Keynes, with extremely low rates of plant utilization, such as existed during the depths of the depression, investment may not be fostered even at a zero rate of interest. It would make little sense for a firm to build a new plant in order to expand output when it is operating the old one at, say, 50 percent of capacity. To induce further investment at this point would require the existence of *negative* interest rates—a logical absurdity.

Furthermore, the expectations of businessmen are subject to wide and frequent fluctuations. As a result, investment expenditures fluctuate widely and, since investment is one element of aggregate expenditures (along with consumer and government spending), aggregate demand tends to fluctuate also. The final result of this is instability in the level of employment. The clear policy prescription in this situation is for the government to vary its expenditures to offset the swings in investment. Such "discretionary fiscal policy" is aimed at smoothing out the cyclical behavior of investment spending and, therefore, to mitigate its disruptive influence on aggregate demand (assuming, of course, that consumer spending remains relatively constant).

The classical answer to the above fluctuations in aggregate demand, should they occur in the short run, was that these movements still do not bring about unemployment. The reason: if demand falls temporarily, the wage rate also falls, thus bringing the economy back to a new equilibrium level of full employment. If wages did not fall, however, there would be unemployment. The policy prescription in this case is also clear: strike down the market power of those institutions (mainly, trade unions) that prevent wages from falling. In this view, the unions—and the government through minimum wage laws—are responsible for the resulting unemployment when demand falls.

The Fallacy of Composition

The observation that wages tend to be "sticky" downward was not new with Keynes, and there was little argument with his restatement of a familiar occurrence. What was new, however, was his contention that *even if* wage rates move downward with a drop in aggregate demand, this does little to help the employment situation. The basic mistake was in falling into the old fallacy of composition: what is true of the parts is true of the whole. The classical school had attempted to observe behavior in one market (or for one firm or industry) and then to generalize from this in order to explain the behavior of the entire economy.

Many times this does not work. With respect to one firm or industry, it may be assumed (correctly) that the wage rate of the persons working in that firm has little effect on the demand for the firm's product since the employees make up only a small portion of the company's customers. Thus, if Bethlehem Steel Corporation lowers its wages, this has a negligible effect on the demand for, and price of, steel.

Such reasoning, however, is *not* true when applied to the entire economy. And herein lies the fallacy of composition. When the average of all wages is reduced, one cannot assume that aggregate demand remains constant, since the total of all wages and salaries amounts to some 70 percent of total expenditures. Therefore, if the average wage level moves downward, this decreases total spending, and there is a further decline in the aggregate demand curve in the product market. As this demand curve shifts to the left, it again implies a further decrease in employment. But further decreases in employment still fail to bring about an equilibrium situation because of the continued interaction this has on the aggregate demand for goods and services.

Even if one makes the heroic assumption of flexible wages and prices, then, there are no assurances that lowering the wage rates will bring about a stabilization. And, when body shops in Detroit were paying men 10¢ an hour and sweatshops in Connecticut paid girls between 60¢ and $1.10 for a 55-hour *week,* as was the case during the Great Depression, even a classical economics enthusiast might legitimately wonder just how low wages would have to go before reaching the bottom.

The Role of Government

If the economy does not automatically operate at, or necessarily work toward, a full employment level of output, the government has the responsibility of taking corrective measures. This was the principal policy lesson to be learned from the Great Depression. Living in a world where man has the ultimate responsibility for his economic lot may not be nearly as comfortable as believing in natural laws or invisible hands. Unfortunately, there seems to be no alternative.

A further lesson of the 1930s is that not all meddling in the marketplace by human hands (that is, the government) is necessarily bad. Indeed, there is a very legitimate role for this intervention when the market is not performing its historic role of turning the pursuit of individual gain into public benefit. The market failed in this respect in the 1930s, and again and again in the 1960s and 1970s. And, if the suggested remedies are not the same, no one should be surprised. Few things have remained constant during the intervening forty years.

What tools, then, may the government use to implement the Keynesian doctrines? Basically, there are two: monetary policy and fiscal policy. Fiscal policy—government taxing and spending actions—was seen by Keynes as the more powerful of the two and, indeed, the only one

A CLOSER LOOK AT UNEMPLOYMENT: THEORIES AND REMEDIES

likely to succeed in a serious depression such as that of the thirties. Although the New Deal attempted to implement such programs, the real vindication of Keynesian theory came with the massive spending of World War II. Then, exactly as Keynes had predicted, the economy surged and unemployment plunged to record lows.

Monetary policy could, it was thought, be counted on to provide a lesser but more finely controlled stimulus. This tool consists of efforts on the part of the Federal Reserve System (FED) to control the supply of money and, thus indirectly, the level of interest rates. The Federal Reserve is able to move these policy levers on a very short-run basis (daily, if necessary), and monetary policy is thus able to react to emerging conditions much faster than fiscal policy.[3]

This reference to monetary policy provides the one instance where Keynes viewed an aggregate wage decrease as possibly leading to increased employment—a process known now as the "Keynes effect" of falling wages. If the supply of money is held constant while all wages and prices are lowered, the amount of money that consumers wish to hold, their "liquidity preference," decreases. This is true since, on average, the population tends to hold a relatively constant fraction of their income in the form of cash. As prices go down, however, the real worth of the money they hold increases so there is a tendency to hold less. Then, as this excess money finds its way into the bond market, it drives the price of bonds upward and, as a consequence, the interest rate downward. The effect, then, is to increase the money supply thereby making investment funds more available to businessmen. This, however, is a very roundabout method of forcing interest rates down and, given the multitude of social and institutional problems associated with lowering wages, it is a very impractical method. Indeed, remarked Keynes, given the difficulties attendant to lowering the general wage level and the result it could be expected to have, only a "foolish person" would "prefer a flexible wage policy to a flexible money policy" (49, p. 268).

Monetary and fiscal policies remain the most powerful weapons available to the government in attempting to carry out the mandate of the 1946 Employment Act. And there is no doubt that they are still extremely useful tools. The tax cut of 1964, which represented the first all-out attempt to adopt Keynesian policy, was a success by almost all standards. Implemented at a time when unemployment was high and tax revenues already low, it stimulated the economy to such an extent that the tax intake as well as employment increased. Later in the decade,

---

[3] The current "monetary school" of economic thought holds that monetary policy is far more powerful—and, hence, more important—than fiscal policy. This is discussed in Chapter 6. Suffice it to say for now that this was not Keynes' view nor is it the view of modern-day Keynesians.

the Viet Nam War buildup again proved the powers of aggregate demand stimulation as a means of reducing unemployment. Unfortunately, there were serious side effects to this method of financing the war, and they took the form of a dangerously high and tenacious inflation.

When Richard Nixon took office and vowed to end this inflationary spiral, the power of the monetary brakes was amply demonstrated. Interest rates rose to record levels in 1970, and the economy went into a planned recession with output falling and unemployment climbing. The tight money policies of 1974 again demonstrated their contractionary ability; the power of monetary policy to pull down an overheated economy cannot be doubted.

The reaction of the price level to these restrictive policies, however, has been puzzling, if not downright appalling. Prices displayed little sign of slowing their rate of increases—let alone leveling out—in 1971. In 1974 and 1975, price mitigation became evident only after extremely high unemployment levels had been reached in response to steep plunges in industrial production. And still the rate of inflation remained high by historical standards. The macro-economic tools of monetary and fiscal policy, as the experience of the 1960s illustrated, had ample power to stimulate the economy and hurl it into an upward trajectory. The application of monetary restraints could also be counted on to turn the economy downward in terms of output and employment, as shown in 1971 and again in 1974–1975. Unfortunately, this prescription did not have a similar effect on wages and prices, both of which reacted extremely slowly to increasing unemployment. Something more than aggregate tools was needed.

In a sense, Keynesian policy has put a floor under the economy. However, propping up wages and prices is naturally easier than forcing them down: large institutions—unions and corporations—are much more prone to accept stimulation than downward pressures. Also, the very success of Keynesian policy has exerted an upward influence on prices and wages. Without the fear of massive and prolonged unemployment as a result of upward pushes on prices and wages, corporations and unions are less inclined to consider the employment effects of wage and price decisions. The possibility of increased union and corporate market power is discussed in more depth in Chapter 6.

THE STRUCTURAL THESIS

The essence of the structural hypothesis concerning unemployment is that various changes are taking place within the economy that are making it increasingly difficult to match the available labor force with the available jobs. That is, structural changes are occurring that are making it more difficult for labor markets to bring supply and demand together. As a result, it is argued, the average rate of unemployment continues to move upward.

An implication of this is that efforts to bring the unemployment level down through aggregate methods (monetary and/or fiscal policy) are frustrated by inflationary pressures developing at successively higher unemployment levels.

The structural thesis first gained credence in the late 1950s and early 1960s when it was observed that after each cyclical swing in the economy, the unemployment rate would bottom out at a higher level than during the earlier recoveries. For three years from 1951 to 1953, unemployment hovered around the 3 percent level reaching a low of 2.6 percent in December of 1952. It then shot up to 6.1 percent in the Fall of 1954 giving the year an average rate of 5.5 percent. With the boom of 1955 the rate again dropped but this time only to a low of 4.1 percent. By 1957 the rate was again climbing and eventually reached a high point for the decade of 7.5 percent in July, 1958. After falling to the 5 percent neighborhood in 1959, it rose once more during the 1960 recession reaching the 7 percent mark in 1961. It wasn't until 1966 that the unemployment rate again dipped below 4 percent, almost ten years since this rate had last been seen. And, even more alarming, after holding steady for the preceding seven years, the wholesale price index then began moving steadily upward.

The Debate

A hotly contested debate of the 1960s revolved around the question of what was keeping the economy from reaching a 4-percent level of unemployment (set as an "interim goal" by the Council of Economic Advisors). Was this a lack of aggregate demand, thus calling for monetary and fiscal stimulation? Or was it an increase in structural adjustment difficulties that seemingly made this goal unattainable? The argument is by no means settled. But, at the risk of taking the always unpopular middle ground, the evidence seems to indicate that both factors were (and are) important. Certainly the 1964 tax cut followed by the Viet Nam buildup in the middle to late 1960s once again demonstrated the ability of aggregate demand stimulation to pull down the unemployment rates. The fact that this was accomplished only at the expense of an intolerable rate of price increases, however, indicates that aggregate demand, by itself, is an insufficient public policy and keeps the structural thesis relevant. The question of how much structural unemployment is present and whether it is increasing is far from settled, but there is little doubt that structural problems do play a significant role in blocking the attainment of lower unemployment levels.

As noted in Chapter 3, there are large discrepancies among the unemployment rates for different sectors and groups. The structural argument is that the changes taking place in the economy are making this situation worse. A number of forces are seen to be operating in this direction, resulting in a higher average unemployment level than in earlier periods which, presumably, were characterized by fewer structural problems.

A primary consideration is the pace of technological advancement. While it is true that technological changes are always occurring and that, as a result, the labor force must always adjust to new demands, the pace of change is much faster today than, say, fifty years ago. And this creates problems. If change is slow, the labor force is able to adjust with a minimum of unemployment. Indeed, if the changes are slow enough, the necessary decreases in employment in the declining sectors can be met solely through attrition with new entrants to the labor force moving into the growing sectors.

As the pace of change increases, however, this is no longer possible, and persons must be laid off in the declining sectors. If they are then unable to obtain employment in the new sectors, they will be unemployed. The problem in this case is not a lack of aggregate demand but the fact that the unemployed persons do not fit the requirements of the new jobs. The essence of the argument is that the demand for labor is shifting faster than the supply, bringing about unemployment. And the faster the demand shifts, the greater the resulting unemployment.

If the new jobs that develop as the economy shifts had the same characteristics as the ones that are being replaced, there would be no problem. Unfortunately, this is not the case. Besides the fact that the declining and growing sectors of the economy may be widely separated geographically, the new positions usually require more skills. The *absolute* number of unskilled jobs in the economy has been declining, which implies, with a growing labor force, that the *relative* number of unskilled openings has been decreasing even more. The fastest growing sectors of the economy are among the professional, technical, and clerical fields where the necessary skill or education level is higher than that of unskilled workers. Where a high school diploma used to be sufficient for a wide range of openings, it is now often a minimum requirement. The net effect of this is to raise the average educational level of the labor force and, as a result, to place the unskilled person even farther down on the occupational ladder than before.

At the same time, the number of young persons entering the labor force with little education and no experience has been increasing. As a result, the supply of labor is growing in precisely those areas where demand is expanding the least or even diminishing. The cumulative effect of these forces has been dubbed the labor market "twist" by one of the leading "structuralists," Charles Killingsworth (50, 51).

The unfortunate result of this twist is that those members of society, namely the unskilled and uneducated, who are least able to afford it, are the ones hurt most. Since minority groups have fewer skills and less education than the white majority, the effect on these groups is particularly pronounced.

While many observers agree that some structural deterioration has taken place and thereby worsened the trade-off between unemployment and inflation, there is still considerable disagreement as to the extent of this process. Indeed, there is some evidence (115) that the twist in the labor market has slowed since the late 1960s and, in some instances, has even reversed itself. This viewpoint coincides with that of many economists who considered the argument to be settled in favor of the anti-structuralists when, in 1966, the unemployment rate dropped below the 4 percent (so-called) interim goal.

Other evidence, however, conflicts with this rather sanguine viewpoint. During the fall and early winter of 1971, the unemployment rates for blacks increased much faster than those for whites and the historical difference of 100 percent was again reached. It is too early to tell whether this represents only a temporary setback or a continuation of earlier trends. The 1974 experience is also inconclusive with black rates hovering near double those of whites during the year.

The 1960s Revisited

Killingsworth has made a strong argument that the decrease in unemployment in the late 1960s was not by any means entirely the result of rapid increases in aggregate demand, and, that by assuming it was, the present high levels of unemployment are not understood. Furthermore, if aggregate demand is not responsible for the earlier decrease in unemployment, then heavy spending cannot be counted on to solve the present problem (50).

There were many structural changes taking place during the 1960s that were in part responsible for the drop in unemployment. These changes, however, were of a temporary nature. First, the increase in demand was largely felt in the manufacturing sector of the economy in response to the war buildup. This meant that the historic shift away from manufacturing (which produces many unskilled jobs) was reversed, and we had a temporary (and artificial) return to a more unskilled job structure. This trend was reversed when the economy later shifted to peacetime conditions. The reversal is now having dramatic effects in the cities, where manufacturing is the basic economic mainstay. Unemployment in these areas is far above the national average.

Second, the war buildup also had the effect of taking out of the labor force a disproportionate number of persons who would have experienced high unemployment rates had they remained in the job market: that is, the young and unskilled who made up a high proportion of those persons entering military service. At the same time, college enrollments sharply increased partly, one suspects, because of the deferments offered to students. These forces, then, were quite apart from the concomitant increases in aggregate demand and, to ascribe all of the decrease in unemployment to this latter factor, would therefore be misleading.

Finally, the manpower programs developed to deal with structural problems played no small part in decreasing the reported unemployment late in the 1960s. Although there is considerable debate concerning the extent of the success displayed by these programs, there is no doubt that the net effect of the various efforts was positive and large. These programs, which provided institutional and on-the-job training for new workers and retraining for displaced workers, contributed to the lowering unemployment rates in a manner again quite separate from the increased federal spending. As an example of the magnitude of these manpower programs, the number of first-class enrollments in programs administered by the Department of Labor increased from 34,000 in 1963 to 1,051,400 in 1970 (118, p. 299). Although not all of these persons would have been unemployed, of course, many of them would have been since they are largely drawn from sectors to the labor force where unemployment rates are traditionally high.[4]

Definitional Changes

Coupled with the real advantages of the manpower programs, there was also a change in the definition of unemployment in 1965 which had the effect of decreasing the visibility of the problem. This was the decision to exclude those persons who were enrolled in job training programs from the unemployment rolls since, it was argued, they are not actually looking for work during the training period. There is no real quarrel with this change, because it can be properly defended as an improvement in the measuring method. It should be recognized, however, that since 1965 we have been using a different measuring stick and that comparisons over time are not, as a result, highly accurate. Also, the larger the manpower programs have become, the more error there is in these time-series comparisons. Another change in the definition of unemployment was made in 1967 when the requirement was added that persons must actively be seeking employment. Again defensible on its own terms, this alteration has the effect of understanding the present problem when compared with earlier time periods.

Killingsworth has presented evidence (50) that the cumulative effect

---

[4] This was especially true during the latter part of the 1960s as the training and retraining programs increasingly focused on the economically disadvantaged.

of these definitional changes has been to lower the stated rate of unemployment by approximately .6 percentage points. This means that with a stated unemployment rate of 6 percent, the actual rate, by earlier definitions, would be closer to 6.6 percent. It also means that part of the apparent success in lowering unemployment in the late 1960s was only an illusion.

Such considerations would have little interest if the only question at stake were that of a proper definition. There is much more than this at stake, however, since the degree of success to be attributed to the increase in aggregate demand is largely measured by the reported unemployment rate. It is the contention of Killingsworth and the other structuralists that this success was much less than is commonly assumed because of these structural and definitional changes occurring at the same time that demand was increasing.

One of the toughest problems facing the science of economics is that of factoring out the important or "causal" variables when many things are happening at the same time. Although it would be nice to "hold other things constant" in order to test the importance of changing one parameter (i.e., aggregate demand) the real world laboratory, unfortunately, does not allow the economic research such liberties.

It is difficult, therefore, to ascribe to aggregate demand any specific amount of the credit for the drop in unemployment in the late 1960s. Certainly there is little disagreement that demand stimulation was extremely important. It does not follow, however, that *all* of the decrease can be credited to expansionary monetary and fiscal policies. A part of it is undoubtedly due to structural and definitional changes occurring at the same time.

Moreover, even though unemployment dropped below 4 percent, for these combinations of reasons, it did so only at the cost of an intolerable inflation. More alarmingly, these inflationary pressures became much more intense in 1973 and 1974 while unemployment remained considerably higher. Part of the explanation for the inflationary pressures undoubtedly lies in the structural bottlenecks that become increasingly apparent as labor markets tighten. The structural elements are not only responsible for unemployment but also for the higher inflationary threshold that appears once the government undertakes to stimulate aggregate demand. Thus, structural problems imply the need for an active manpower policy designed to alleviate bottlenecks in the labor force that occur as the markets tighten. Controls on wage and price hikes would be inefficient without concomitant efforts to mitigate structural mismatches. Correspondingly, manpower programs would be ineffective (and misleading) without the demand stimulation necessary to provide jobs. Manpower policy, demand management, and wage and price controls are complementary, not contradictory, policies.

The Teenage Situation

Structural mismatches are the most serious, and the most obvious, with respect to teenage—and especially black teenage—employment and unemployment. A look at this situation illustrates the seriousness of labor demand and supply moving in opposing directions, a situation that is the most acute in the inner cities. Here the black teenage population increased by a stunning 75 percent in the decade of the 1960s while the number of white teenagers rose by only 14 percent (118, pp. 85–96). At the same time, the demand for labor in the cities has been increasingly of a skilled nature with few jobs opening up in the unskilled categories. New businesses in the cities have been mostly in the nature of services—banking, insurance, real estate, and the like—and the jobs thus created have been predominantly of a white-collar, skilled type.

The results are as one would expect: the unemployment rate for black teenagers stood at a disastrously high level of over 40 percent in early 1975, and this undoubtedly understates the true figure which many observers place at over 50 percent! And this is the total figure; the rates in central cities are even worse. To comprehend the seriousness of this situation, one might recall that at the lowest point of the Great Depression, it is estimated that approximately one-fourth to one-third of the labor force was unemployed. One can hardly expect these destitute citizens to be enamored with the beauty of the invisible hand which is supposedly creating jobs for everyone who wants to work.

A Short Note on Automation Unemployment

With unemployment levels gradually increasing since the 1950s, much concern has been expressed over the effect of automation on the level of employment. Specifically, it is feared that automation will replace workers and, as society becomes more advanced technologically, unemployment will become an increasingly vexatious problem. At the same time, it is frequently argued that the jobs replaced by machines will be unskilled ones and that the remaining demand will be for highly trained technicians. A "reserve army of unemployed" would therefore develop, much in the manner foreseen by Karl Marx. How much truth is there in such arguments?

First, one must specify whether he is speaking of deficient demand or structural unemployment as the result of automation. The most serious case is that of deficient demand where the forces of automation limit the total number of jobs in the economy. This is the effect usually referred to by those persons most alarmed by the prospects of automation. Fortunately, there is little economic justification for so glum a view. The economy would only find large numbers of persons superfluous to the productive process if and when wants became satisfied to the degree that increased output is unwanted. Such a time is certainly in the far, far distant future. The demands to limit pollution, eliminate poverty, and increase other "public goods" put a great strain on our productive capacity, let alone the tremendous number of private wants that remain unfilled. If we ever arrive at the happy state where economic wants are completely satisfied, we can worry about the problem of finding things for people to do other than work. In the meantime, we should pursue economic policies that avoid the serious problem of deficient demand.

The structural aspects of automation, however, are not so easily dismissed. As noted, the increasing speed of technological change can increase the problems of adjusting supply to demand. At the same time, there is evidence that the *net* effect of technological advancement is to increase the skill requirements of jobs, although, in many *specific* instances, skill requirements may be decreased. These structural problems, like others, can be dealt with by an active manpower policy while at the same time holding the overall level of aggregate demand high through monetary and fiscal policy.

Further Policy Implications

While aggregate demand stimulation is not a sufficient condition to ensure full employment, there is no doubt that it is a necessary condition. It makes little sense to spend large amounts of time and energy training people for jobs that do not exist. About the only advantage of such a policy is that it spreads the remaining unemployment more evenly thereby promoting, in a certain sense, equality. Equalizing poverty, however, is a poor substitute for eliminating it.

A more productive policy is to vigorously pursue manpower training and retraining programs while at the same time adopting policies designed to keep aggregate demand high. The condition of adequate aggregate demand not only makes manpower programs more successful, but also makes many of them unnecessary. Structural problems do not disappear with demand stimulation, but, during such times, private employers act in such a manner as to help reduce them. While structural changes may have *caused* the unemployment, demand stimulation will help *cure* it.

Consider job training. Any employer is reluctant to train an unskilled person for a job if he is able to hire a skilled person instead. And, with high unemployment rates, this is exactly what he is able to do. Thus, there is little training taking place in the private sector during times of low economic activity. Furthermore, such times are also characterized by low profit margins so that hard-pressed companies can hardly be expected to maintain costly training programs for skilled personnel they don't need. As a result, such programs are among the first to be discarded as the economic outlook worsens.

Now suppose that the government stimulates aggregate demand to the point that labor becomes scarce, profits grow, and unfilled orders begin to accumulate in the company's sales offices. In an effort to expand employment, the employer must accept persons with less training than before (the skilled employees are already working again) and, if necessary, train them himself. Training, which is in the public good, has now been undertaken by a private employer because it is also in his good. Indeed, this is one of the best criteria for public policy: to make the private gain of individual and businesses coincide with the public interest.

The same effect is apparent with respect to other structural problems. Suppose there is a geographical mismatch between effective demand and available supply. With markets becoming tighter, employers are forced to enlarge the area in which they search for available talent, and, if necessary, to promote increased mobility through the provision of moving allowances. Such actions serve to make the labor market more efficient while, at the same time, reducing the level of structural unemployment. Again the public welfare is served by individuals and firms following their private interests.

Aggregate demand stimulation also works to reduce employment discrimination against racial minorities, as well as other groups such as women, older persons, and disabled persons. It does this by making it economically unprofitable to pursue discriminatory practices and, while it may be objected that this is not the loftiest of motives, one can rightly argue that this is an area where results are of greater importance than motives.[5] When labor markets become tight, an employer, wishing to expand, can continue to discriminate only at the cost of being unable to hire additional employees. When such a choice must be made, the barriers to equal employment opportunities quickly come down.

As the experience of the 1960s demonstrated, however, there are problems associated with demand expansion, the most overwhelming one being the inflationary pressures that develop. Thus, while structuralists and anti-structuralists alike recognize the desirability of maintaining a high level of aggregate demand, such a policy soon becomes impossible to maintain as the price level moves upward. And, to the extent that structural factors are making the unemployment problems more serious, the jobless level at which inflation becomes serious moves upward.

---

[5] It should be noted that many of the "anti-structuralists" of the 1960s did not deny the fact that structural unemployment was important. Instead, they argued, along the above lines, that demand stimulation was the suitable means for attacking the problem.

Thus, aggregate measures of monetary and fiscal policy become increasingly unable to effectively deal with the inflation/unemployment dilemma. In a study undertaken by the Urban Institute, the authors argue that on the basis of their statistical model, increasing structural problems does indeed result in a worsening of the unemployment inflation trade-off. They recommend, as a method of reversing this, increased emphasis on manpower programs designed to help labor markets operate more smoothly. Present programs, they argue, are insufficient in scope to effectively lower this trade-off (47).

At this point, some type of incomes policy to deal with wages and prices may become necessary. By restraining wage and price pressures, aggregate demand can be increased to a point where there are sufficient jobs. Employers themselves will then begin to attack the structural problems. While aggregate demand alone cannot solve the problem of unemployment, keeping it at a high level is a necessary condition. But only if the lid can be held on inflation can demand be kept high. At the same time, it is clear that manpower programs designed to facilitate labor market adjustments must be undertaken.

A caveat is in order here. To imply that wage and price controls enable the government to decrease unemployment with massive increases in total spending is clearly wrong. History provides ample evidence that no type of controls can long restrain prices and wages in the face of massive spending, the experience of 1973 being the latest example. Also, the speed at which total spending increases bears upon whether a given amount of demand is inflationary. The faster the spending increases, the less chance there will be for supply to adjust—and more structural problems, in both labor and product markets, develop. In short, wage and price controls cannot provide a substitute for responsible and effective monetary, fiscal, and manpower policies.

THE ATTEMPT TO REACH NON-INFLATIONARY FULL EMPLOYMENT

5

> If you took all the economists in the world and laid them end to end, they still wouldn't reach a conclusion.
>
> G. B. Shaw

It is difficult to dispute the power of those Keynesian policies designed to control the level of aggregate demand. Although one may dispute the ability of mortal man to pull the right control levers at the right time—no mean feat—there is little doubt as to the direction of the effect. World War II demonstrated what massive increases in spending could do to pull the economy out of a deep depression, just as the war buildup in the late 1960s proved that demand stimulation could still be counted on to reduce unemployment. The engineered slowdown of the early 1970s and again in the mid-1970s, on the oher hand, illustrated the effectiveness of restrictive policies to work in the other direction.

At the same time, it is clear that there is no feeling of general euphoria in the economics profession. No one is currently saying, as Professor Paul Samuelson said in 1966 that, "In connection with stabilization policies for the contemporary American economy, we economists are at the moment riding very high" (93, p. 3). That moment has passed. In the mid-1970s, economics is again being viewed as the dismal science, and to the public, if economists aren't actually responsible for the current economic mess, at best they seem incapable of doing much about it.

So what happened? The tax cut in 1964 was surely a victory of logic over ideology, and the profession gained in stature as the success of this innovative policy change became apparent. Keynesian doctrine was again vindicated as spending increased, unemployment decreased, and the combination of low unemployment and stable prices made Americans feel rich, optimistic, and generally pleased with their economic lot. Economists became the high priests of society.

By 1970 this happy era had ended. The Viet Nam War, never popular, had become an increasing source of social unrest during the late 1960s and, in addition, was now taking its toll on the domestic economy. Massive deficit spending had initiated a tenacious inflation that, in spite of efforts to reduce it during the first two-and-a-half years of the Nixon Administration, failed to abate. Nor did the restrictive policies adopted after the collapse of the control program have the desired effects. To be sure, the economy slowed to the point of producing the most severe post-war recession to date, but price increases moderated painfully slowly. The public's esteem for economists fell as rapidly as inflation advanced.

In large part, this state of affairs can be attributed to the extreme difficulty of reaching the goals of full employment and price stability simultaneously. To understand the difficulties in achieving these dual goals, we must examine more closely the nature of the inflationary problem and the effects that the aforementioned structural and institutional changes have had on the dilemma.

Inflationary Full Employment

Consider Figure 5–1 which represents a modified supply curve for the economy. The vertical axis represents the price level and the horizontal axis the level of real (deflated) gross national product. Since the amount of employment is largely dependent upon the level of total output (GNP), the horizontal axis also depicts the level of employment.[1] Thus, as we move to the right we increase GNP and employment and *decrease* unemployment. At some point we reach a level of output coincident with full employment; that is, unemployment reaches some absolute minimum. Let this point be depicted as Q_F, indicating that this level of output implies full employment.

Suppose now, that the level of total output is such that there is a good deal of unemployment, say level Q_1, which corresponds to an aggregate

---

[1] This is not strictly true, since through increasing productivity output can (and does) increase while employment remains constant. This presents no problem for the analysis. In the short run, technological changes are few, and even when they are present, GNP must increase in order to increase employment—only now it must increase more. The important point is the direction of the effect and this remains the same: greater employment means greater GNP.

THE ATTEMPT TO REACH NON-INFLATIONARY FULL EMPLOYMENT

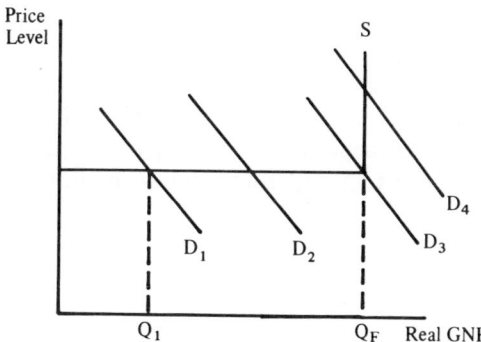

Figure 5–1. Aggregate Supply and the Price Level

demand of D_1. Given this framework, in conjunction with the Keynesian policy referred to above, the obvious need is to increase aggregate demand, say to D_2. By doing so, GNP increases and unemployment decreases. In the simple model depicted here, prices do not move upward at all with the increase in demand.

Stable prices at this point are in line with the classical view of perfectly competitive markets. There is no reason why prices should increase until full employment is reached; at this point, excess demand pulls them up.[2] Such is the case at our hypothetical level of full employment output shown as point Q_F. A further dose of aggregate demand increases real output to this level (Q_F) and completely does away with unemployment. Further increases in demand, however (D_3 to D_4), are only inflationary. Real output does not increase; instead, the price level shoots upward. Given a perfectly competitive world, the only inflation would be of the demand-pull variety, and we would not arrive at this point until full employment were reached.

The Meaning of Full Employment

A part of the problem, it can be seen, revolves around the concept of "full employment"—an issue that has been conveniently sidetracked until now. "Absolute" full employment is reached when everyone in the labor force is working as much as he desires (no economic part-time employment), and there is no further movement into the labor force in response to increased jobs. At such a point, there is only a minimum level of "frictional" unemployment as people move from one job to

---

[2] The supply curve in the figure is a "modified" classical supply curve since it allows for a condition of less than full employment. A "true" classical supply curve is completely vertical, thus implying full employment (and making an analysis of unemployment unnecessary).

another; and even this is eliminated, theoretically, as the adjustment speed approaches infinity.

Absolute unemployment, of course, is never reached, nor even approximated, and as a result, we need a more workable and realistic definition of full employment. In the 1960s, the Council of Economic Advisors set 4 percent as an "interim" goal—"interim" mainly because no one wanted to admit that this might be the best we could ever do. (Since then, the thinking has changed so much that many question whether the 4 percent level is far too optimistic.)

The difference in levels, influencing the manner in which the unemployment and inflation "cures" are considered, is more than one of semantics. For example, one could arbitrarily define the "normal" unemployment level to be 7 percent. There would then be little structural problem, since aggregate demand could take us to this level without an appreciable rise in the price level. Moreover, since 7 percent would be considered "full employment," any inflation after this point could be attributed to irresponsible monetary and/or fiscal policies. Thus, one can conveniently define away the nasty problems of adjustment difficulties and market power and, in the process, the possibility of structural unemployment and cost-push inflation. Moreover, should the parameters change by, say, the appearance of inflation at a higher unemployment level, the "full employment" rate could simply be revised upward and the problem dismissed on the basis that a "normal" level of unemployment is, like taxes and death, unavoidable.

Such convenient sophistry, however, cannot disguise the fact that with higher unemployment rates—normal or otherwise—the level of personal suffering and social waste is correspondingly increased. The whole purpose of attempting to improve economic tools and policies is to reduce this normal rate, that is, the unemployment rate associated with a given rise in the level of prices.

Since the level of full employment is an elusive concept, the 4-percent interim level will be adopted here for the purpose of discussion. Given this target goal of 4-percent unemployment, we can now ask, in terms of Figure 5–1, how much demand must be increased in order to reach this level. Or, what level of gross national product is necessary to achieve this unemployment level? This is similar to the way in which the problem was viewed during the 1960s by the Kennedy-Johnson economic advisors when the important question became the size of the gap between actual GNP and the GNP necessary to achieve full employment.

During this time, economic advisor Arthur Okun estimated that for every 1 percent that real GNP was increased, unemployment would drop by one-third of 1 percent (77, p. 17). By this reckoning, reducing the level of unemployment by three percentage points would require a 9-percent increase in real GNP. In 1975 this would have amounted to an increase of approximately $135 billion in the nation's total output. For those who easily dismiss the significance of two or three percentage points of unemployment, this look at foregone output may be revealing. To forego $135 billion of output at a time when many city and state governments, businesses, and private citizens are on the brink of bankruptcy is a high price indeed.[3]

Moving Closer to Reality

Of course, Figure 5-1 is an unrealistic representation of the nature of price increases. In truth, inflationary pressures begin to be felt long before full employment is reached. Figure 5-2 is more realistic.

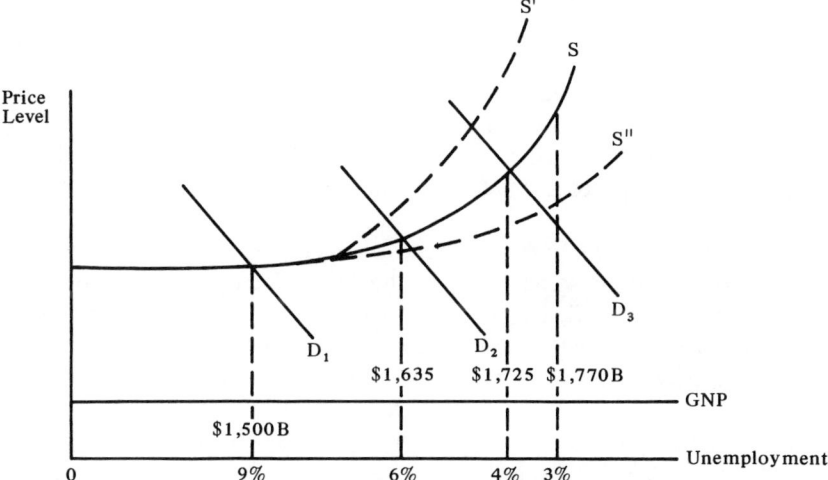

Figure 5-2. Modified Supply Curve

Here too the price level is shown on the vertical axis, whereas real GNP and unemployment are shown on the horizontal axis. Decreasing unemployment (moving to the right) is associated with increasing output. (Data representative of 1975 are included.)

GNP of $1,500 billion is associated with unemployment of 9 percent and GNP of $1,725 billion with unemployment of 4 percent.

We will examine the reasons for the upswing in the S curve before full employment is reached. Note first, however, that the actual curve

---

[3] At this writing, it appears that unemployment during 1975 will *average* around 9 percent. The GNP loss between this and an unemployment level of 5 percent amounts to approximately $225 billion in 1975 dollars.

may actually be somewhat worse than that of S in Figure 5–2. That is, it may now look more like S', thereby indicating that the price level increase associated with any given level of unemployment is worse than it used to be. The purpose of policy, and especially of wage and price controls, is to move the S curve downward somewhat in the direction of S''. If this can be done, it is possible to reach lower levels of unemployment and inflation simultaneously.

Labor Market Imperfections

As noted in Chapter 4, a wide band of different unemployment rates lies behind any given average. That is, certain sectors of the economy reach full employment before others. In 1974, for example, the unemployment rate for white-collar workers stood at 3.3 percent and that for blue-collar workers was 6.7 percent. (The national average at the time was 5.6 percent.) In fact, the differential was even more acute: the rate for professional and technical workers was 2.3 percent (considered to be quite high for this group) while that for nonfarm laborers was 10.1 percent. Within the blue-collar category itself there were such differences as the 4.4 percent rate for craftsmen compared to the 10.1 percent for laborers.

As a result of this uneven spread of unemployment rates, shortages begin to appear in some parts of the labor force even though other groups are still experiencing high rates of joblessness. The labor market can adjust to this condition to some extent by increasing the utilization of unskilled workers when skilled workers come into short supply, but this mechanism is far from perfect. In many fields it is difficult to alter production methods (especially in the short run) in response to changing labor market conditions.[4]

Moreover, an employer may be able to utilize more unskilled labor if he is unable to obtain the necessary skilled labor. For example, suppose that the production process of a given firm requires two skilled workers for each unskilled employee (a close approximation in many construction projects). Now, suppose that the demand for the firm's output increases as the result of an overall expansionary policy on the part of the federal government. As the demand for the product increases, the firm's labor requirements increase; so it begins hiring. With the differential rates of unemployment (available supply), however, the market for skilled labor will become tight while that of unskilled labor remains slack. As demand continues to expand, the firm may be unable to hire more skilled workers and, since the 2 to 1 ratio may be relatively fixed

---

[4] In technical terms, production coefficients are relatively fixed in the short run.

in the short run, this effectively limits the firm's demand for unskilled labor.

At the same time, because of the shortage of skilled labor, upward pressure is put on the wage rates of these people. The net result is continued unemployment among unskilled workers while wages move upward for skilled employees.

This type of inflationary pressure (illustrated, for example, as an increase in demand from D_1 to D_2 in Figure 5–2) is the result of increased demand, but it occurs before full employment is reached due to structural imbalances in the economy. If there were no structural mismatches, the increased demand would coincide with the available supplies and inflationary pressures would not be experienced before full employment.

These structural adjustment problems (moving from one equilibrium position to another) are reflected in the fact that mobility is much less than perfect with respect to movements among occupations. Were this not the case, unskilled workers could quickly become skilled and thus alleviate labor market bottlenecks as they developed. In reality, however, job training frequently takes a long time, thereby creating impediments to occupational mobility.

Part of the inflationary pressure, then, is created by the combination of structural imbalances coupled with relatively fixed ratios among different types of labor. Although these ratios change over time in response to labor market movements, the adjustments are sluggish and thereby contribute to the problem of rising prices at less than full employment.

Introducing Economic Power

An institutional or "power" factor that adds a cost-push element to the process furthers the foregoing inflationary tendency. Unskilled wage rates may be tied institutionally to the skilled rates—a not unlikely situation. In that case, *both* wage rates can exhibit signs of upward movement, with the skilled occupations pulling the unskilled ones along. This must be termed a power factor since, in the absence of market power, the unskilled rates would not move upward in these circumstances. Furthermore, this has the effect of discouraging the very movement toward unskilled labor that would mitigate the original bottleneck. With wages moving upward in both areas, there is little incentive for employers to attempt to substitute unskilled for skilled employees.

The Speed of Change

Structural adjustment problems also influence the *speed* at which demand changes can be made in order to reach a given unemployment/inflation level. The faster the growth in demand, the less chance there is for the necessary adjustments to be made and, as a result, the more inflationary the process.

Referring again to Figure 5–2, different supply curves will result from different *rates* of increase in demand. (The demand and supply functions under this view are not independent of each other.) With a very rapid expansion of demand, the result might well be a movement along S' with much of the increased output consisting of price increases. A slower rate of expansion, on the other hand, will give the labor markets (and other factor markets) a better chance to adjust through occupational and geographical mobility. This will result in a greater share of the increased output being represented as real increases in GNP and less pressure will be exerted on the price level.

Implications

The policy prescription for these structural matters is to institute manpower programs designed to increase the efficiency of the labor markets. Another productive policy is to reduce artificial barriers that inhibit the free flow of resources, including human resources. Unions, for example, that construct artificial entry barriers, by means of racial quotas or unnecessarily long training periods, further the structural mismatch between supply and demand. Similarly, government policies that restrict competition (that is, supply), from such sources as foreign countries have the same effect. In either case, the market is thwarted from performing its necessary function of allocating resources in an efficient manner, and the result adds to the inflationary pressures that develop before full employment is reached.

Collective Bargaining Pressures

Part of the upward movement in prices as the economy nears full employment is due to cost-push elements. Powerful unions (including professional associations) are able to demand pay increases as economic conditions improve. At the same time, large sellers are increasingly able to pass the increased costs on in the form of price hikes.

At any given time, the ability of a union to extract a large wage increase from management rests upon two factors: management's *ability* to pay and its *desire* to pay. Both factors increase as the economy moves toward full employment. Compare, for instance, the position faced by the typical company as the economy moves from a period of stagnation to one of surging activity. As business picks up, orders begin to accumulate, stockpiles (inventories) go down, and profits swell. (This is especially true during the initial stages of the upswing as productivity increases rapidly.) Thus, the company becomes increasingly able to meet the union's demands.

At the same time, with orders coming in and business (at last) picking up, the last thing the company wants is a strike. Therefore, the *desire* of the company is to settle increases, and labor is able to strike a better bargain. Furthermore, in the face of improved conditions, management knows it has a better chance of successfully increasing the price of the product; so it has less to fear from a wage increase. The net result is that both the union and the company are in a better position to flex their economic muscle as the economy moves toward full employment.

Is this demand-pull or cost-push inflation? Actually, it is both. The increase in demand is responsible for improved economic conditions but these in turn allow the unions to increase wages and management to push up prices. Thus we are led to an extremely important consideration: with a given amount of monopoly power, it becomes easier to exercise this power as economic conditions tighten. We will have cause to examine this phenomenon further.

Productivity Changes

As the economic upswing continues, productivity increases slow down. During the first phases of recovery, productivity gains are abnormally large since the increased output lowers per unit fixed costs, and for a while management can increase output without adding to its labor supply. That is, increased output comes from the slack that has accumulated during the previous downturn.

As the recovery continues, however, this slack disappears and additional labor must be hired. Oftentimes, this labor is of lower quality than the existing work force and, as a result of this and other inefficiencies, productivity increases begin to taper off. At the same time, wages are beginning to move upward for the reasons noted previously.

Forces soon begin to operate that push upward on the price level. The closer the economy moves toward full employment, the less chance there is that productivity gains will keep pace with wage gains. As a result, per unit labor costs begin to rise. Then, in an attempt to maintain profit levels, management raises prices. The inflationary spiral is on its way.

The Range for Controls

It is in the context of market power on the part of unions and corporations that the case for controls on wages and prices is the strongest. Otherwise, only with respect to a relatively small band of economic activity do they make sense. Attempts to hold down prices and wages while indiscriminately expanding aggregate demand is unquestionably foolish as well as ineffective. Unless market controls are extremely strict and involuntary, they simply will not work in the face of massive demand pressures.

Aggregate demand pressures intensify greatly, for example, as the economy approaches (or passes) the 4-percent unemployment level in Figure 5–2. At the same time, when unemployment is extremely high (say, about 8 percent in Figure 5–2), there is little, if any, need for controls. At this point there is enough slack in the economy to moderate prices and wages. At a 9-percent unemployment rate, aggregate demand could be increased in an effort to stimulate employment without seriously affecting the price level. Only within a certain band characterized by imprecise limits can controls have a useful, albeit limited, role to play. Recent experience indicates that the width of this band may be increasing. Wage increases continued at high levels in 1975 in the face of unemployment rates unseen since the Great Depression.

Effective controls allow less discretionary wage and price changes on the part of monopolistic labor and product market forces. If the economy were perfectly competitive, there would be no need for controls. No unions or companies would possess market power, and they would be unable to push wages or prices up. It is only because we have imperfect—perhaps increasingly imperfect—markets that controls can serve a useful function under certain circumstances.

THE TRADE-OFF BETWEEN UNEMPLOYMENT AND INFLATION

The foregoing analysis suggests that a trade-off exists between inflation and unemployment and that by adjusting aggregate demand (as in Figure 5–2) through monetary and fiscal policies, we can choose the combination of the two that we prefer. Depending upon the predilections of the policymakers at any given time, we could have a combination of high unemployment and stable prices or a lower unemployment rate accompanied by rising prices. Take your pick.

The problem, however, is not so simple. Ever since the publication of an article by A. W. Phillips in 1958 (86), economists have argued about the existence—or lack thereof—of a *Phillips curve* and its implied trade-off between unemployment and inflation.

Figure 5–3 presents an Americanized version of the Phillips curve; that is, the vertical axis represents price changes (inflation) rather than the rate of change in money wages as depicted in the original Phillips version.

The curve represents the trade-off between unemployment and inflation by showing that, as unemployment is decreased (movements to the left on the horizontal axis), prices increase at increasing rates. This is

THE ATTEMPT TO REACH NON-INFLATIONARY FULL EMPLOYMENT

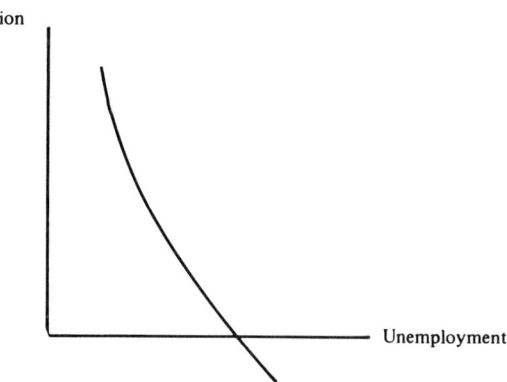

Figure 5-3. The Phillips curve

the same basic relationship that is shown in Figure 5-2, and it occurs for the same reasons: as labor markets become tighter (lower unemployment), structural and power forces begin to produce inflationary pressures.

As unemployment becomes *very* low, these forces combine with demand-pull elements to make price increases extremely rapid. Figure 5-3 also makes it apparent that when unemployment is low, the cost (in terms of inflation) of reducing it still further is great. Or, put another way, a small increase in unemployment will greatly reduce the speed with which prices increase.

The Logic behind the Phillips Curve

Logically, the basic Phillips curve relationship seems straightforward enough—a reasonable relationship to expect between price changes and unemployment changes. One might wonder, then, why this concept has been the subject of such intense debate among economists.

Basically, there are two areas of dispute concerning the Phillips curve. First, the relationship between inflation and employment is close, and at any given time, an increase in one variable may not produce an immediate decrease in the other one. Specifically, Figure 5-4 illustrates the relationship between unemployment and price changes for the past twenty-five years. Although a line fitted to these data lies in the direction indicated by the Phillips curve, the fit is obviously not close.

Second, a problem has arisen in formulating a satisfactory theoretical explanation of the Phillips curve in terms of labor market behavior. A perceived drawback is that the Phillips curve relationship depends upon imperfect markets. Theoretical explanations that do not admit to market imperfections have had to resort to strong assumptions concerning labor

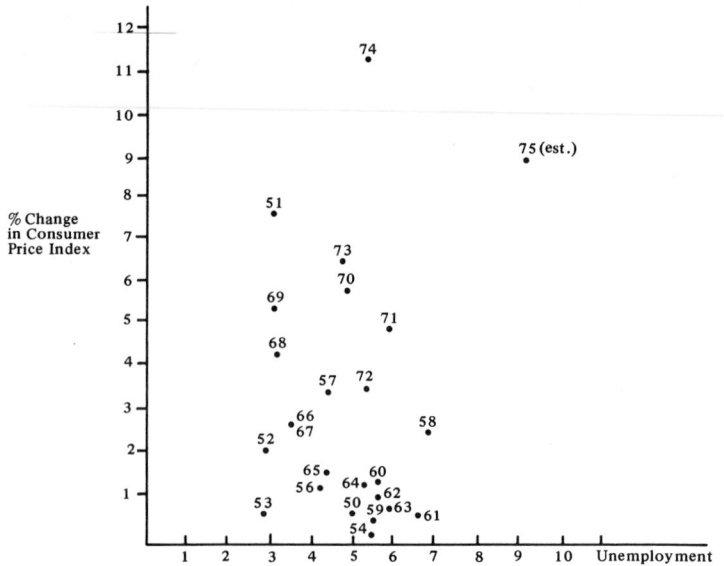

Figure 5–4. Unemployment and Inflation, 1950–1975

market conditions. And these assumptions, along with the theoretical constructs built upon them, have failed to stand up to rigorous analysis.

Once market imperfections are introduced, however, the relationship makes sense. Unions and corporations have the power to extract higher wages and prices as unemployment decreases. At the same time, structural adjustments run into increasing bottlenecks as markets tighten. A theory that fails to recognize the existence of market imperfections can hardly be expected to explain a relationship based upon these imperfections.

Problems with the Curve

The lack of an exact functional relationship between unemployment and inflation, however, has caused serious questions concerning the applicability of the Phillips curve to the United States. When models are constructed to measure the change in inflation (or the change in money wage rates) associated with changes in unemployment, the association is often quite loose, thereby suggesting that there is little relationship between the two variables.[5]

On the other hand, part of the difficulty in finding solid relationships between unemployment and inflation is the result of technical statistical

---

[5] A problem is that when regressing the rate of change in money wages (a proxy for inflation when combined with productivity) against the unemployment rate, the coefficient of multiple determination (R^2) is low.

problems and, in particular, the problems of choosing appropriate measures of unemployment and price changes. By introducing various lag structures into the equation and different wage and price series, it is possible to construct an almost infinite number of Phillips curve relationships with widely differing statistical properties.

In spite of these difficulties, Professor Lowell Gallaway (36, pp. 76–88) has presented the evidence that the explanatory power of these models is greatly improved by more careful selection of the data. While noting that very different results can be obtained for the United States by slight changes in definition, Gallaway makes a strong case for the existence of a Phillips curve relationship for the United States in both the short and the long run.

Most empirical studies of the nature of the Phillips curve phenomenon have used the change in money wages as the dependent variable, rather than inflation itself. This is because a strong causal relationship exsits between the rate of change in money wages and the change in prices. In particular, it is usually assumed that the amount of inflation (change in prices) is equal to the change in money wages *less* any increase in productivity.

For example, if wages go up 5 percent and productivity increases 3 percent, according to this formulation there will be a price increase of 2 percent.[6] This definition of inflation seems to hold quite well over the long pull; but the hidden assumption that labor is unable to increase its *share* of total output by extracting a part of the increased wages from capital should be noted. (This seems to be empirically true; wages have increased only slightly as a percent of total output in the past seventy years and much of this is due to sectoral shifts in the economy toward areas that are more labor intensive, such as services.) In addition, the commodity-based inflation of 1973 and 1974 illustrates the inappropriateness of Phillips curve analysis to some types of inflation.[7]

Fitting the curve to the U.S. Data

Given the fact that the Phillips curve relationship is far from exact, what does it look like for the United States? Figure 5–5 is based on the

---

[6] If wages and productivity both increase by the same amount, say, 3 percent, this does not imply that labor has received all the gains of the increase in productivity. Returns to capital, in this case, will also increase by 3 percent.

[7] The inflation of 1973–75 has focused attention on areas other than unit labor costs that are capable of sustaining a general price rise. Thus, capacity pressures and raw materials bottlenecks, along with an effective oil cartel, are now seen to be important sources of inflation as well as labor costs.

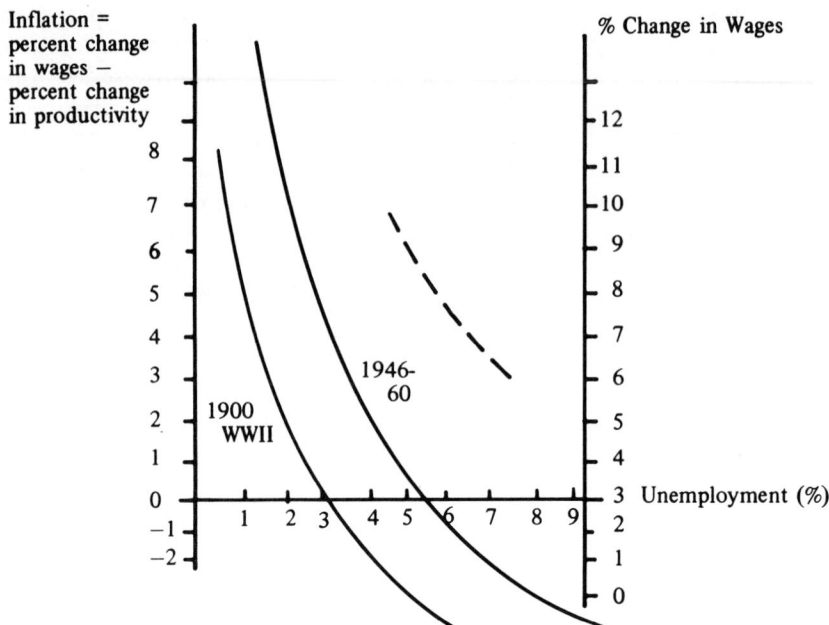

Figure 5–5. Modified Phillips curve

work of Samuelson and Solow (92) in fitting a curve to the American data. On the left vertical axis is the rate of inflation; that is, the average annual price change. On the right vertical axis is the rate of change in money wages. The assumption here is that productivity is increasing at an average of 3 percent per year. (Samuelson and Solow used a productivity rate of 2.5 percent in the calculations, whereas the Council of Economic Advisors later adopted a rate closer to 3 percent.)

Two different curves have been considered representative of the United States data. The first is for the early part of the twentieth century, whereas the curve to the right represents the Phillips curve since World War II. With respect to the modern Phillips curve, the implication is that stable prices are possible with approximately 5.5-percent unemployment while wages are increasing with the assumed productivity improvement of 3 percent. Other combinations can be read off in similar fashion. Wages increasing at an average rate of 6 percent would be consistent with a 3-percent rise in the price level and approximately 3.5- to 4-percent unemployment.

At the extremes, if wages are increasing at an 8 percent annual rate, unemployment is pushed down to 3 percent but prices will be rising at a rate of 5 percent. On the other hand, stable wages are consistent

THE ATTEMPT TO REACH NON-INFLATIONARY FULL EMPLOYMENT

with a falling price level (deflation) at an average unemployment rate of 8 to 9 percent.

The Policy Options

These apparent relationships, then, seem to be the ones on which we should base our choices. But what is the reality? In 1970 the unemployment level stood at an average level of 4.9 percent but prices rose by 5.9 percent. In 1975 unemployment reached 9 percent and inflation continued at 9 percent. These are much worse trade-offs even than those predicted by the modified Phillips curve. The policy choices implied by the curve in Figure 5–5 appear extremely attractive as opposed to the realities of recent experience. The reason, of course, goes back to the closeness of fit of the data to the curve: this is very imprecise, and at any given time a set of observations may be quite far from the curve. On balance, however, some sort of trade-off between unemployment and inflation apparently *does* exist and, within bounds, a policy choice is available between the two. Certainly, given enough unemployment, prices will moderate. If "enough" implies a depression, however, it becomes a matter of more theoretical, than practical, interest.

The ideal policy, of course, would be to shift the entire curve to the left rather than moving up or down a given curve. This would be exactly analogous to pushing the S curve down as in Figure 5–2 and would require the same policies. This is the purpose of an incomes policy. To the extent that controls can hold down wages and prices while allowing increases in aggregate demand to decrease unemployment, the entire Phillips curve will move to the left. Whether this is possible is an unsettled question, whereas the hoped-for effect of the policy is not.

Shifts in the curve

It is interesting to note that the Phillips curve for the years since World War II is further to the right than the curve representing the earlier part of the century. Thus, for any given level of unemployment we must now pay a higher price in terms of inflation. This is due to a number of factors, including additional market power on the part of unions and corporations and increases in the severity of structural roadblocks in the path toward full employment.

Professor Gallaway (36, pp. 85–88) provides evidence that the long run Phillips curve has actually moved slowly to the *left* as labor markets *increase* in efficiency due to advances in communications, transportation, and other factors that improve mobility. However, he argues that there was a sharp shift to the *right* during the 1930s. He attributes this to the rapid increase in collective bargaining at the time which, in turn, increased the institutional rigidities in the labor market. The net result has been to make the present trade-off less favorable since one policy goal can be purchased only by giving up increasing amounts of the other goal.

The Validity of the curve

The experience of the late 1960s to mid-seventies has led many observers to the conclusion that the Phillips curve relationship is no longer valid, if, indeed, it ever was. Powerful reinforcement for this viewpoint is the failure of Richard Nixon's economic policies, in which unemployment was deliberately increased (via restrictive monetary policy) to halt the rapid increases in prices. The object was to move down on a given Phillips curve. If this is valid concept we are discussing, why did prices fail to respond to this treatment by decreasing? And when they did respond, why did it take so long for so little?

Such evidence does not dissuade the true believer. He answers that the policy (the old-time religion) will work if it is left alone. The Phillips curve, it must be remembered, is not an exact relationship. And, since inflationary expectations were very strong during the 1970s, it may simply have taken longer to change these expectations and thereby to bring down prices via increased unemployment.

This argument is analogous to the proverbial rain dance. If you believe that dancing while you pray to the rain gods will bring rain, the facts cannot prove you wrong. If it rains, the theory is borne out. If it doesn't, you can always claim that you haven't danced long enough or there simply wasn't faith. Thus the fault is not with the theory; it is with the impatient observers who do not give it a proper trial. So it is with inflation in the 1970s. It can be argued that by continuing to suffer high unemployment for a longer period of time, prices will eventually decrease. Indeed, this may be true; prices did begin to moderate in 1975 in response to restrictive monetary and fiscal policies. The social costs of this policy, however, proved to be extremely high.

Refinements in the Relationship

The reason for the lack of a close fit between the change in wages (and consequently inflation) and the level of unemployment is largely that wages depend on many things beside the tightness or looseness of the labor market. As a result, many observers have attempted to improve the Phillips curve relationship by adding other variables. Hopefully, if one can explain with greater precision the reasons behind wage changes, the chances of improving our anti-inflation policy will be improved to a commensurate degree.

In 1962 Otto Eckstein and Thomas Wilson published an influential article (31) in which they put forth the thesis that, among other things, wage rates are set in bargaining rounds (cycles) of from one to five years and that certain key industries are extremely important in impact on the wage rates in other industries. That is, there is a good deal of institutional connection between the wage rates in these key industries and the wages in the other sectors of the economy. Thus, if we can explain the changes in the key areas, we will have gone far toward explaining the entire process of wage change and, therefore, of inflation.

Furthermore, they found that most of the wage changes in these key industries can be explained by the use of two variables: unemployment and profits. Unemployment, they reasoned, provides a measure of the looseness or tightness of the labor market while profits serve as a proxy for product market conditions. Their results proved to be very significant, statistically as well as practically. By using the concept of wage rounds determined by collective bargaining (the length of the contract) in place of annual data, and by including profits along with unemployment as an explanatory variable, the predictive power of the model was greatly improved.[8]

In a major study published in 1966 (45), George Perry also linked the change in wages to other variables in addition to the level of unemployment. Specifically, he included the cost of living (since many contracts include this), profits (a measure of the ability and/or resistance to grant wage increases), and "expectations," for which he used the *direction* in which profits were moving. As expected, the degree explanation is much greater in this model than when unemployment is used as the sole explanatory variable.

Of particular interest is the fact that profits were again found to be an important determinant of wage changes. From this, Perry constructed a family of Phillips curves moving from left to right. Each curve represents a different (higher) level of corporate profits. The conclusion is that any given rate of unemployment will imply a faster rate of price increase the higher profits are. The implication is that by lowering profits, the trade-off between unemployment and inflation can be lowered.

Perry was careful to state, however, that policies that attempt to lower profits may lead to inflation by other means. For example, increasing corporate taxes may have the effect of directly increasing prices as companies pass the taxes on to the consumer. Then too, such taxes may

---

[8] Regressing average annual increases in straight time earnings in the key group against profits and unemployment for the five wage rounds from 1948–60 produced an R^2 of 0.9975 significant to the 0.01 level.

impair investment, which will lead in turn to a slower growth rate of productivity and thus to higher levels of inflation.

An alternate policy, suggests Perry, is to change the institutional structure in an attempt to alter the wage equation. Such policies as breaking up unions and corporate power structures would do the trick, but these options are, of course, extremely unlikely to be undertaken (and may, for other reasons, be undesirable as well).

A further possibility, he suggests, is to apply restraints to wages and prices within the present institutional framework. Although Perry was referring to the wage-price guideposts of the 1960s, the same reasoning applies to the Price Commission and Pay Board of the 1970s. Once again, the policy implications are to push the Phillips curve downward in an attempt to better the trade-off between unemployment and inflation. Market controls are an attempt to achieve this without resorting to the drastic (and much more difficult) option of breaking up large conglomerates of power.

An improvement in the basic Perry model was made in 1968 by Normal Simler and Alfred Tella (100) with the introduction of their labor reserves model. Unemployment, they argued, provided only a crude measure of the tightness of the labor market since it failed to take into account changes in labor force participation rates *in response to* changes in unemployment. In particular, as unemployment rates move lower, participation rates increase as more persons enter the labor force in response to the improved job situation.[9] On the other hand, as unemployment increases, people will drop out of the labor market, thereby creating a reserve of workers who will rejoin the labor force once conditions improve. Thus, as unemployment goes down, there are reserves of workers who begin to seek employment again. This provides a restraining influence on the increase in wage rates.

As employment conditions continue to improve, however, these reserves dwindle and wages begin to move up more rapidly. The result is to make the model that includes a labor force reserve factor more accurate in predicting the wage changes associated with given changes in unemployment.

The upshot of these and other studies is that unemployment alone is insufficient to explain changes in wages and, hence, inflation. As usual, a single-causation theory is inadequate and the case of inflation is no exception. There is little doubt, however, that a Phillips curve for the United States does exist; that is, there is an inverse relationship between unemployment and price movements. While differing in detail, the re-

---

[9] This is the "discouraged worker" effect. See the Appendix to Chapter 3.

sults of these studies point in the same direction—as unemployment decreases, inflationary pressures mount.[10]

Further Questions

An unanswered but extremely important question is the reason for the lack of recent data to conform to the Phillips curve data depicted in Figure 5–5. Since the inflationary period of 1968, the observed levels of unemployment and price change have been consistently to the right of the projected curve. This may simply reflect the fact that there is a time lag between increasing unemployment and decreasing price levels. On the other hand, it may represent a shift to the right in the Phillips curve such as that depicted by the broken line in Figure 5–5. There is increasing uneasiness and concern over this latter possibility.

In other words, were the Nixon-Ford economic programs simply not given enough time, or has there been an increase in structural or power factors that could have shifted the true Phillips curve eastward? As mentioned, Samuelson and Solow noted a shift to the right after World War II and Gallaway in the 1930s. Also, Gallaway presents further evidence (36, p. 88) that a Phillips curve for 1968 would be somewhat to the right of the Samuelson and Solow version, especially with regard to high unemployment rates.

Even these data, however, fail to take into account the very high unemployment and inflation rates of 1973, 1974, and 1975. It seems increasingly clear that the Phillips curve has indeed been shifting to the right, thereby making any achievable combination of inflation and unemployment more painful.

The evidence indicates that there is, to a limited degree, a trade-off between the goals of full employment and price stability. Experience indicates, however, that attempting to engineer movements along the curve is extremely precarious. An active incomes policy, structural reforms, and manpower programs may be able to move the curve to the left. Controls, which enable aggregate demand to be increased while restraining wages and prices, are attempts to lower this trade-off. It is not clear even after the experience of 1971–74 whether such policies can be effective. It *is* clear, however, that the economy is not working well without them.

---

[10] Numerous additional studies have been undertaken in an attempt to develop more reliable wage and price equations (55, 56, 57, 58, 58–A, 61), a number of which are discussed in Chapters 10 and 12.

THE EXTENT OF MARKET POWER

6

> The world will always be governed by self-interest. We should not try to stop this, we should try to make the self-interest of cads a little more coincident with that of decent people.
>
> Samuel Butler

The market power of labor unions and business firms has been referred to, to justify the imposition of wage and price controls. In this chapter we examine the nature of this power and the extent of its impact.

Basically, market power as used here, is the ability to raise or maintain prices—either in labor markets or product markets—at levels above those that would prevail in perfectly competitive markets. That is, market power means that businesses and unions are able to exercise a degree of *discretion* in setting prices and wages. They do not simply have to accept them as a given, as in perfectly competitive markets. A primary purpose of wage and price restraints is to limit discretionary powers in both markets. If no power exists, there is nothing to limit.

No business or union, of course, possesses absolute power. Even with respect to the largest of these institutions, there are limits to their ability to set prices. Competition is still effective, even for large firms and unions. The question, like so many, is a matter of degree.

In the real world, as opposed to the world of competitive economic theory, economic power is a fact of life. Business firms are able to push prices up in the face of slack demand, and unions possess the necessary power to demand and get wage increases during periods of substantial unemployment. Neither of these situations would be possible under perfectly competitive conditions.

THE MARKET POWER OF BUSINESS FIRMS

Market power is much easier to speak of, and even to define, than it is to measure. To exert power, a business firm must be large enough to *set* the price at which it sells its output and not merely *take* the price as a given. Of course, no firm has the power to set its price completely independent of competitive forces; there are always some constraints. But, even though a business enterprise may not possess absolute power (none do), they may possess some power. And it is the extent of this ability to set prices that we refer to as market power.

Conditions for Power

Given the importance of market power to the applicability of market controls, what are some of the determinants of this power? Willard Mueller, a recognized expert on monopoly power in the United States, cites three sources of market power: (1) the degree of buyer or seller concentration; (2) the condition of entry into the industry; and (3) the degree of product differentiation (72, pp. 11–20). Large businesses exhibit all three of these sources to a considerable extent. And, to a similar extent, they are able to set prices in product markets with diminished concern for demand conditions compared to their counterparts who operate in more competitive markets.

There have been numerous attempts to measure the extent of concentration in American industry. This index of market power refers to the share of business, in a particular market or the economy as a whole, that is conducted by the largest business units. For example, one measure of concentration is the percentage of all business conducted by the top 500 corporations.

Professor Lee E. Preston, in refining the measures of concentration, has found it useful to distinguish between *economic concentration* and *market concentration,* the former referring to aggregate, or economy-wide, concentration and the latter to the amount of concentration in a particular market (88, p. 66).

Although these are different measures, Preston notes that the two types of concentration are likely to go hand in hand for several reasons. Being large enough to play a part in aggregate concentration usually implies that the business firm is also large in relation to the particular market in which it operates. As Preston cites, "General Motors and Standard Oil (New Jersey), the two largest industrial firms in the economy in terms of sales and assets, respectively, are also the largest firms in their principal industries—automobile manufacturing and petroleum refining" (88, p. 7).

Furthermore, although there is disagreement about the extent of change, the evidence clearly shows an increase in the amount of economic concentration. Professor Mueller states that "the level of aggregate concentration in American manufacturing has risen substantially since World War II." Since the absolute size of the economy has expanded greatly since the war, this means that the top firms have not only cut themselves a larger share of the pie but, in addition, are now enjoying a larger share of a much larger pie. In fact, Mueller further points out that, with respect to the assets of manufacturing corporations, "by 1968 the top one hundred companies held a greater share than that held by the top two hundred in 1947" (72, p. 26). Preston confirms this judgment with respect to aggregate concentration. "The conclusion," he writes, "that aggregate concentration within the industrial sector of the economy has increased over the past two or three decades seems inescapable" (88, p. 8).

In terms of market concentration, the trend is much less clear. About the most conclusive one can be is to state that there is no indication of lessening, nor of increasing, market concentration in recent years. Professor M. A. Adelman expands upon this latter point and argues that whatever increases there are in *superconcentration* (mergers, conglomerates, and "bigness"), they imply little in the way of evidence for monopoly behavior in individual markets (2).

If one considers the concentration of *control* with respect to American business firms, there appears to be greater evidence of increased concentration. In a series of studies concerning the degree of ownership and control of banking activities, the House Banking Committee under the chairmanship of Wright Patman has uncovered a strong trend toward financial control of manufacturing activities by major banks. Furthermore, the concentration of ownership among banks is extremely high (79). Although the trend toward diversification of *ownership* of American industry continues, with larger numbers of persons owning shares of stock, evidence indicates that the *control* of business enterprise is becoming increasingly concentrated in fewer hands.

The Exercise of Power

It is one thing to say that American industry is becoming more concentrated and the number of controllers fewer, and quite another to argue that this control is used to push up prices. It may be used, and undoubtedly is used, to determine the direction in which new investments will be made, to facilitate long-run planning, and to spread costs over a large base. This does not necessarily imply, however, that market power is used to increase prices above levels they would attain without market power. Moreover, in view of the tremendous number of simultaneous changes and innovations occurring within the economy at any given time, it is extremely difficult to pinpoint a direct relationship between the degree of market concentration or concentration of ownership and the act of increasing prices. The problems of measurement are myriad.

To say that something is difficult to measure, however, is not to deny its importance. And, in spite of measurement difficulties, the increased concentration of industry does make it possible for prices to be pushed upward in a more independent fashion. When many "competitors" are owned (or controlled) by the same interest groups, they are less likely to worry about the reaction of the "competition" than when degree of ownership concentration is smaller. To assert that pricing decisions have not become more independent of market forces in the face of increasing industrial concentration is to assert that power exists but is not used. To so state is to declare that companies have an increasing ability to charge higher prices—or resist lower prices—but that they fail to do so either because of benevolence or ignorance. Such a reaction seems unrealistic. To claim either disinterested benevolence or undocumented ignorance on the part of American business is to underestimate both the aggressiveness and the shrewdness of the businessman. Power of any sort rarely exists in a vacuum.[1]

The Decline of Price Competition

It is plausible that the competition engaged in by large businesses will tend to be in areas other than price. Competition in terms of styling and advertising is one thing; cutting prices in order to lure new business is quite another. Indeed, price competition, which forms the heart of the perfectly competitive model of economic behavior, is increasingly viewed as unfair competition! Price competition has become a "price war"; it is to be avoided wherever possible.[2]

Why are firms so reluctant to engage in price competition? Basically, because no good can come from it—at least for the businesses in ques-

---

[1] It is interesting to note that denial of the *use* of such monopoly power on the part of the business firm is sometimes done in *defense* of the competitive system. Such a denial is itself a contradiction, since a basic premise of price theory is the profit-maximization principal. And profit maximization implies increasing prices whenever this will lead to greater profits. It cannot go both ways.

[2] Price cutting as a means of increasing business was widely observed during the severe recession of 1974–75. This was taken by many observers to be proof that price competition still exists. It does. The question, of course, is whether it is necessary to have an 8 to 10 percent level of unemployment in order to observe this "competitive" behavior.

tion. Cutting prices in order to gain a larger share of the market will necessitate a similar action on the part of the competition. For example, when Inland Steel refused to go along with industry price increases in the face of presidential wrath in 1962, other steel firms had no alternative but to roll back their increases. Similarly, price cuts by an oligopolist can be expected to bring about retaliatory measures on the part of other firms in the industry. If, as is usually the case, the total industry demand is fairly inelastic—meaning that total sales will not increase substantially with a given decrease in price—every firm will be worse off than before the price cut. It takes only a few such instances to prove to the firms involved that such price competition is simply poor business. And it does not require any overt collusion—such as that prohibited by antitrust statutes—to prevent such price wars in the future.

Corporate Planning

John Kenneth Galbraith contends in the *New Industrial State* that firms have, as their major goal, planning for the future, in which case the likelihood that price competition will not be resorted to increases. Power, argues Galbraith, is passing to a new factor of production, the organized intelligence of those individuals who make up the technostructure of the emerging society. The principal function of this new class, he holds, is to plan for the future. Furthermore, Galbraith argues, such planning requires size.

The modern corporation has obviously achieved this size. For example, Galbraith points out that "in 1965, three industrial corporations, General Motors, Standard Oil of New Jersey and Ford Motor Company, had more gross income than all of the firms in the country. The income of General Motors, of $20.7 billion, about equalled that of the three million smallest firms in the country—around 90 percent of all firms. The gross revenues of each of the three corporations just mentioned far exceed those of any single state. The revenues of General Motors in 1963 were fifty times those of Nevada, eight times those of New York, and slightly less than one-fifth those of the Federal Government" (34, p. 76).

The overriding reason for attempting to gain such size, argues Galbraith, is to gain a control over markets in order to expedite the planning process. In order to plan effectively, the firm must reduce the number of uncertainties. Growth is the most effective way to do this, at the same time spreading the risks of the remaining uncertainties. One big uncertainty that the rational firm will want to minimize is that of price fluctuations. The cold winds of perfectly competitive markets with their rapidly and continually fluctuating prices may forge strong-willed individuals out of small producers; they most decidedly will not facilitate the planning of large corporations. Here, changing prices—especially those fluctuating downward—are a threat. If possible, they are to be eliminated.

Of course, even with the most astute advertising program, it is impossible to isolate oneself completely from the exigencies of the market. No one seriously contends that the large corporation is able to set prices or to make other decisions with complete disregard for external constraints. Again, it is a matter of degree. The important consideration is the limits within which the large firm is constrained. The evidence indicates that these limits have been widening. And, to the extent that large firms are increasingly able to isolate themselves from market forces and thereby to enlarge the discretionary limits within which they act, they are able to set prices above those that would prevail in a perfectly competitive market.

One can view this process in a slightly different manner. Where competition prevails, the business firm is "controlled" by this competition with respect to its pricing decisions. As the firm grows, however, and increasingly isolates itself from market forces, this control diminishes. As a result, it becomes possible to raise prices (that is, cause inflation) because of market power. Public intervention, then, can be designed to replace the earlier restraints provided by the market, with overt constraints provided by a public agency. This is not to say that such a policy always works or even that it can possibly work. It is simply to say that this is one of the considerations concerning the imposition of market controls.

The Steel Industry

Actions of the steel industry in recent years provide an example of the exercise of market power on the part of business firms. Throughout the 1950s, prices for steel continually increased in spite of the fact that utilization rates in the industry were decreasing. From 1951 to 1960, the wholesale price index moved up by a total of only 4 percent for the entire period. The price of metals, which reflects largely what is happening to the price of steel, increased by 25 percent throughout this same period. At the same time, manufacturing utilization rates *decreased* from 94 percent to 81.5 percent.

This can hardly reflect demand-pull inflation. Instead, it provides clear evidence of market power in the steel industry. Not only was the industry able to hold prices constant in the presence of falling demand, it was able to *increase* prices. Surely this is not the type of behavior one would expect in competitive markets characterized by a lack of market power. Indeed, profit *margins* in the steel industry were actually increasing during the 1950s.

More recent figures display similar trends. From 1966 to 1970, capacity utilization rates in manufacturing continually moved downward from a high of 90.5 percent in 1966 to a sluggish 76.6 percent in 1970. During this same period, however, wholesale prices for metals rose by slightly more than 18 percent while the total wholesale index rose only 12 percent. The difference is hardly as dramatic as that recorded earlier, but the trend is the same—and steel prices led the pack. The record is much the same for the period since 1970. From August 1970 to August 1971 when the wage-price freeze was imposed, the wholesale price index rose by 4 percent. During this period, however, the price of iron and steel went up by 8 percent—double the average rate—and steel mill products increased in price even more. From August of 1971 through December of 1972, during Phases I and II of the price-control program, wholesale prices increased at an average annual rate of 5.7 percent. The steel and iron price indexes went up at an annual rate of only 2.5 percent during this period. Over the next twenty-four months, however, while wholesale prices increased at an incredible 18 percent rate, steel and iron prices increased at a 25.6 percent rate. Furthermore, this latter period was characterized by a declining capacity utilization rate in the primary processing industries from 89.6 percent in the first quarter of 1973 to 68.8 percent in the first quarter of 1975.

Walter Adams, an expert on the steel industry, confirms these impressions. Speaking before a Senate subcommittee, Professor Adams stated that, after World War II, "there was an almost unbroken climb in steel prices, in good times and bad, in the face of rising or falling demand, increasing or declining unit costs. Prices rose even when only 50 percent of the industry's capacity was utilized" (1, p. 246).

This is real market power. And it means, among other things, that the companies in question are able to shield themselves from the winds of competition to such an extent that losses are seldom, if ever, incurred. Gardner Means notes that during the second half of 1960, United States Steel Corporation had a net income after taxes of $111 million. At this time they were operating at 47 percent of capacity. Indeed, Means, along with break-even specialist Fred V. Gardner, estimates that the break-even point for U.S. Steel would have been reached, in 1959, at only 30 percent of capacity! Furthermore, the $111 million profits earned by U.S. Steel in the second half of 1960 represents an *annual* rate of $222 million or "nearly as much as it made after peacetime taxes in 1953 when operations were at the rate of 98 percent of capacity" (64, pp. 147–48).

Galbraith has neatly summarized this implication of market power in a passage from the *New Industrial State:*

> The American business liturgy has long intoned that this is a profit and loss economy. "The American competitive enterprise

system is an acknowledged profit and loss system, the hope of profits being the incentive and the fear of loss being the spur." This may be so. But it is not true that organized part of the economy in which a developed technostructure is able to protect its profits by planning. Nor is it true of the United States Steel Corporation, author of the sentence just cited, which has not had losses for a quarter of a century (34, p. 82).

The evidence from trends in price movements as well as from analyses by several careful researchers all points in the same direction: the steel industry is able to push prices up even when demand is low and falling further. It is even able to increase profit margins during such periods because prices increase faster than costs. As a result, losses are seldom incurred while the price indexes are pushed steadily upward. And this is the essence of market power.

Price Movements

The debates concerning market power and the ability of firms to become protected from market forces have hardly subsided over the past forty years. Professor John M. Blair, a leading proponent of the market power thesis, has provided perhaps the most exhaustive study of the issues in *Economic Concentration* (8). His work contains detailed analyses of the evidence and the arguments surrounding his hotly debated and important subject (see especially pp. 418–466).

While Blair's presentation of the evidence of "administered prices"[3] is highly persuasive, other researchers remain less convinced. Phillip Cagan of the National Bureau of Economic Research has meticulously analyzed pricing behavior of the post–World War II years and concludes that a major reason for the increasing lack of responsiveness of prices to recessions has to do with the greater general anticipation of inflation in recent years. "The decisive influence on price response," writes Cagan, "appears to have been a general adaptation of economic units to inflationary prospects rather than structural developments . . ." (73, p. 93).

Means, however, draws opposing conclusions from recent price history which, he agrees, confirms the administered price thesis:

> . . . In spite of a large budget surplus, almost complete cessation in monetary growth, and a substantial decline in real demand, wholesale prices rose in 1969 and 1970 *faster* than in any of the preceding five years . . . The real problem was the new type of

---

[3] Originally used by Gardner Means in 1935 in *Industrial Prices and Their Relative Inflexibility*.

industrial inflation, one that arises from the market power of big business and big labor and that cannot be controlled by the traditional prescription of limiting demand (63, pp. 52–53).

At issue in this continuing debate is the degree to which market power on the part of business firms is responsible for the observed decline in price flexibility in the face of declining demand. What is *not* at issue is the price rigidity itself. The material presented by Cagan (73) leaves little doubt that prices are much less responsive to slack demand than was previously the case, and there is little argument with this viewpoint.

Just *why* prices fail to respond to recessions is still an open issue. Undoubtedly, a part of the explanation lies in the market power thesis while inflationary expectations also play a part. But whatever the proper division among these and other explanations, the fact is clear that recessions are an increasingly futile and expensive means of attacking inflation. With increasingly rigid prices (in a downward direction), throwing the economic machine into reverse to reduce inflation becomes correspondingly less effective and more expensive. The lesson seems clear: working by themselves, macroeconomic tools can be expected to be an increasingly less effective means of promoting general price stability.

THE MARKET POWER OF LABOR UNIONS

Nowhere does the debate over market controls generate more heat than with respect to the power of labor unions. Union critics maintain that the increased inflationary pressures evident in the economy are entirely the result of the ability of large monopolistic labor unions to blackmail employers into excessive wage increases. Defenders, on the other hand, argue that unions have only been trying to keep up with the cost of living and that, in spite of their efforts, they have been unable to keep up with inflation, let alone cause it.

As usual, both sides can marshal data to support their cause. Critics point out that average weekly earnings have increased every year since 1947. In addition, with the exception of 1955 and 1963, unit labor costs have also risen in every year since 1947. And this is in spite of the fact that the economy experienced recessions in 1949, 1954, 1958, 1960, and 1970. Wages simply do not move downward in the American economy.

From labor's viewpoint, however, the wage situation does not appear so sanguine. For a representative family of four, average real, *spendable* weekly earnings (which consists of weekly earnings less social security and income taxes) were lower in 1974 than in 1971. In view of this fact, it is difficult for labor supporters to see how wage increases can be responsible for inflation.[4]

The argument concerning union impact on wages is neither new nor resolved. And yet it is of central importance to the debate concerning wage controls since controls are at least partly based upon the assumption that labor unions possess market power. Wage controls are justified, in large part, on the premise of cost-push inflation. And this type of inflation, by definition, requires the exercise of market power on the part of labor unions.

The Question of Causality

One might reasonably wonder why there should be any question about the ability of unions to push wages (and, therefore, costs) up. Anyone who glances even occasionally at a newspaper can easily see that labor has been demanding and getting large wage increases. The question lies not so much in *the size* of a wage increase as in *the cause* of an increase. And it is not at all clear that the sole cause is union power.

It is understandable that the public should attribute a given pay raise to the union in question. Certainly, the union does little to discourage this notion. But the fact is that some, if not all, increases may have come about without any union. After all, nonunion wages have been increasing too. The problem, then, is to factor out that part of the wage increase that can rightly be attributed to union power from the part which would have been granted anyway. The result indicates the degree of union power.

Measuring Union Power[5]

Studies that attempt to measure the impact of unions on wages have generally been of two major types. The first method is to measure the

---

[4] Average weekly earnings takes into account two variables: hourly wage rates and the length of the workweek. Therefore, it is possible for wages to increase substantially without any increase, or only a slight one, in weekly earnings if the workweek is shortening. This occurred with the slowdown which began in 1969. Thus, labor's critics prefer to use hourly data. Labor's defenders cite average weekly earnings.

[5] The following discussion concerning the role and impact of unions addresses itself only to their *economic* impact. Many observers have argued that the most important role of labor unions has been in the area of industrial government—dispute settlements, grievance procedure, and so on. The *economic* impact, however, is the factor of direct concern to the debate over market controls.

extent to which unions have been able to increase their wages in relation to nonunion employees. In this case, the *differential* between organized and unorganized workers is the important factor. The second method is to measure the extent to which labor organizations have been able to increase the total share of national income allocated as wages and salaries. That is, the attempted determination is whether unions have been able to increase the factor share of total income that goes to labor as opposed to that which goes to capital. Unfortunately, the results of both types of studies have been extremely imprecise. As with so many other areas of economic analysis, the major problem is that "other things" cannot be held constant in order to see the effect of unionization alone.

Union-Nonunion Wage Differentials

Consider the question of wage differentials. Broadly speaking, there are two main lines of attack in attempting to discern union impact in this area. One is to engage in *cross-section analysis,* which involves looking at different firms or industries that display different degrees of unionization. This is done at a specific time in order to minimize the effect of changes in the nature of demand, production techniques, and other variables that change over time. Then, after adjusting for differences in the firms or industries *other* than the degree of unionization, the remaining wage discrepancy is attributed to union power. Conceptually, this method is sound.

The problem, however, and it is a very serious one, comes when adjusting for the "differences other than unionization." These adjustments may be impossible to make with any degree of precision and, in the final analysis, are the result of value judgments made by the investigator. As a result, the accuracy of the final estimate of union influence may be considerably less than that implied by a number carried out to the third or fourth decimal place. For example, how does one adjust for the differences between auto manufacturing (heavily unionized) and the textile industry in the South (largely unorganized)?

In an effort to minimize these interindustry difficulties, other researchers have undertaken *time-series analyses* of the problem, in which a given industry is studied over a period of years. Usually, this involves analyzing the wage trends in the industry before it becomes organized and noting changes (increases) in wages after extensive unionization of the industry. Again, after adjusting for other variables that might have influenced the observed change, the remainder is attributed to the presence of the union. Once again, the problem is clear. It is very difficult to adjust for all the other things that have been happening to the industry over the period in question, such things as shifts in demand, the introduction of new production techniques, or increased (or decreased) competition. Thus, the results must again be viewed as rough estimates of union impact rather than precise, scientific findings.

The most detailed study of union impact is that provided by H. Gregg Lewis (60). In it, he concluded that unions affected the wages of nonunion as well as union employees and accounted for a differential between the two groups ranging from 10 to 15 percent. Lewis notes that the impact of unionization has been different for different groups at different times, thereby making generalizations difficult. For example, unionization usually has a fairly large immediate impact on wages, which then tapers off as increases fall more in line with those in nonunion areas. Also, some unions (such as the United Mine Workers) have been extremely effective in gaining pay hikes for their members whereas other organizations (such as the Amalgamated Clothing Workers Union) have had little effect.

Because of these differences in union power along with the many other complicating variables, the exact extent to which organized labor has been able to increase the union-nonunion differential is extremely difficult to determine. Most researchers, however, would agree with Lewis' conclusion that the overall impact has probably been 10 to 15 percent, with certain groups (construction trade unionists) achieving a differential of 20 to 25 percent.

Is this really very much to attribute to union power? The public is probably apt to attribute a much larger impact to unions, perhaps as much as a 50-percent differential. This notion results from the fact that large settlements are the ones that make the news and the tendency is to attribute to all unions the same degree of power associated with the most powerful ones. Moreover, as Milton Friedman has observed, "given a labor union, any wage increase will come through the union, even though it may not be a consequence of the union organization" (32, p. 123).

Relative Shares

The other major line of analysis used to evaluate the wage impact of trade unions asks whether unions have been able to increase the total share of output that goes to labor. In other words, has the return attributed to wages and salaries been increasing at the expense of capital? Historically, this was considered a crucial measure of the well-being of the working class as well as a useful measure of labor power.

The interest in this measure undoubtedly springs in large part from the Marxist challenge to capitalist theory that holds that *all* income should accrue to labor. This conclusion is reached by reasoning that labor is the only real factor of production (the *labor theory of value*).

What has been happening? In contrast to Marxist prediction, the share going to labor has been *increasing* slightly rather than decreasing. Labor's share of total income has gone from approximately 60 percent in 1930 to slightly over 71 percent at present (37, p. 224). Figures differ depending upon measurement definitions and procedures, but most estimates agree substantially with this one.

What are we to conclude from this with respect to union power? Unfortunately, not much. Most economists place little stock in the labor theory of value since it is now generally recognized that there are other legitimate factors of production. But even on its own grounds the relative share idea indicates little concerning either labor's power or its well-being. Concerning the well-being of the working man, a glance at the data will show that in times of recession or depression the *share* going to labor *increases* as prices (and profits) fall faster than wages. The reverse is true in times of prosperity, when profits increase and wages decrease as a share of total income.

According to the exploitation theory, one would be forced to argue that labor is better off in recessionary times and worse off in times of recovery. Such a theory has little appeal to economists and even less to the working man, who knows that good times mean higher wages and better living conditions. His concern is more with the level of wages than the share of total income that is accruing to labor.[6]

Even though the share of income going to labor has increased slightly, this is not necessarily due to union power. As with wage differentials, many things were happening at the same time. The fact that union size and labor's share of income were increasingly simultaneously does not imply that one caused the other. Indeed, there is good reason to believe that the causal effect of union size (power) on labor's share of total income has been small, perhaps nonexistent.

Sectoral Shifts

More important than union power has been the shift in sectors of the economy from agriculture to industry and, more recently, from industry to services (including government). Only a small portion of agricultural output is attributed to labor; the rest is apportioned as returns to cap-

---

[6] This helps to explain the lack of sympathy Marxists have traditionally found among the American working man. While the Marxian socialists continue to view labor's lot as tied to the share of total output they receive, the working man sees his well-being as tied to the size of his pay check. His wages continue to be of greater concern to him than the "surplus value" he is producing. In large part, the degree of "exploitation" and the level of wages depend upon different forces and, indeed, tend to move in opposite directions.

ital, including land. Manufacturing, on the other hand, displays a large share of return going to labor since there are many more wage and salary employees than in farming.[7] At the other extreme, the less capitalized service and government sectors have even larger shares of income attributed to labor. The proportion reaches 100 percent in government since the value of governmental output *is measured* by labor inputs.

As the society evolves, then, from primarily an agricultural economy to one in which the emphasis is on manufacturing and services, one would expect to see an overall increase in labor's share simply because of these sectoral shifts. (Emphasis here means in terms of employment, not "importance." Food is still just as important as ever and so are physical goods. They can simply be produced with less manpower than before.) These changes, then, are much more important in explaining the slight increase in labor's share than is the impact of unionization. There is fairly widespread agreement that organized labor has had little effect on trends concerning labor's share.[8]

Spillover Effects

Despite repeated attempts to compute the influence of unions on wages, the extent to which unions can push wages beyond productivity increases, and thereby contribute to inflation, is still unresolved. One reason for this is that a given union may have a very marked influence on the wage rate of the nonunion firm or industry. As a result, the union-nonunion wage differential may greatly understate the power of organized labor to increase wage rates.

Suppose, for example, that a union is able to organize one-half a given industry. Predictably, the union would begin its organizing with those firms within the industry it deemed the most susceptible to unionism. The remaining firms, in the union's estimation, may consist of the "tough nuts to crack." In fact, the remaining firms may be adamant in

---

[7] Part of the problem here is one of measurement. Conceptually, a farmer's income is partly a return for his labor and partly a return on his capital investment. That is, his income consists of both wages and profits. In practice, however, it is extremely difficult to divide these returns. As a result, all of his income is considered profits. The same is true of small individual proprietorships where all returns are considered profits. As these businesses continually account for a smaller portion of the total transactions in the economy, the relative returns to capital continually diminish while those to labor grow. And this is quite independent of how "well off" anyone is.

[8] The solid union supporter, of course, will not let the fact that labor's share has not been increasing in the union sector deter his enthusiasm. He will simply argue that, had it not been for unions, the share going to labor would have decreased much more in this sector. To this there is no answer.

their objections to seeing their work force organized and may go to great lengths to avoid unionization. This may involve paying their employees the union wage rate or even slightly more in order to convince them that there is no reason to organize. In this event, the union has exerted an influence on wages much greater than the relative differential between the union and nonunion firms will show. Indeed, there could be little or no differential and it would not mean that the union was ineffectual. It could mean that it was extremely effective in increasing overall wages.

The foregoing example illustrates the spillover effect of unions on the wage level. This constitutes a prime reason for the difficulties in measuring union impact since it is very difficult to measure the extent of this spillover. For the same reason, this constitutes a major reason for the continuing debate concerning the impact of unionization. Once again, it would be nice to hold other things constant in order to measure the extent of this spillover. And, once again, this is impossible.

Furthermore, spillover can affect different sectors of the economy as well as different firms within the same industry. How much impact, for example, does a large wage increase in the construction industry have on union demands in other sectors? It would be a mistake to assume that demands in various sectors and industries are independent of each other. Also, how much does the going rate of pay in the private sector (which may be unionized) effect what different governmental agencies are willing to pay in the public sector? It is impossible to assume independence among the wage structures in these different sectors since, even without unionization in the public sector, wages cannot be set with total disregard for comparable wages in the private sector. Indeed, public wages are often explicitly tied to those for "comparable work" in the private sector. Thus, the effects of labor unions' market power are felt far beyond the firms and industries in which this power is directly exerted. The question, then, is the extent to which this power is felt on the entire level of prices. Furthermore, increased technological and communications advances in conjunction with an increasingly mobile society has undoubtedly increased the degree of wage emulation throughout the economy. The future shock of wage movements is much greater than it once was.

The Cost-push Mechanism

For purposes of analysis, we can divide the economy into two sectors: union and nonunion. Wages and employment, even in the nonunion sector, need not conform completely to the competitive model. However, we will assume that there are fewer market restrictions in this area than in the union sector.

Given this situation, suppose that the union (or unionized sector) is able to bargain a substantial increase in wages and that, in turn, the companies increase their prices. Two possibilities then present themselves.

Case I

First, suppose that demand is highly inelastic in the union sector so that just as much output will be sold after the price increase as before. (This is the strongest assumption, that is, perfectly inelastic demand.) In this case, there will be no decrease in employment in the union sector since output will remain constant.

Consumers, however, will now have less money to spend in the nonunion sector; so there will be a drop in demand here. Two events are then possible in this sector. If wages are flexible downward, they will move to a lower equilibrium level and there will be no decrease in employment. In this case, the union sector was able to increase its wages by depressing those of unorganized workers.

However, it is unlikely that wages will be completely flexible in the nonunion sector since many social factors other than unionism mitigate downward wage flexibility. To the extent that wages do not fall in the face of declining demand, unemployment will be the result. In this case, the union wage increase will be responsible for an increase in nonunion unemployment.

Case II

The second, and more realistic, possibility for the original union wage increase is that as prices rise in this sector, output will decrease; that is, demand will display some degree of elasticity.[9] In this case, the wage hike will result in a loss in employment in the union sector as output is decreased and unemployed union workers are forced to look elsewhere for work—namely in the nonunion sector. But spending will still be unable to keep pace with the decrease in employment in the union sector if the money supply remains constant. As a result, there will again be downward pressure on nonunion wages. If they do move down, this sector will again have paid for the increase in union wages by accepting lower rates of pay. If they do not move down, unemployment will again

---

[9] Readers with a background in price theory will recognize that even if the firm is a complete monopolist it will, if attempting to maximize profits, operate at a level of output where demand elasticity is greater than one, since, at lower levels of output, marginal revenue is negative. This does not necessitate an elastic demand for labor, but one of the determinants of demand elasticity for labor is, of course, the elasticity of demand for the final product.

increase in the nonunion sector. This time, however, some of the former union members who have moved to this sector will also share in the resulting unemployment.

Effects on Allocation

Regardless of the employment effects in the union sector, the resulting reallocation of resources will be less favorable than the pre-union allocation. Prices will be higher in the union sector than they would be in the absence of market power and, as a result, resources will be redirected into areas less desired by consumers. The nonunion employee, therefore, gets hit from two directions: First, his wages have gone down (or, more likely, have failed to go up as fast as they would have without the union influence); and second, the price he pays for union-made products has gone up. The same can be said for the nonunion consumer in general.

Problems of Observation

It may be objected that wage increases in the union sector are unlikely to decrease nonunion wages and, furthermore, that there may be no noticeable employment effects. Indeed, as is often the case, wages and employment may rise simultaneously. Thus, it is often concluded that union pressure on wages is not responsible for either lower nonunion wages *or* unemployment. Therefore, the argument goes, the preceding theoretical reasoning must be wrong.

Although it is true that employment and wages often increase at the same time, it does not follow that the effects of a union increase as depicted above are untrue. It must be remembered that this analysis of union impact attempts to hold other things constant. And the "other things" that are assumed constant include the demand for the product. Oftentimes, demand increases for the final product at the same time that wages are moving upward. In this case, the demand effect may outweigh the higher labor costs and employment will increase *in spite of* the increased wages. (The shift in the demand curve has, in this case, more than compensated for the upward movement along the demand curve.)

Furthermore, since demand is constantly changing in all markets, union and nonunion alike, it is very difficult to isolate the influence of a wage change. This is precisely why it is difficult for most union members (and many other people) to see an increase in wages as the cause of unemployment. Many times, because of demand increases, the two are not associated with each other.

Thus, the effects of union power are often masked by other conditions that are changing simultaneously. *Relative* changes, however, are as important as *absolute* changes. Union wage pressures will make increases in employment in the union sector less than they would have been in the absence of the union; but this will not necessarily bring about an *absolute* decrease in employment.

The same is true for wages in the nonunion sector. Although it is unlikely that wages will move *down* in this sector as a result of union activity, it is likely that they will move upward more slowly than they would have in the absence of the union increase.

Further Spillover

At the same time, the possibility exists that wages will move up faster in some nonunion sectors as a result of union activities. This will be the case where the spillover effect is strong. In this case, an increase in the union sector will trigger a chain reaction in the nonunion sector that will cause wages in the unorganized sector quickly to follow those in the organized markets. The result will be increased unemployment in both sectors.

As an empirical fact, there appears to be a good deal of spillover in the economy. In addition, there are indications that the degree of spillover is *expanding,* which implies greater unemployment as a result of a given wage increase. Although this subject is discussed later, note that to the extent that the spillover from large wage increases *is* greater than it was earlier, the employment (and inflationary) results of the increase will be more pronounced.

Unaided Cost Push

Since the crux of cost-push inflation is that movements such as those discussed above lead to general price increases, one might ask if this is the necessary conclusion from the union-nonunion sector analysis. The answer is no. By itself, such a mechanism would fail to produce a prolonged inflation. This may appear contradictory to the discussion presented above, but it is quite consistent with it.

If wages and prices rise in the union sector, with a constant supply of money and a stable velocity of money (meaning that it doesn't change hands more often), this will mean that less spending can take place. Supposing the extreme, if consumers buy as much from the unionized markets as they did before the price increase, they will necessarily be spending more money in this sector. With a given money supply in the economy, they must then be spending less in unorganized markets. The result will be a decrease in demand in the latter sector and further unemployment.

To the extent that consumers spend less in the union sector as well, some unemployment will be shifted to this area. In either case, with a constant money supply, the result will be unemployment and not serious inflation. There may be *some* inflation if prices fail to come down in the nonunion sector as demand decreases, but this will soon level off. The cost-push pressures in the union sector would, if left alone, lead to enough employment and underutilization of resources and capacity so that further upward movements in the price indexes would be curtailed. At this point, whatever inflation had been caused by union power would be halted.

The Critical Role of the Money Supply

While this mechanism undoubtedly stops any inflation that resulted from excessive wage demands, it is just as certain that such an event is unlikely to occur. Again, other things cannot be assumed to remain constant and this time the changing variable is likely to be the money supply. In order for the wage increases to bring about the unemployment necessary to stop the inflationary pressures, it is necessary to assume that the supply of money is constant. Should it be increasing, however, it would be possible for prices to move upward in the union sector without any decrease in spending in the nonunion sector and, hence, with no decrease in employment. Indeed, should the money supply increase fast enough, there could be employment *increases* in the nonunion sector.

This action, however, will turn potential unemployment increases into price increases. The Federal Reserve, by increasing the money supply, is ensuring that excessive wage hikes will not result in unemployment but that they will, instead, result in inflation.[10] Indeed, it can be argued that both unions and management are aware that a drop in demand (and hence in employment) is unlikely to result from an increase in wages and prices. Increases in the supply of money will prevent this from occurring.

Thus, each party to the bargaining table is less likely to consider the employment effects of its actions. Indeed, in the extreme case, there is no employment effect but only a price effect as the Federal Reserve continues to inject enough money into the economy to prevent unemployment from becoming serious.

This ensures that the inflationary spiral will continue since it makes little sense for anyone to forego a possible wage increase because of the threat of unemployment. Nor does it make sense for management to risk a strike because of fear that demand for its product will drop after a price rise. The logical action for both parties becomes attempting to

---

[10] While "excessive" is a value-packed term, it can be defined in a more operational manner as an increase in wages above the increase in productivity. Such incrases, when widespread, are inflationary.

increase wages (and prices) enough to stay ahead of the continual upward price movements. And this is the essence of an inflationary spiral. In short, cost-push inflation would be largely nonexistent were it not for the fact that the monetary authorities legitimize excessive wage and price increases by increasing the supply of money.

Why, then, does the Federal Reserve persist in increasing the supply of money to the point of inflation? Or, turned around, why do the monetary authorities not allow the resulting unemployment to cure the inflationary process by itself? The answer lies in the mandate, both social and legal, for the federal government to maintain a full-employment economy. And, although many years have passed since the passage of the Employment Act in 1946 when full employment was not reached, the thrust of federal policy has still been in this direction. Indeed, for the most part, monetary authorities have been criticized for being more concerned with inflation than with unemployment and for deliberately following tight money policies which have resulted in relatively high unemployment rates (relative, at least, to most Western European countries). Thus, there is little doubt that, left alone, cost-push inflation would bring about its own demise through increased unemployment. But this option, if allowed to operate, is deemed by most Americans (as well as by most economists) to be too high a price to pay for price stability.

In a sense, then, one can say that it is the monetary authorities in the foregoing chain of events, not union or corporate power, that is responsible for the inflation. But this requires a rather curious twist of the facts. The money supply was increased to mitigate the unemployment triggered by excessive wage and price increases. And this was done because the resulting unemployment was deemed to constitute an extremely serious problem. To blame the price rises on Federal Reserve policies, then, rather than the union and corporate power that made these policies necessary is completely to negate the importance of unemployment. It would also seem to be a rather nearsighted view of causality.[11] Thus, to hold monetary authorities responsible for inflation caused by market power on the part of labor unions seems misplaced. Only if large increases in unemployment are held to be an acceptable condition of price stability does this view of the situation seem credible. Hopefully, the amount of unemployment that would be necessary to provide price stability in the absence of market controls will continue to be considered excessive by the public as well as by the policymakers.

---

[11] Of course, if one holds that unions do not have the power to push wages up in the first place, any inflation can be attributed to demand pull elements made possible by increases in the supply of money. Whether this power exists, however, is an empirical question and, as such, does not negate the logic of the cost-push thesis. Rather, it denies the premise; namely, that of market power, upon which the idea of cost-push inflation rests.

The Trade-off Again

This brings us squarely back to the trade-off among unemployment, inflation, and free markets. If a part of the inflationary bias of the economy is the result of market power on the part of unions and corporations, as appears to be the case, policies that restrict the exercise of this power can mitigate inflationary pressures. The idea behind market controls is just that; to decrease the range in which discretionary wage and price increases can take place.

Limiting wages and prices, however, involves the loss of some market freedoms on the part of both labor unions and business firms. Thus, there seems to be no easy way out of the three-pronged dilemma of full employment, stable prices, and free markets. Any two can be achieved, at least partially, at the expense of the third. Attempts to reach all three, however, require trade-offs among them.

The "Old" Versus the "New" Economics

A part of the price-employment dilemma arises precisely because of the *success* of Keynesian policies. Most economists no longer accept the view that recessions are somehow necessary to "keep everyone honest" and, more precisely, to ensure that high rates of inflation will be unable to persist. At the same time, the public is committed both socially and legally (through the Employment Act of 1946) to the goal of full employment. Indeed, with economists teaching that high levels of unemployment are unnecessary, the public has a right to demand that its elected officials follow full-employment policies. And this in itself builds an inflationary bias into the economy since, as market power is flexed and unemployment results, corrective actions are taken that, as a side effect, produce a rising price level.

One option, of course, would be to revert to the old economics and give up the idea of smoothing out the business cycle in an effort to eliminate large-scale recessions. Indeed, such a policy has many advocates. They point to the current inflationary recession as proof of the fatal flaw within the full-employment policies of the new economics. The degree of unemployment in 1975 in response to their old-time religion should at least make one wonder just how much of a recession it now takes to achieve a semblance of price stability.

To accept such a conclusion belies the very substantial gains that have been made in the science of economics within the past several years. And, in addition, it represents a defeatist attitude toward the solution of serious social problems. The public should not tolerate high levels of unemployment, and it should not tolerate high rates of inflation. Nor should the public accept rigid and inflexible controls on the markets that completely thwart the pricing system. A policy mix, however, should be accepted where *some* market power on the part of private interests is sacrificed for the public interest.

The choice is not between perfect competition and government intervention. Market power is a fact of life and could not, even if one desired it, be swept away. A substitution of some public power for private monopoly power can, if applied cautiously and thoughtfully, have a beneficial effect. The result will not be completely stable prices at low levels of unemployment. Such a state of affairs, along with perfectly competitive markets, is utopian. If a better trade-off can be achieved, however, (that is, a movement of the Phillips curve to the left), the policy that engenders it deserves at least to be tried out.

Evidence of Union Power

The existence of cost-push inflation, through the mechanism described above, rests upon the assumption that unions are indeed able to push wages and prices up in the absence of strong market pressures working in this direction. The process described above was assumed to have started with the ability of unions to obtain wage increases larger than would have been achieved in their absence. What evidence is there that this is indeed the case? And, even more fundamentally, what type of evidence would be necessary to demonstrate the existence of substantial market power?

With respect to the latter question, two types of evidence can be important. First, we can examine the extent to which wages increase in times when the market clearly displays no excess demand. That is, if wages are going up during periods when there is substantial unemployment, this may be considered evidence that market power is present. In a powerless economy characterized by perfect competition (see Chapter 2), wages would be going *down* during these periods, not up. Second, we can examine the extent to which unions are able to increase, or at least maintain, the wage differential they enjoy over their nonunion counterparts. It was argued above that an increase in wages in the union sector will lead to downward pressure on wages in the nonunion sector. If true, this should lead to greater wage differentials between the two sectors.

Wages, Prices, and Employment[12]

Observing the period when cost-push inflation first began to be seriously considered—the late 1950s—evidence points to the existence of cost push forces in operation. Consider, for example, the 1957–58

---

[12] Again, unless otherwise stated, the data presented in this and later sections are from U.S. Department of Labor sources.

period when unemployment was high and moving higher. It averaged 6.8 percent in 1958; a peak of 7.5 percent was reached in July of that year. At the same time, both the consumer and wholesale price indexes continued to move upward. In addition, unit labor costs continued to rise while corporate profits were falling.

It is often argued that these increases were simply due to momentum from earlier periods of lesser unemployment. Furthermore, when unemployment remained high in the early 1960s, price indexes (especially the wholesale index) did stop their increases. The fact that this momentum was unable to make itself felt, however, is a solid indication that strong institutional forces with the power to push prices upward existed.

Recent evidence is even more dramatic. Consider 1970, a slack year by all measures. Unemployment continually increased, reaching and exceeding the 6 percent level by the end of the year. Labor markets became very loose, utilization rates dropped, and the economy slid deeper into the planned recession of 1969. Prices and wages, however, did not drop in the face of this. They did not even stop rising. In fact, they continued their relentless increases at even faster rates! Surely if ever the classical laws of supply and demand failed to operate, this was such a time.

Nor can all this simply be attributed to "left-over agreements" from the late 1960s when demand-pull elements started the inflationary process. Collective bargaining agreements that were reached *during* 1970 exhibited no tendency to show any respect for the fact that unemployment rates were high. That is, market conditions seemed to have little, if any, influence on the wage and benefit increases obtained by organized workers.

Consider more recent history. In 1974 unemployment moved steadily upward during the year as the economy slid into the worst decline since the Great Depression. From a low of 5.0 percent in April, unemployment rose to 7.2 percent by December and to 9.2 percent in May 1975. Classical wage theory suggests that this would be a period of declining wages and prices. Such, of course, was hardly the case. Consumer and wholesale prices continued to sizzle along in the double-digit range, while wage increases continued at near-record levels. Compensation per man-hour in the private nonfarm economy rose at an annual rate of 8.1 percent in the first quarter of 1974, 11.3 in the second, 10.2 in the third, and 9.4 in the fourth. And what about the union sector? Here negotiated first-year increases rose dramatically throughout the year *in spite of* rapidly increasing unemployment. In the first quarter of 1974, first-year settlements average 6.9 percent; in the second quarter 9.2; in the third 11.9; and in the fourth 14.6![13] It may well be that such in-

---

[13] Data are from Department of Labor sources.

creases were "justified" in terms of the burning inflation, but the fact that such increases were possible in conjunction with rising unemployment strongly suggests that demand was not *pulling* wages upward; unions were *pushing* them up. And this is the essence of labor market power. One might wonder just how long unemployment would have to continue at this level or how much higher it would have to go before the size of these settlements would decrease substantially.

If market forces are still working, they are doing so only with significant time lags, and then only marginally. Furthermore, when one considers that these major agreements form the basis for scores of smaller settlements, their inflationary nature becomes even more apparent.

Further Inflationary Settlements

Construction wages head the list of large increases. First-year changes in wages (*excluding* fringes) for contracts negotiated during 1970 averaged over 18 percent. And this is an industry where productivity increases are generally thought to be small. By 1971 the rate of increase in construction wages was abating with first-year settlements averaging 13.7 percent. 1972 and 1973 saw dramatic improvements with first-year settlements averaging 6.7 and 6.1 percent, respectively. Much of this decrease, however, can be attributed to the Construction Industry Stabilization Committee, which proved to be a forerunner of the Pay Board. Most observers believe that this committee was highly successful in mitigating the inflationary nature of construction industry settlements. In 1974, after controls ended and in the face of sharply rising unemployment in construction (from 8.2 percent in January 1974, to 15 percent in January 1975 to over 20 percent by mid-year), first-year settlements in this industry again took off—from 7.1 percent in the first quarter of 1974 to 9.2 in the second, and 11.2 and 10.3 in the third and fourth quarters, respectively.

When considering the trends in productivity, the above settlements appear even more inflationary. The average rate of increase for the total economy is about 3 percent per year in output per man-hour. Considering that the inflationary nature of a wage settlement consists of the wage increase minus the growth in productivity, it can be seen that increases such as the ones under discussion are highly inflationary.

Recent productivity increases have been even less than the trend. In 1973, for example, productivity rose by only 0.73 percent, and in 1974 productivity *declined,* due to the recession, by 3.6 percent. The result was an increase in unit labor costs of 7.4 percent in 1973 and an explosive 14 percent in 1974.

This disparity between wage increases and productivity increases continued to take place in the face of increasingly high unemployment rates and low levels of industry capacity utilization. One is hard-pressed to find an explanation for such increases in the form of excess demand. And although high and prolonged unemployment rates may eventually pull down these increases—no group is entirely isolated from market forces—the social and personal costs represented by the necessary length and severity of the unemployment would be unacceptable. While the foregoing evidence may not "prove" that unions are able to push wages above the level that would exist in a more competitive market, it should at least make one highly suspicious.

Another Look at Wage Differentials

The second major source of evidence concerning union power is the question of union-nonunion wage differentials. As discussed, the evidence indicates that unions have been able to increase their relative earnings by an average 10 to 15 percent. Of particular interest, however, is the extent to which they are able to *widen* the lead they enjoy over nonunion employees. As many researchers have noted, the percentage differential between nonunion and union employees has not been increasing and, therefore, organized labor has not been able to increase its *relative* advantage. From this it is often concluded that increased union power has not been a source of cost-push inflation.

Such evidence, however, can be misleading. First, if one looks at union versus nonunion wages in manufacturing, the increases are clearly larger in the union sector. For example, in 1970 union wage increases in manufacturing averaged approximately 7.8 percent. During this same period, increases in nonunion manufacturing firms averaged approximately 5.7 percent. Admittedly, such evidence is only suggestive, but it is consistent.

The major point concerning wage differentials between union and nonunion employees, however, is that these differentials would not *have* to be increasing for cost-push inflation to be occurring. This is because of the close connection between wage movements in the union sector and those in the nonunion sector; that is, the spillover effect. There is hard as well as impressionistic evidence that such effects are substantial and, indeed, may be increasing. The Eckstein-Wilson study cited earlier (31) concluded that all manufacturing wages tended to follow closely the movements in certain key industries. In addition, Professor George Hildebrand has argued persuasively that these spillover effects are now built into the economy in such a way as to ensure that there exist increased wage rigidities. The result is a greater inflationary bias to any large settlement (45).

In particular, Hildebrand argues that collective bargaining has built into the entire economy—nonunion as well as union sectors—the expectations that wages will increase year after year regardless of market conditions. Hildebrand argues:

> Employees throughout the economy "now expect and can insist upon regular annual increases in total money compensation per unit of work performed, whether they are represented by unions or not, wherever they work and whatever their occupation, and regardless of any level of unemployment . . . ." (45, p. 18).

Given such a state of affairs, it would not be necessary for the union-nonunion wage differential to increase for wage increases to be responsible for inflationary pressures.

Professor George Perry, who has studied extensively the wage-price relationship, agrees with Hildebrand concerning these spillover effects. He admits, however, that they are difficult to demonstrate theoretically. "Although the concept lacks theoretical elegance," writes Perry, "I am persuaded that inflation is now perpetuated to an important degree because of high 'habitual' rates of wage and price increases" (80, p. 446).

The Success of Collective Bargaining

As with Keynesian policy, the very success of collective bargaining as an institution may be responsible in part for the seeming increases in the spillover effect. As unions have become firmly entrenched as a part of the American industrial relations scene, employer resistance to their existence, as well as to their demands, has declined. And with unionists able to demand and obtain annual wage increases, nonunion employers as well as their employees have increasingly gone along with this arrangement. Indeed, the many unorganized employers that fear an invasion by the union can hardly "afford" not to give approximately the same increases as those negotiated in the union sector. The demonstration effect works on both employees and employers.

Furthermore, a part of the ability of the union to extract large and consistent increases from the employer depends upon the ability of the employer to raise his prices in turn. The power of corporations to do this may well be increasing, and to the extent that it is, they have less to fear from wage increases. Indeed, in many instances union wage demands become the justification for price increases that *more* than cover the increased wage costs. When the firm is able to pass on the wage increase and even go beyond this, it has little to fear from union demands.

Annual wage increases, then, have become an institutionalized feature of the American economy. And with the high visibility of large union increases, nonunion employees increasingly view these settlements as the norm, as well as the target, for their own increases. Furthermore, everyone can legitimately claim to be attempting to catch up as they continually chase the ever elusive leader. And as resistance from nonunion employers decreases—(regular increases become the thing to do)—the spillover effects become more pronounced, thereby increasing the ripple effect of union wage demands.

In an other-things-equal world, this would lead to high unemployment rates. In the real world, however, where the government must pursue full-employment policies, this leads to inflation. Thus, without some kind of income policy to moderate discretionary wage and price increases, the normal rate of unemployment associated with a given rate of price increase may well continue to rise.

The fact that there is little evidence of an increase in the relative union-nonunion wage differential does not, therefore, negate the probability of cost-push inflation. Because of these spillover effects, there is no reason why this differential would have to be increasing in order to support the cost-push theory of inflation.

Absolute or Relative Wage Differentials?

Lowell Gallaway (36, pp. 99–108) has presented an interesting and persuasive argument for considering the *absolute* wage differential between union and nonunion employees as the relevant one. Briefly, Gallaway's argument is that in a growing economy characterized by increasing real wages, there is no reason to assume that if two occupations remained proportionately attractive, their *relative* wage differentials would remain constant. Indeed, since some of the costs of relocating and/or retraining could be expected to decrease in real terms, we might expect to see the relative wage differential shrink. After citing a number of implications from formal economic theory as well as empirical evidence concerning the movement of wage differentials in a pre-union economy, Gallaway concludes that absolute differentials constitute a more appropriate measure of union impact than relative differentials.

While all of this may strike the observer as being not too meaningful and, indeed, somewhat tedious, the implications are quite significant. For if absolute differentials are the important consideration, it can be shown that unionized sectors of the economy have continually been increasing their wages in relation to nonunion sectors. The difference in the two measures (relative versus absolute) results from the fact that heavily unionized sectors of the economy (construction, transportation, manufacturing, and mining industries) started the post-war era with much higher wage rates than those in less unionized sectors (service, retail, and wholesale trades). Thus, even though these latter sectors have been receiving increases on a par with the unionized sectors percentage-wise, the result has been continuing increase in the absolute differential. This lends support to the contention that unions are able to increase their wages at the expense of nonunion workers.

Further Evidence of Union Power

Additional evidence of union power is the fact that the large wage increases evident in unionized sectors of the economy have come at a time when employment in these same sectors has been decreasing in a relative and, in some instances an absolute, sense. For example, durable-goods manufacturing employment has grown very little in the past twenty years and, indeed, was slightly greater in 1953 than in 1965. After 1965 employment rose in this sector but this was largely a result of the movement toward manufacturing as a result of the Viet Nam War buildup and not due to the normal growth pattern of the economy. The results of this artificial demand increase became very apparent as the economy moved into the 1969 recession and, because of defense cutbacks, employment was sharply curtailed in manufacturing. By December of 1970, employment in durable-goods manufacturing was down by well over a million persons from the peak of 11.97 million it reached in September 1969 and was almost back to the 1953 level. In 1960 durable-goods manufacturing employment accounted for 13.5 percent of the civilian labor force. In 1968, at the peak of the Viet Nam War, this figure had increased to 15 percent. After 1969, however, employment in durable-goods manufacturing decreased in *absolute* terms as well as relative terms and by 1974 again represented only 13 percent of the labor force.

There is no way in which durable-goods manufacturing could be termed a growth industry, except, perhaps, with respect to wage rates. Hourly earnings in this field rose from $1.86 in 1953 to $3.56 in 1970. By 1974 this rate was up to $4.68 an hour, a 31-percent increase from 1970.

Consider mining, which is, of course, another heavily unionized industry. Here, the total number of nonsupervisory workers *decreased* by 25 percent from 1950 to 1974, whereas wages rose from $1.77 to $5.20, by over 90 percent. Other examples could be cited. Classical economic theory would indicate that in an industry that is declining in absolute, as well as relative, employment terms, we would expect to see a leveling out of wage increases and possibly even some decreases. Such has hardly been the case. As George Hildebrand noted when referring to similar figures for an earlier period, "These are end-year comparisons and are at most only straws in the wind. But there is not much doubt about how the wind has been blowing" (45, p. 23).

Summary

There can be little doubt that powerful unions are able to keep wages up for their members and, indeed, even increase them substantially in the face of high unemployment and declining demand. Such occurrences in the present magnitude would scarcely be possible in a more competitive economy and, as a result, this provides clear evidence of substantial market power. Furthermore, even if one contends that relative wage differentials are the relevant measure of organized labor's power to better itself in comparison with unorganized labor, there is good reason to believe that unions have been quite successful in preserving the differential, if not in widening it.

If one holds to the idea of absolute differentials as being the relevant criterion of strength, union power becomes even more impressive. Starting with higher base rates, unions have been able to maintain—and in many cases increase—the percentage increases in pay. As a result, the *absolute* level of their pay has continued to climb faster than that of nonunion employees, and therefore the differential has increased.

Finally, the use of either measure of wage differentials understates the true union impact because of the large amounts of spillover from wage actions in the union sector. There are reasons to believe that the degree of spillover—an impossible variable to measure—is increasing. To the extent that this is so, rigidities in the wage structures are increasing. And this leads to a worsening of the unemployment-inflation tradeoff.

THE WORSENING TRADE-OFF 7

> The first panacea for a mismanaged nation is inflation of the currency; the second is war. Both bring a temporary prosperity; both bring a permanent ruin.
>
> Ernest Hemingway

The persistence of continually worsening combinations of unemployment and inflation during the 1970s raises a very important question: Is this simply a temporary phenomenon that will right itself once inflation is brought under control, or have the structural and institutional factors changed the basic nature of the economy in such a way as to make it more inflation-prone? In other words, has the Phillips curve shifted to the right, or are we simply observing unemployment and inflation combinations that lie, temporarily, to the right of the actual, long-run curve? The question is of crucial importance since policies must be based upon an assumption concerning the temporary or permanent nature of the current problem. If one holds that the current worsening is only a temporary matter, he may view market controls and structural reforms as unnecessary or, if necessary, only for short periods. On the other hand, if there have been basic changes in the economy, this may imply the need for longer-run incomes policies and, at the same time, policies aimed at altering structural problems.

The position taken here is that there has, indeed, been a permanent worsening of the inflation/unemployment trade-off due to basic changes in the economy. These changes are seen to consist of increases in the structural adjustment problems caused by continuing changes in the labor supply and in the demand for labor as well as increases in the power factors that allow unions and corporations to exhibit more inflationary pressures than before. The existence of these two factors—structural imbalances and market power—provides the basic reason why prices increase before full employment is reached. If, then, one holds that these factors are moving the economy (reality) further from the perfectly competitive model, the result will be a continually worsening inflation/unemployment trade-off. And this is precisely what appears to be happening.

The problem in marshalling evidence of this proposition is that there are forces inherent *within* an existing inflationary situation that give it a momentum of its own and that could, therefore, explain the observed worsening in the trade-off. Furthermore, if this inflationary momentum is the cause of the poor trade-off, the problem will subside once the price rises are mitigated.

Undoubtedly, much of the problem *is* the result of this momentum. Few economists hold market power or structural changes responsible for starting the current inflationary spiral, which was largely brought about by demand-pull forces in the second half of the 1960s and again in 1972 and 1973. Before examining the possible reasons for a shift to the right in the Phillips curve, we will look at the reasons why both unions and corporations are better able to flex their marketplace muscle in times of rising prices.

Inflation as the Cause of Inflation

Many observers believe that unions and managements do not have the power to *start* an inflationary spiral but, once started by other forces, they are able to keep it going. This seems to be true. The implication is that somehow a given amount of market power is better able to increase either wages or prices during times of inflation than in times of stable prices. That is, the existing inflation is able to cause further inflation. Why might this be so?

First, with respect to unions, there is the overriding fact that inflation—especially serious inflation—means a decrease in purchasing power. Indeed, this was the case in the second half of the 1970s when real (deflated) earnings were actually less in 1975 than in 1970. Such an occurrence produces a strong justification for demanding not only a wage increase but a further increase to catch up with the cost of living. At the same time, the frustrations brought about by continual increases in prices lead to increased militance on the part of all groups and, therefore, an increase in the determination to get the necessary increases. Nor is the union sector the only one affected. Frustrations become widespread and everyone demands to catch up with rising living costs. Moreover, to the extent that unions are able to protect themselves from rising prices by obtaining sizeable wage increases, other sectors will increasingly view this as a further justification for their own increases. That is, the spillover effects of large union increases will be greater during a period of mounting frustrations brought on by the inflationary spiral. And, of course, no one can really be blamed for attempting to keep pace with the cost of living.[1]

On the other side of the bargaining table, there will be less incentive for management to resist a large wage boost during inflationary times. First, many managements simply agree that the rising costs of living are beyond the control of their employees and that their wage increases should reflect these additional costs. The equity argument is very strong.

More important, however, is management's belief that it will be easier, during times of inflation, to increase prices in order to pay for the wake hikes. With everyone raising their prices, there is less reason not to, since the public comes to expect rising prices and companies find it easier to get away with the increases.

Therefore, on the one hand the business firm is faced with an increasingly militant union demanding to catch up with the cost of living. On the other hand, it may not be too difficult to finance the wage increases by hiking prices; so there is less resistance by management. Greater militancy and decreased resistance are the very ingredients necessary to ensure larger wage increases. And larger wage increases provide just what is necessary to ensure the continuation of an inflationary spiral.

Oligopoly Theory and Momentum Inflation

The theory of oligopolistic behavior on the part of business firms and the probable reactions of this behavior can show, in somewhat more theoretical terms, why inflation is able to develop a momentum of its own. An explanation for the observed stickiness of prices with respect to large, oligopolistic firms is often given in terms of a kinked demand curve. Figure 7–1 illustrates the demand curve facing such a firm.

The demand curve is kinked at the going price, P_1, because of the expectation of the firm concerning the probable response of competitors to possible price changes the firm may make. In particular, the firm believes that if it *lowers* its price, competitors will be forced to follow. For this reason the demand curve below the existing price is relatively inelastic, thereby indicating that the firm would not be able to gain a larger share of the market by lowering its price. With everyone following the price decrease, they would all share in the expanded market but no one would have a larger share of the new market.

---

[1] Econometric models of wage changes now nearly all include price changes as an explanatory variable for wage changes. The chain of causality generally worked in the opposite direction in earlier models.

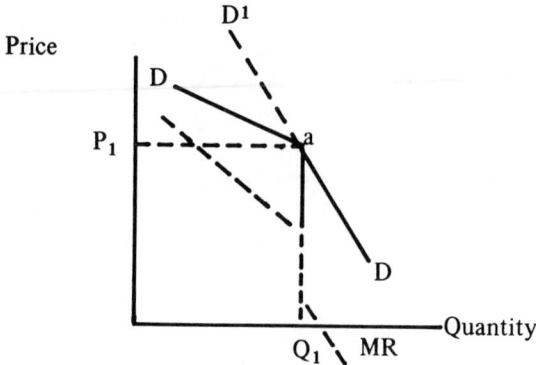

Figure 7–1. The Kinked Demand Curve

On the other hand, if the firm attempts to *raise* its price, there is no reason that competitors would have to go along and, indeed, the assumption is that they would not. In this case, the firm's share of the market would *decrease* as other firms gained at its expense. This is indicated by the upward section of the demand curve (*Da*) faced by the firm when considering a price increase. In sum, the kinked demand curve arises because the firm assumes a different reaction on the part of its competitors to a price rise than to a price decrease. As a result of this kink, there will be a break in the marginal revenue curve *at the going price*. Thus, costs can fluctuate within this break without implying any change in either price or quantity since marginal costs will continue to equal marginal revenue.

Consider now the probable change in the belief of the oligopolist concerning the behavior of his competitor during a time of inflation. In particular, the assumption that the competitor will not follow his price rise will cease to be true. During periods of continuing increases in the general price level, it would be much more realistic to assume that one's competitors will shortly initiate their own price increases. If this is the case, the firm need not worry about losing a share of the market by increasing prices and, as a result, the general inflation can be expected to result in a swing to the right of the top portion of the firm's demand curve. This indicated by the government from *Da* to *D'a* in Figure 7–1.

At this point, the demand curve no longer displays the familiar kink and the break in the marginal revenue curve disappears. Any cost increases, then, will lead directly to an increase in the firm's price.

This change in expected behavior is observed by the union as well as management. During times of increasing prices, the union feels that, if necessary, the firm can simply increase prices to pay for an increase in wages. And, given the above framework, the chances are that the union is correct in this belief. Furthermore, since the price increase in the firm's product will mean, by itself, only a small decrease in the purchasing power of the firm's employees, there is little reason to expect the union to forego such increases.[2]

At the same time, the company is also aware of the implications of this inflationary impact. Since the feeling is that the competition will also be increasing prices (if it hasn't done so already), there may appear to be little reason not to grant the wage increase, especially since there is already a feeling that employees deserve to catch up with the price level. At this point, all the necessary conditions for a price and wage increase are present: the union has more power to demand an increase and has become more militant about these demands, and management has a decreased resistance to the increases. Thus, the inflationary spiral develops an inner logic and momentum of its own and can continue in spite of the fact that there may no longer be demand-pull elements present in the economy.

Changes in the Economy

If the above analysis accounted for all of the worsening in the observed Phillips curve relationship, there would be little reason to be concerned with long-term controls. Once the inflationary pressures are brought back into line, the kink will again become apparent in the oliogopolist's demand curve, price increases will slow down, and the situation will correct itself.

Unfortunately, there also appear to be underlying changes within the structure of the economy to indicate that the Phillips curve is indeed to the right of where it stood during the earlier post-World War II years. It is impossible to quantify this precisely, however, since no one can be sure of how much the present situation is the result of the momentum factor discussed above. Also, some of the suggested reasons for the worsening in the trade-off are impressionistic and do not easily lend themselves to quantitative measurement. With these caveats in mind, we will now examine some of these structural and institutional changes.

A. Structural Changes

The basic arguments concerning structural changes in the economy were presented in Chapter 4 and will not be repeated here. Of concern,

---

[2] The union, of course, will be under intense pressure during an inflation to fight for higher wages regardless of whether it believes management can increase prices. The union's *motive* will be to recoup lost purchasing power and to gain something above this. The lack of a kink in the firm's demand curve will facilitate the achievement of this goal.

however, is the extent to which these changes are *increasing* in scope and significance and, in the process, leading to a more inflation-prone (or unemployment-prone) economy.

It has been observed that the structure of the economy is moving in such a way as to increase the relative proportion of some groups in the labor force while other groups are decreasing in proportion. In particular, the percentage of women and teenagers in the labor force has been increasing due to a host of demographic and cultural reasons. At the same time, as observed in Chapter 3, the unemployment rates for these groups are consistently higher than the average unemployment level. George Perry has constructed a model of labor market tightness that takes these changes into account. He concludes that, because of increasing dispersion in the different unemployment rates that make up the average rate, any given level of unemployment is now associated with a higher degree of labor market tightness than was previously the case (81, 82).

In the Phillips curve relationship, the unemployment rate is taken to be a proxy for the degree of tightness in the labor market. Thus, at low unemployment levels, labor markets are tight, therefore leading to increased inflationary pressures. The significance of Perry's findings is that, due to the structural changes in the make-up of the labor force, any given level of unemployment now implies a greater degree of tightness and, hence, inflation, than was earlier the case.

In an attempt to measure this change, Perry weighs different unemployment rates by their importance in the overall level and finds that "compared with the official unemployment rate, the weighted unemployment rate gives a picture of a progressively tighter labor market in recent years relative to earlier periods" (82, p. 70). Translating these findings into a Phillips curve framework, Perry illustrates how the current trade-off between unemployment and inflation has shifted to the right since the 1950s.

This finding holds significant implications for the probable course of the inflation/unemployment dilemma in the 1970s since there is little likelihood of these structural changes reversing themselves. Thus, one must either look for methods by which to reduce this trade-off through public policies or simply accept a higher noninflationary level of unemployment. A method Professor Perry and others suggest for lowering the trade-off is to concentrate on manpower programs designed to reduce the unemployment disparities among the different groups within the economy.

Other evidence supports this contention that the trade-off between unemployment and inflation is becoming worse because of structural changes within the economy. Charles Schultze has confirmed Perry's findings by using an alternative measure of labor market tightness, namely, the quit rate (the degree to which people voluntarily quit their jobs) (95). Observing that the quit rate has sharply increased in recent years in relation to a given amount of unemployment, Schultze concludes, as does Perry, that a given rate of unemployment now implies tighter labor markets. The reasoning is that the quit rate is really a better measure of labor market tightness than the unemployment rate since it indicates the degree to which people are willing to give up a job they currently hold in search of a better one. As labor markets tighten, employees are more willing to take this risk, and hence, the quit rate moves upward as the unemployment level goes down. Thus, the fact that higher quit rates are now associated with a given level of unemployment indicates that markets are now tighter at higher unemployment levels.

As with Perry's analysis of unemployment dispersions among different groups, the conclusion Schultze reaches is that the economy is now more inflation-prone than earlier. Based upon the results of his regression model, Schultze depicts three different Phillips curves: one for the 1950s, one for the 1966–70 period, and one for the 1969–70 years. In each successive period the trade-off has worsened; that is, in each period a given level of unemployment has higher levels of price increases associated with it. For example, in the mid-1950s Schultze found a 6-percent unemployment rate consistent with an annual increase in the price level of approximately 1 percent. By the 1966–70 period this had increased to about 2 percent, and by 1969–70 a 6-percent unemployment rate implied an average annual price increase in the neighborhood of 2.5 percent.

Although they rely upon different variables as a measure of labor market tightness, the Perry and Schultze studies both point to structural changes as making the trade-off between unemployment and inflation worse. Because of changes in the groups that constitute the labor force, structural mismatches between available labor supplies and the demand for labor are increasing. The clear implication is that not only are these problems serious, they are becoming worse. And as a result, the amount of unemployment necessary for price stability is becoming increasingly more severe.

B. *The Role of Productivity*

The inflationary impact of a given wage change will depend largely upon the rate of productivity increase that will act to offset the wage increase. If productivity increases (output per man-hour) keep pace with total compensation (wages plus fringe benefits), there will be no upward pressure on prices from the cost side since unit labor costs will have remained constant. Similarly, when compensation is increasing faster than productivity, unit labor costs are rising and upward pressure is placed on the price level. Thus, although there are substantial short-run variations, in the longer run a good measure of inflation is the difference between wage increases (more accurately, total compensation) and productivity gains.

During the early 1960s, productivity gains kept pace with pay increases, resulting in fairly stable per-unit labor costs, which led, in turn, to relatively stable prices. Beginning in the late 1960s, however, employee compensation increased at a much faster rate than productivity. The results were a sharp increase in per-unit labor costs, upward pressure on prices, and declining profit rates. Indeed, the Bureau of Labor Statistics estimates that unit labor costs for the total economy increased by more than 6 percent in 1969 and 1970. This compares with an average increase of approximately 2 percent a year since World War II. At the same time, productivity increases have slowed down, averaging only 2.1 percent per year from 1965 to 1970 as compared with 3.9 percent from 1960 to 1965 and 3 percent from 1950 to 1970.

These movements have become even sharper in the seventies. Output per man-hour (productivity) has been declining since 1973, whereas unit labor costs have been sharply rising. During 1974, for example, productivity *declined* at an average rate of 3.6 percent while compensation per man-hour increased at an average pace of 9.9 percent. The result was an average increase in unit labor costs of 11.9 percent. And in spite of this, *real* earnings continued to decline!

To further emphasize the connection between productivity and prices, Table 7–1 illustrates the relationship between these two variables from 1958–68. Although there are many exceptions, the trend is clear: high rates of productivity growth imply slower price increases and, in several cases, actual price decreases.

Given the overall importance of productivity, what is the outlook for the future? As a result of the structural changes taking place with respect to both labor supply and demand, the future increases in employment are going to be mostly in the service sector—a trend already strongly apparent. In terms of productivity growth, this continuing trend is disturbing since the growth in output per man-hour is lower in this sector than in either agriculture or industry. Thus, while the U.S. economy is becoming more service oriented, it will become increasingly difficult for productivity increases to offset wage increases, thereby furthering the inflationary bias of the economy.[3] This structural change, of course, did not suddenly appear in the last couple of years and thus

---

[3] Categorized broadly, "industry" consists of mining, manufacturing, and construction, whereas "services" consists of transportation, communication, public utilities, trade, finance, government, and miscellaneous services such as recreation and private household work.

THE WORSENING TRADE-OFF   139

Table 7–1. Percent change in output per man-hour
139 manufacturing industries, 1958–68

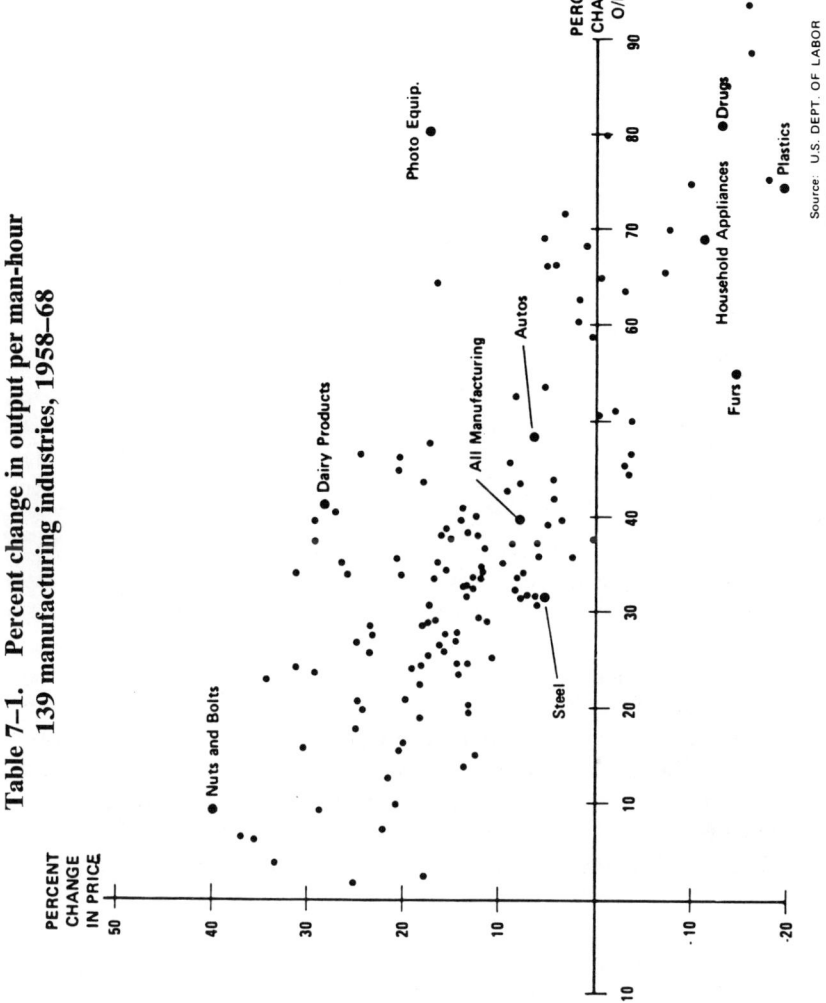

Source: U.S. DEPT. OF LABOR
BUREAU OF LABOR STATISTICS
Bulletin 1710

cannot be blamed entirely for the worsening trade-off between unemployment and inflation. It is, however, a change that will continue to make it more difficult to reach noninflationary full employment in the future.

Finally, as BLS economist Constance Sorrentino has illustrated (105), the United States is not the only country undergoing the shift from agriculture to industry to services. The U.S., however, has led in this movement and, until 1958, was the only country with over half its labor force employed in services. As a result, many other countries are only beginning to experience employment shifts that, when combined with considerations of productivity, have already become severe in this country.

Sectoral shifts provide further evidence, this time of a more long-run nature, of a movement to the right in the Phillips curve. This movement also emphasizes the crucial importance of efforts to increase productivity in these new sectors. In the final analysis, the only hope for continuing to increase the standard of living for the entire population lies in continuing improvements in productivity. This is the one factor that can provide increased real wages and mitigate inflationary pressures at the same time.[4]

C. Increases in Market Power

The important changes in the structure of the economy tell only part of the story. A further reason for the worsening trade-off between inflation and unemployment is the increasing market power on the part of unions and the groups they bargain with. Market power, and the deviation from the competitive model that it represents, is not only present, it is growing. Not all of this growth can be measured in precise terms. Even more difficult is the attempt to discern the differing degrees of influence on increased market power that various factors have had. Once again, some of the evidence is circumstantial—but it is strong circumstantial evidence.

The most significant development during the 1960s that resulted in

---

[4] It is interesting to note that in times of severe unemployment, productivity increases are equated with automation and cursed as an evil affliction upon society. Alternatively, during times of inflation productivity is lauded as providing the only real answer. As discussed above, there is no inherent reason why productivity improvements (automation) must create long-term unemployment—at least not until all of society's needs are met; and this happy day is a long way off. The responsibility rests with society to provide the structural mechanisms necessary to provide for smooth transitions in the face of a rapidly changing technology. The costs of such changes should be borne by the entire society, not only by the people who experience the immediate unemployment.

an increase in market power was the very rapid and dramatic unionization of government employees on all levels. As the Bureau of Labor Statistics has noted, "The last half of the 1960's witnessed a remarkable and largely unexpected expansion of labor-management activities at all levels of government. Union membership among government employees increased dramatically and was characterized by labor leaders as the new frontier of union growth" (116, p. 1).

This occurred at the very time when government employment was rapidly increasing as a percentage of all employment. From 1948 to 1968 federal, state, and local government employment (public-sector employment) doubled, from 5.9 to 11.8 million. Four-fifths of this (5.2 million persons) consisted of increases in state and local government employment. And, whereas union membership in private industry increased by about 5 percent from 1956–68, government unions grew in membership by 135.5 percent (18, pp. 15–16)! By 1968, state and local government unions boasted a membership of 804,000 persons, with 662,000 of these members belonging to three large AFL–CIO affiliates (the American Federation of Teachers, the International Association of Fire Fighters, and the American Federation of State, County, and Municipal Employees).

This growth in public employee union membership, impressive though it is, does not tell the whole story. At the same time that membership rolls were increasing, tactics and strategies were changing, which had the effect of changing public-sector organizations from "professional associations" to bona fide collective-bargaining agents. Furthermore, as Harry P. Cohany, Chief of the Division of Industrial Relations, BLS, and Lucretia M. Dewey, BLS economist state: "It should be emphasized that all of the figures discussed refer to union *members* only. Not infrequently, the number of workers represented by unions far exceeds those on their books. Thus, union bargaining strength is in many jurisdictions far greater than is apparent from membership figures alone" (18, p. 17).

Furthering this power is labor's ultimate weapon, the strike. Although illegal, this weapon began to be employed by public employees with impressive results during the 1960s. Indeed, the more militant organizations gained at the expense of the others, resulting in increased pressures from all sides for higher wage demands.

And these demands were met. Today, the wages of state, local, and federal employees many times not only meet but exceed that of their counterparts in private employment. Since public salaries were, only a short time ago, substantially below private levels of compensation, this implies a very rapid increase in public employee compensation. Wages, then, have been increasing the fastest in precisely that area where productivity is the most difficult to improve (or even to measure). The result has been not only an upward push in the price level but also an upward thrust in state and local taxes, since employee compensation is by far the largest component of government spending.

Nor can the recent increases in public employee wage levels be attributed to market forces. For the first time in memory, we hear of a surplus in public school teachers. Competitive price theory tells us that this is precisely the time when wages in this area should be decreasing —or at least failing to increase. Not so. Wages have been moving upward for teachers at the very time when these surpluses are appearing. Obviously, there is something more at work here than market forces. There is market power.

What is true in the government sector is true, albeit to a lesser degree, within other service areas. Increased unionization along with an increased awareness of bargaining power has substantially increased wages in these areas within the past few years.

A look at wage trends in the service sector (including government) indicates the extent to which these increases have been occurring. Between 1964 and 1970, weekly earnings in the service sector rose from an average of $70 to $98, a jump of some 40 percent. During this same period, manufacturing earnings went from $103 to $134, an increase of 31 percent. Not all of this, of course, can be attributed to market power. Significant expansions in government employment occurred during these years, and as a result, we would expect to see wages going up somewhat more rapidly in these areas. The supply of labor available to these new jobs was also growing rapidly, however, and, as pointed out with respect to teachers, the supply often increased faster than demand. Thus, there were institutional factors in addition to market forces causing the increase in earnings.

The late sixties and early seventies, then, witnessed the combined effect of structural changes in the direction of services along with an increase in the organizational and market power of employees in these fields. As a result, wages began moving up rapidly, especially in government occupations, where productivity continues to increase only slowly. In addition to the inflationary pressures inherent in such a situation, it has also produced a crisis of major importance concerning the financing of state and local governments.

This does not imply that the organizational upsurge along with the concomitant salary increases is to be regretted. Service-sector employees should be entitled to the same job protections, grievance procedures, and bargaining representatives as the traditionally unionized sectors. Also, there can be little argument that the pay scales in the area of government employment, retail and wholesale trade, and a host of other service sector areas were woefully low for years in relation to, say, manufacturing or construction work. On equity grounds, it would be difficult to justify this traditional discrepancy.

The two-sector model discussed in the preceding chapter suggested that the unionized sectors of the economy may be able to gain increased wages at the expense of the nonunion sector. With increased unionization of traditionally low-paying occupations, this is becoming less likely. That is, to the extent that industrial union employees were able to gain at the expense of nonunion service employees, they could increase their wages in a noninflationary manner. This is no longer as likely, however, since the service unions are also able to force their wages upward. Put another way, if some sectors are able to increase their wages faster than the overall growth-rate in productivity, this will not be inflationary as long as wage increases in other areas are less than productivity increases. When all wages rise faster than productivity, however, inflation is the inexorable result.

The spillover effect of large wage settlements is felt among various unions as well as among the union-nonunion sector. Often, public-employee unions set the wage and salary increases negotiated in the private sector for their goals, and with the power many have amassed, they are often successful in obtaining these increases. Furthermore, since it is often difficult to deny the legitimacy of these demands, negotiators for governmental units often do not strongly resist the demands of their employees. (Also, many times governmental bargaining units are not directly responsible to their constituency with respect to granting wage increases.) Indeed, many of them sympathize with the fact that their employees have, for years, been working at substandard wage rates. It seems likely, then, that the spillover effects of large increases in the private sector are increasing as the new employee organizations, both public and private, use these increases as targets for themselves. The wage settlements of large organizations have ripple effects that extend beyond the immediate groups that are parties to the collective-bargaining agreements. It is very likely that these ripples are now extending further and possessing greater force as we move into the last years of the 1970s.

The Combined Effect

The evidence is very strong that a combination of factors has been operating to make the unemployment/inflation trade-off less favorable during the latter 1960s and early 1970s. That is, what we seem to be observing is a shift to the east in the Phillips curve and not, unfortunately, only scattered instances of observations to the right of the real curve.

The Phillips curve relationship arises because of two major deviations from the perfectly competitive model: structural imbalances and market power. Both of these appear to be increasing and together are responsible for the worsening trade-off. At the same time, however, it should be remembered that inflation itself can also breed further inflation. For this reason, the real trade-off may not be quite so bad as the experience of the 1970's would suggest.

It is unlikely that these trends concerning structural changes and market power will diminish or reverse themselves in the foreseeable future. As a result, efforts to reduce unemployment through demand stimulation will require larger and faster jumps in the price indexes.

The prospect of either of these choices is not encouraging. The dilemma, cruel as it is, cannot be avoided. It is increasingly being felt in this, and other, market economies and, as a result, the search for acceptable forms of income policy designed to mitigate the dilemma continues with increasing urgency. In light of these structural and power considerations, we now turn our attention to the rationale for these income policies and the inherent problems they present. In an imperfect world, nothing worthwhile comes easily. So it is with efforts to reduce the unemployment/inflation dilemma.

ARGUMENTS SURROUNDING CONTROLS   8

> When a thing ceases to be a subject of controversy, it ceases to be a subject of interest.
>
> William Hazlitt

The cost to society in terms of unemployment is very high if restrictive monetary and fiscal policies are adopted in an effort to maintain stable prices. At the same time, the cost in terms of inflation is unacceptable as a means of maintaining low levels of unemployment. An alternative is the imposition of market controls in an effort to minimize both evils. Such a policy, however, is not without its own costs. Indeed, there are many who believe the cure to be worse than the disease.

Almost no one likes controls *per se*. They are cumbersome, inequitable, inefficient, and intellectually messy. On top of this, they may not even work. Indeed, President Johnson's Council of Economic Advisors stated that

> The most obvious—and least desirable—way of attempting to stabilize prices is to impose mandatory controls on prices and wages. While such controls may be necessary under conditions of an all-out war, it would be folly to consider them as a solution to the inflationary pressures that accompany high employment under any other circumstances. They distort resource allocation; they require reliance either on necessarily clumsy and arbitrary rules or the inevitably imperfect decisions of government officials; they offer countless temptations to evasion or violation; they require a vast administrative apparatus. All of these reasons make them

repugnant. Although such controls may be unfortunately popular when they are not in effect, the appeal quickly disappears once people live under them (20, p. 119).

Such objections are strong and convincing. They cannot be overlooked or sidestepped in an attempt to promote cures for the unemployment/inflation dilemma. And if, in addition to all these objections, controls will not work, imposing them becomes even more repugnant. Therefore, the objections and alternatives must be closely considered.

The Natural Death of Inflation

If left alone, would inflation continue to accelerate or would it burn itself out? Almost surely it would diminish at some point, and perhaps even stop—and this would happen without governmental interference in the marketplace. How? To answer this, one must examine the impact of rising prices on the level of demand for goods and services along with their further impact on the demand for labor.

As prices and wages go up, spending will also increase since people have larger incomes. However, there will be, in Charles Schultze's terms, certain "indirect effects" of rising prices and wages. First, because of progressive income taxes, a greater proportion of the rising incomes of consumers will be taken by the government. This will dampen consumption spending and put downward pressure on prices and, eventually, wages (94).

Also, if the government does not act to increase the supply of money, higher prices will have the effect of lowering the real supply of money, which will lead to higher interest rates and, in turn, to decreased investment. That is, as prices go up, consumers will increase their dollar holdings in an attempt to hold constant real balances of money. With a fixed supply of money in the economy, this leads to less money in capital market, increased interest rates, and decreased investments. The result is further deflationary effects that will mitigate the price and wage increases.

However, as Schultze points out, all this depends on how *sensitive* wages and prices are to changes in demand. If they are not very sensitive, the decreases in demand will lead to unemployment and reduced capacity rather than to lower wages and prices. Writes Schultze, "The responsiveness of prices and wages to changes in demand is thus the central issue" (95). As noted in Chapter 6, this responsiveness is not great. As a result, unemployment begins to develop before prices and/or wages begin to move downward.

Of course, if this process were allowed to continue long enough, the inflation would abate. In practice, however, it is very difficult for a government that is committed to full employment to allow unemployment to increase to the necessary level. As a result, expansionary monetary and fiscal policies are usually adopted in an effort to bolster demand and, therefore, employment. Furthermore, if, as argued previously, the responsiveness of prices and wages to changes in demand is *decreasing* because of increasing structural problems and market power, the unemployment necessary to halt an upward climb in price levels will continue to become greater.

Most observers believe the necessary cost of achieving stable prices in terms of unemployment is too high to pay. What, then, are the alternatives? Otto Eckstein, speaking of the wage and price guidelines of the 1960s, cites two possibilities (28). First, he says, in reference to inflation, we could "relax and enjoy it." All wages and transfer payments could (conceivably) be tied to a cost-of-living index so that no one would be hurt. This, however, is a practical impossibility.

Eckstein points out two further difficulties. One involves the balance-of-payments problems that such a policy would and, indeed, did, engender. With domestic prices climbing steadily, American products become less and less attractive to foreign buyers whose goods, in turn, become increasingly competitive in this country. The result is exactly what the U.S. experienced throughout the late 1960s and early 1970s—a continuing balance-of-payment deficit as imports exceed exports. Eventually, this can lead to a currency crisis, as it did in 1971, to a devaluation of the dollar, as it did late in the same year. The shift to floating exchange rates in 1973 has mitigated this effect of inflation as currencies continually adjust by appreciation or depreciation.

Furthermore, as Eckstein notes, it may not be possible to have a continuing inflation that does not, by itself, become worse. That is, suppose everyone is successful in tying his income to a cost-of-living rise of, say, 5 percent. This would then cease to have the expansionary effect on the economy that an unexpected 5-percent price rise does, and everyone would again try to get ahead by insisting upon even greater wage and price increases. At the same time, the unemployment level would adjust to the 5-percent inflation level as if there were no price increases and, in an effort to reduce joblessness, monetary and fiscal policies would be forced to contribute to an increasing upward spiral. In other words, it is highly doubtful that a 5-percent rate of price increases would represent a stable situation. To have a stimulative effect, inflation must be largely unexpected. Certainly this has not been the case in recent years.

Assuming that we cannot simply relax and enjoy it, then, what possibilities are there for lowering the unemployment/inflation trade-off other than the imposition of market controls. The second option, which has many supporters, is to break up power elements in both product and labor markets and thereby do away with one of the principal causes of the economy's inflationary bias. Since an atomistic economy of perfect competitors would not exhibit the inflationary tendencies that the present mixed economy does, a return to this type of society would do much to moderate the current dilemma.

Such a policy recommendation holds a good deal of appeal to many people who are strongly attracted to the perfectly competitive model of the economy. It also appeals to the nostalgic instincts of many who, quite naturally, would like to return to the so-called simpler life of an earlier era. Unfortunately, such a return is impossible even if such a life ever did exist. If there ever existed an atomistic economy of perfect competition, it is fairly certain that we could not reach it today through legislation.

Even if such a policy were a viable option, it may not be a wise one. There are advantages to a world of large businesses and unions, and it is not at all clear that the benefits in price stability would outweigh the costs in efficiency and output that could result from dismembering these large groups. This is not to say that antitrust efforts should be forsaken as useless. Moreover, many firms are beyond any size that can reasonably be justified in terms of "technical efficiencies." It is necessary to recognize the reality, however, that it may be extremely difficult to break up existing power forces, especially in the short run.

A more promising approach would seem to consist of recognizing that large power forces do exist in the U.S. economy and that they are likely to exist into the foreseeable future; therefore, it is wise to formulate policies around this realization. A reasonable policy must deal with this power directly; and this implies, in essence, some type of market intervention. It is not so much that controls are intrinsically attractive; rather, it is that the other possibilities are so unattractive.

The fact is that unemployment and inflation both exist in undesirable and unacceptable quantities in an economy characterized by structural mismatches and significant quantities of market power. In such a situation market restraints are, in economist Robert Solow's terms, "the type of policy you back into as you search for ways to protect an imperfect behavior" (104, p. 41).

The Cost of Controls

If we reject, at least partially, the idea that the price of no controls is too high and that the policy options are fairly unattractive, we must consider the costs of controls themselves.

By far the most serious criticism of any kind of governmental interference in the marketplace is that this intervention will destroy the pricing system. And this system has proven to be highly efficient as a means of allocating resources in a complex economy. This argument is both logical and forceful. It would be a serious mistake, even in an economy characterized by large power groups, to contend that the pricing system does not, for the most part, perform admirably. Indeed, given the extreme complexities of allocating resources in a highly developed economy, it is doubtful that any other system could hope to approach the market system as a means of efficiently allocating resources. Thus, if one wishes to contend that controls are useful, he must show that they will not destroy the essential mechanism of the price system.

The Impact on Allocation

Those who argue most strongly against controls usually base their arguments on the contention that if the restraints are effective they will destroy the market mechanisms, and if they are ineffective it is useless to implement them. Consider, for example, how the imposition of controls could frustrate the market from performing its function of allocating society's output according to proponent of a "no-controls" philosophy. Begin with consumer demand. If the demand for a certain product increases because a new product is introduced (the example of low-calorie scotch in Chapter 2), the price will be bid up as consumers "vote" for this product with their expenditure patterns. As a result of the increasing price, more producers move into the area in an attempt to reap the expanded profits and by so doing they provide society with more of what it wants. Furthermore, as output increases, the price will drop as produces compete with each other.

Now, if there were controls on the price of this new product that prevented it from moving up in response to consumer demand, the whole process would be thwarted. Instead of an increased price signaling the need for expanded output, the result would be shortages that would make it necessary to ration the available supplies. This rationing would most likely be done on the basis of favoritism or political power rather than by channeling goods into their most productive uses through the pricing system. It can readily be seen how this could lead to a messy, bureaucratic nightmare. This argument can be, and usually is, extended to cover the entire allocative mechanism.

If controls were to put the economy into such an allocative straitjacket, the results would be extremely harmful. However, most advocates of market restraints, whether the guidelines of the 1960s or the yardsticks of the 1970s, do not envision such rigidity. Furthermore, the example cited above is a clear case of demand-pull inflation. That is, the price of the product rose because of an autonomous increase in spending. This type of price increase is not the sort of thing that is amenable to controls. Indeed, most economists would agree that controls are harmful if applied rigidly in the face of the tight market conditions characterized by demand-pull inflation. The allocative function of price increases is seen by almost everyone as one of the real advantages of the market economy. This function should not be interfered with by the imposition of controls on prices, whether these controls be in product markets or labor markets.

It is fallacious, however, to attempt to characterize *all* price movements as the result of shifts in demand. As noted in Chapters 6 and 7, many price and wage increases appear in the face of substantial amounts of unemployment and unutilized capacity. During such times, shortages of goods or labor are not the problem and, as a result, rationing would not become necessary. Most observers who favor market controls would agree that only within a relatively small but highly important range is their application desirable. This range lies between high unemployment levels, where controls are unnecessary, and very low unemployment levels (tight markets), where controls will reduce efficiency. At this latter point, controls *do* restrict the allocative function of the market and the need is to institute monetary and fiscal restraints.

By examining only the type of demand-pull inflation that the whiskey describes, the problems of cost push and structural adjustments are conveniently overlooked. And market controls are simply not an efficient method for dealing with demand-induced inflation. They may, however, be effective in dealing with the inflation that occurs *before* product and labor markets become tight and thus before shortages begin to develop.

Controls and Capacity

The argument is perhaps clearer in reference to a product market. Suppose that plant capacity in a given industry is operating at a level of 70 percent, which is considerably below peak efficiency. When prices move upward at such a time, it is difficult to see that as the result of excess demand, especially if utilization rates are moving *downward* rather than upward in this period. In this case the price of the product could be influenced (controls adopted) *without* shortages appearing, as long as the controlled price still covered costs.

Indeed, in cases of oligopolistic market power, controls may sometimes *improve* market efficiency rather than destroy it. One of the features of the market system is that the price of a product, under perfect competition, will just reflect the necessary costs of producing it. However, this need not be the case with respect to monopolistic (or oligopolistic) situations where profits can be increased by restricting output and raising prices. Furthermore, this latter behavior is exactly what one would expect from a firm (or union) that possessed market power. In this case, controls on the price would prevent output from being deliberately decreased since restriction (or expansion) of output has no effect on a controlled price. In these circumstances, moreover, as long as a controlled price is not so low that production is stifled, it can lead to a price and quantity more in line with the levels in a competitive market.

Controlling the Heat

According to Milton Friedman, controlling prices to stop inflation is like breaking the thermometer to control the heat. In both cases the measuring mechanism or the symptom has been attacked rather than the cause itself. He then goes on to say:

> A much closer analogy is a steam-heating furnace running full blast. Controlling the heat in one room by closing the radiators in that room simply makes other rooms still more overheated. Closing all radiators lets the pressure build up in the boiler and increases the danger that it will explode. Closing or opening individual radiators is a good way to adjust the relative amount of heat in different rooms; it is not a good way to correct for overfueling the furnace. Similarly, changes in individual prices are a good way to adjust to changes in the supply or demand of individual products; preventing individual prices from rising is not a good way to correct for a general tendency of prices to rise (33, p. 20).

The key assumption in this oft-cited analogy is that the furnace is running at full blast to begin with. An economy that is running full blast runs at a very low level of unemployment. At this point, there is excess heat in the economy and the inflationary process becomes one of excessive demand. Attempting to shut off price rises in various sectors of the economy by instituting controls under these circumstances would simply shift the spending (heat) to other sectors and thereby fuel the flames of inflation in adjacent areas. At some point it becomes necessary to turn the heat down. Few advocates of direct market controls would take issue with such a prescription.

Returning to the analogy, what if the whole house is not overheated but one or two rooms are? In this case the proper course of action is to close the registers in the hot rooms without fear of overheating the entire building. Indeed, if other rooms are cold, as may well be the case, this action helps to direct the heat in their direction. So it is with the economy. Some areas have the power to display rising prices and wages while other areas are still "cold"; that is, they exhibit unemployment and underutilized capacity. In such a situation, controlling the amount spent in some areas will have the effect of channeling the spending into other areas. In the process, unemployment may diminish along with the diminution of inflationary pressures.

Assuming that all overheating comes from the economy running at full blast, then, denies the possibilities that some market sectors may have the power to channel a disproportionate share of the available heat toward them at the expense of the rest. Market controls, in this case, may be able to reallocate some of the heat before the economy gets to the point where it is operating full blast.

A Close-up View

Consider the chain of events which could be expected to follow from the imposition of controls on certain sectors of the economy. Assume that prices and/or wages are rising rapidly in the face of substantial unemployment. Furthermore, suppose that there are no apparent shortages either of labor supplies or physical supplies in these sectors; that is, unemployment and unutilized capacity are both apparent. This is a fair description of much of the U.S. economy in the late sixties and mid-seventies and therefore provides a more accurate model of reality than does the theory of perfectly competitive markets.

Starting with this situation, price and wage controls are now imposed on an oligopolistic sector in an attempt to limit the degree of price and wage increases. What will be the ripple effects? First, with high unemployment and the underutilized plant capacity, no shortages will develop. This will negate the imposition of a rationing mechanism, which will, in turn, obviate the development of black markets, under-the-table deals, and the like.

Second, with prices in this market below what they would be in the absence of controls, a greater part of a fixed supply of money can be spent in other areas. Now, if there existed the condition of full employment—as in the furnace example cited above—this would lead to a shifting of the inflationary pressures into other areas. But this, by definition (and in fact), is not the case. In the case at hand, the increased demand in other areas can be expected to increase output and employment in these sectors.

Ripple Effects

A further ripple effect of the controls will be to hold down the prices that other firms, which use the products of the controlled industries, must pay. This, in turn, will mitigate the inflationary pressures they face from the cost side of the equation. Since all firms do not possess market power, controls in the more competitive areas will be unnecessary. But, as the cost of supplies to these competitive firms goes down (or fails to increase) because of controls, the prices that they charge will also rise less rapidly. That is, there is a direct connection between the prices charged by large, powerful, oligopolistic producers and the prices charged by the smaller, more competitive firms. Holding prices down for the large firms, then, will produce results beyond these particular industries and will result in a lessening of inflationary tendencies in the more competitive sectors of the economy as well. Spillover effects work on the downswing as well as on the upswing.

Finally, the controls on prices will, by themselves, have a mitigating influence on wage increases. One consideration in a negotiated wage settlement is management's *ability* to grant an increase, which often depends upon whether it believes that a price increase is feasible. Indeed, many times wage increases are used as justification for price increases that more than cover the cost of the collective-bargaining settlement. With effective price controls, management can be expected to display greater resistance to wage demands than when it knows in advance that it can raise prices. In short, price controls on large industries can have the effect of stiffening the resistance of these firms to labor's demands at the bargaining table. And this can have the effect of substituting public power for private power when this private power is no longer controlled effectively by market forces.

The above consideration lies at the heart of the matter. Imposing controls on large firms and large unions is not the same as imposing controls on a competitive industry. Often, when arguments are made against any market interference, a subtle but very important assumption is made; namely, that we have a competitive situation upon which the controls are imposed. This can then produce a misallocation of resources, inefficiences and failure. Since perfect competition is, by definition, perfect, interference with it can only make things worse.

We do not, however, live in a perfectly competitive society. And, as Otto Eckstein, one of the architects of the guidelines of the 1960s remarked, "No incantation of the theories appropriate to an atomistic society of tiny business enterprises and unorganized workers is going to solve this problem [of simultaneous unemployment and inflation]" (28, p. 383).

The impact of a reduction in the level of wage increases will have another ripple effect that might be termed a *reverse spillover effect.* Since the large, organized, key industries frequently set patterns for wage settlements in more competitive sectors of the economy, reducing the level of wage increases in the former sectors will tend to promote lower settlements in the latter. Indeed, if, as suggested earlier, the amount of spillover is *increasing,* the key settlements will be of even greater importance in stabilizing wage increases throughout the economy. This is an important consideration in evaluating the effectiveness of the wage controls of 1971–74.

The Extent of Controls

To what extent would the entire economy have to be controlled in order to bring about price stability? A favorite argument against the imposition of *any* controls is that they will quickly lead, by necessity, to the extension of controls to all sectors of the economy. This chain reaction is said to move along the following lines. Controls are put into effect in a sector of the economy where prices and wages are rising rapidly. As a result, inflationary pressures increase in other parts of the economy as the heat is shifted. Prices in these areas then move upward, thereby necessitating the imposition of controls in these sectors. The process continues until what started as a small attempt to control specific prices and wages results in a sprawling, complex, and inefficient attempt to control the entire economy. Therefore, the argument goes, it is impossible to control only a relatively small segment of the economy and achieve a reduction in the overall level of price increases.

Such a scenario is a real possibility and would have unfortunate consequences. But a possibility does not become, ipso facto, a necessity. For creeping controls eventually to engulf the entire economy requires, once again, the assumption that the cause of the overheating is always a furnace running full blast. In addition, the implicit assumption underlying such reasoning—indeed, a fundamental assumption of the perfectly competitive model—is that no unemployment exists. If the economy is operating at full employment, any shift of spending will simply produce inflationary pressures in the recipient sector. But with substantial unemployment, this need not be the case.

If one begins with an economy characterized by substantial unemployment, market power, and large spillover effects, the outcome of controls in only key areas appears quite different. In this case, controlling only some sectors will have ripple effects far beyond the areas of immediate applications, and this will obviate expanding the scope of the controls. Policymakers would, in this case, be using the spillover effects of wage and price movements to their advantage. Of course, this assumes that the controls in the key areas will be effective. If they are not, the effects will be quite different. But in the context above, controls are taken to mean *effective controls,* not simply ineffective attempts at restraining wage and price behavior.

Market Controls and Individual Freedom

Control and *freedom* are contradictory concepts. By definition, market controls require individuals and institutions to act in a manner other than normal. Furthermore, as Friedman so eloquently and persuasively argues (32), economic freedom cannot be expropriated without a concomitant reduction in political liberty.

The degree to which market controls limit individual freedom involves the extent of such controls and the degree to which they subsume or subvert the private decision-making role. An assessment of *extent* and *degree,* however, depends, once again, upon one's view of the structure of the American economy. If the competitive model is assumed, effective controls will necessarily grow until they pervade the entire economy, thereby completely subverting the pricing mechanism and virtually destroying many traditional freedoms.

If the economy is seen to consist of large power groups, the costs in terms of real freedom need not be excessive. Of course, large firms and unions will lose the freedom to arbitrarily set wages and prices with little regard for market conditions. But this loss of liberty is not socially detrimental. Nor, in fact, is it a loss of a freedom that exists in the perfectly competitive system. *No one* has the power (freedom) to set prices or wages in perfectly competitive markets but instead must take them as a given. The "freedom" to set prices comes only when this competitive system breaks down and is replaced by market power on the part of unions or business. Thus, even if controls were *completely* rigid (which no one seriously advocates), they would limit the freedom to set wages or prices no more than does the perfectly competitive system when it operates most perfectly.

Consider, further, the "freedom" of those who adopt the wages and prices that are set in the key industries. In following a lower, controlled wage settlement, these smaller firms and unions have lost no more freedom than they lose when adopting a higher wage. In either case, they are simply following what has been done by the leading industries.

The same reasoning applies to the prices paid by competitive firms for the products of controlled firms. The prices paid will be less, which implies a lower price for their own products. This in no way diminishes the freedom of the competitive firm to respond to its production costs by adjusting the price of its products.

The loss of freedom entailed by a not-too-rigid incomes policy involves a loss in the discretionary power of large interest groups to set wages and prices independent of market forces. It is the loss of a freedom that has been gained to the extent that elements of power have replaced elements of competition in the economy. And, since much of the economy is still characterized by substantial degrees of competition, it will not be necessary to extend controls over the entire economy in order to reduce the general price level. In short, there is no inherent reason for creeping controls to become galloping controls.

It is important to note the basic justification for free markets. The essence of the market mechanism, as viewed by Adam Smith and virtually every economic thinker since, is to translate the quest for private gain into the public good. That is, the market has been seen to work in such a way that when everyone follows his own selfish desires the result can be the best of all possible economic worlds. This ideal of the invisible hand is the principal justification for the private market system. And, to a large extent, the system still works.

But there are areas where private economic decisions lead to the public detriment rather than the public good. Inflationary price and wage behavior is one of these areas. In instances where unions and businesses possess considerable market power, they have some capacity to set prices and wages independent of market forces. In these cases, the market is unable to function in the manner necessary to ensure that private gain will result in public good. Indeed, in such circumstances, the quest for private gain may simply result in more private gain at the expense of the public good.

In such situations the private decision-making process loses its traditional market justification, and public controls make philosophical, as well as economic, sense. Indeed, controls in this sense (and it is a very real sense) can be seen as attempts to force business firms and labor unions to act the way they would be forced to behave if competition *were* all-pervasive. That is, public controls, inefficient and clumsy as they may be, can rightly be seen as substitutes for market controls which, because of the growth of large power blocks, are no longer effective.

Private Gain and Public Good

Public policies should be designed to *ensure* that the public good will be furthered by individuals and institutions as they pursue their own private goals. To rely upon private benevolence and altruism in place of public policy is dangerous as well as foolhardy. This is not to say that benevolence and altruism do not exist or that motives and actions based upon them are not to be commended and, indeed, encouraged. Certainly there is a place, and an important one, for social responsibility on the part of individuals, businesses, and labor unions. But to rely extensively on these motivations has serious deficiencies. First, regardless of the good intent of some, not all individual businesses share these motivations. Second, because formidable competition still exists within the business world (a contention that most businessmen will surely find an understatement), the person who decides to ignore the public good will hold a competitive advantage.

The example of pollution is relevant here. If one or more firms decide to stop polluting the water or the atmosphere, they may be unable to do so unless *all* other firms adopt equally expensive policies. In this case, a law *requiring* the adoption of antipollution devices will be favored by those firms that would like to adopt them but cannot do so for competitive reasons. A policy that rewards nonpolluting behavior, then, and punishes polluting behavior, would force firms to act in the public good while pursuing their private gain. Furthermore, it would allow the firms that want to act in a socially beneficial manner to do so without fear of losing their markets and their reason for existence.

The same reasoning applies to labor unions and corporate managements. Even if individual unions could be convinced that their actions resulted in furthering an inflationary spiral, they would be unable to halt such behavior. They would view (rightly) their actions as being only a small part of the inflationary mechanism. Should they moderate their demands while everyone else continued theirs, inflation would continue and they would be the losers. Indeed, they might accurately be described as the suckers in such a situation. But if everyone were to limit demands —unions and business firms as well—inflationary pressures would subside and everyone could benefit.

A further reason for developing public policies that rely upon selfish interest for compliance is simply that this is a tremendous motivating force. The fact that the mixed capitalist system has provided a legitimate outlet for motives of self-interest and ambitions has released tremendous amounts of the energy necessary to build an affluent society. Therefore, these motives should be incorporated into the framework of public policies.

Controls and Profits

Market controls, if wisely constructed, can operate to promote the public good through the encouragement of private gain—something that occurs "automatically" in a perfectly competitive economy. Consider the goal of maximizing profits. There are, in general, three avenues available for the firm that is attempting to increase its net revenue. First, it can increase output, which, with a given margin of prices over costs, will increase profits. Second, it can cut costs, which, with a given level of output, will increase profits. And finally, it can increase prices, which, if output does not decrease *too much,* will increase profits. The first two options are open to the firm operating in perfect competition as well as to the more powerful producers. The third possibility, however, arises only when market power is present. The small competitor must take the price as a given and will lose his entire market if he attempts to increase it above the going rate. The same is not true for the large producer.

Furthermore, the *first two* options for increasing profits will result in benefits for the *entire society*. Increasing output will provide the economy with more of the product, and cutting costs will provide society with a given amount of output for fewer resources. In both cases, the public good is tied to private gain.

The third possibility for increasing profits is a different story. If a firm is powerful enough to increase prices in the face of steady or decreasing demand for its product (see Chapters 6 and 7), it is able to create a private gain at public expense. Pushing prices up implies restricting output—a condition that is possible only if the firm is large in relation to the market in which it is selling. (If it is not large, reducing its output will have little effect on total output and, therefore, will not result in higher prices.) As a result of this action, the firm will be selling at a higher price than before, output will be less, and a "monopoly profit" consisting of the difference between the average cost and the selling price of the product will be realized by the firm. In this case, the public good was not furthered by private gain; indeed, just the opposite.

An effect of market controls in this situation is to limit the extent to which the third possibility—raising prices—becomes a viable option in the attempt to increase profits. If this option is reduced, the firm's capacity to act as a monopolist and restrict output in order to increase prices (or, in the usual sequence, to raise prices and then adjust output accordingly) will be at least diminished. The effect of controls will be to hold down prices, which will result in a larger output sold and fewer monopoly profits realized. And this, of course, is more in line with the public good *as well as* more in line with the competitive model than is the aforementioned behavior. This is precisely the type of behavior that a public policy should encourage, whether it be income policy or tax proposal.

Market Controls and Socialism

It is sometimes asserted that market controls represent the first step on the road to socialism, and that once begun, there is no turning back. The rise of socialism is often cited as a danger accompanying any governmental interference in the marketplace. Unfortunately, the implications of this argument are not entirely clear. Indeed, it means many things to many people since few people agree on any definition of socialism.

If socialism is taken to mean direction by the state of the means of production, there appears to be little reason why limited controls should lead to this. The purpose of an incomes policy is to mitigate price and wage increases, not to redirect the flow of productive goods.

A more common criticism is that the government is seldom able to interfere with the market to a limited degree; this interference usually grows until free markets are virtually destroyed. This can happen when demand pressures are great. Instituting controls in one area in this circumstance only shifts the pressures to other areas and thereby necessitates the imposition of new controls as pressure is felt in these new sectors of the economy.

This view of market controls is valid only for an economy *entirely* devoid of competitive elements. Actually, many areas of the economy still respond fairly well to the competitive model and, as a result, will respond to policies based upon this model. In particular, although it may be necessary to limit the wage and price setting behavior of large unions and business firms because of the market power they possess, this does not imply that *all* institutions must be controlled since not all of them have this kind of power.

There exists a somewhat dangerous tendency to view the American economy as representative of a single market structure. Either it is perceived as entirely competitive or entirely monopolistic. Such a viewpoint may be intellectually or emotionally pleasing, *but it is simply not accurate.* In many areas competition will continue to guard against arbitrary price and wage increases.

A real danger of expanding governmental intervention arises from political as well as economic considerations. Once the government imposes market restraints, there is a natural desire to see these policies work in the intended manner. However, if the government is unable to hold down price increases in the areas of the economy characterized by large power blocks, the policy will be unsuccessful. Should this happen, government officials may impose controls on other sectors of the economy in order to make the policies work, or appear to work.

Suppose, for example, that a powerful union and business firm settle on a large wage hike and an increase in prices. Assume, also, that the price and wage control authorities go along with this settlement. If this happened in a key industry, the ripple effects are such that competitive firms find *their* costs going up because of the higher prices they have to pay. At the same time, the wages paid by these smaller firms may be tied, formally or informally, to the settlement of the larger firm. In this case, the price and wage behavior in the competitive firms will also be inflationary, not because of any market power they possess, but simply because they are followers. At the same time, the competitive industries (or firms) quite probably possess less political power than their larger counterpart and, as a result, they become natural targets for the price and wage authorities. In an attempt to control inflation the authorities may, therefore, turn to these fragmented segments of the economy. This would be a serious mistake. Controlling these sectors would be unwise since they are price takers. Furthermore, such actions would be unnecessary if the proper policies were instituted in the first place. Devising such policies is not easy. The recent experience of both the Pay Board and the Construction Industry Stabilization Committee indicates, however, that flexible controls that recognize spillovers, catch-ups, tandem relationships, and other institutional arrangements can be devised.

Two features of an incomes policy are necessary in order to minimize the risks of extensive controls. The first is the recognition that, because of the nature of power groups in society, only limited controls are *needed,* let alone desirable. The second necessary feature is the assurance that prices and wages in the desired sectors are, indeed, controlled. If the "controls" turn out to be ineffective on the large power blocks, the temptation will be great to extend them to other areas of the economy. Such a result would be unfortunate.

An interesting and useful parallel can be drawn between the imposition of incomes policies of the 1960s and 1970s and the development of the New Deal of the 1930s. During that time, and later, one heard the assertion that Franklin Roosevelt was replacing American free enterprise with socialism. Because of this, Roosevelt and the New Dealers were, and still are, despised by many conservatives. At the same time, socialists have traditionally disliked Roosevelt for *saving* capitalism! Thus, on the one extreme Roosevelt is blamed for destroying capitalism and on the other for saving it!

The same argument can be applied to the final quarter of the century. A limited incomes policy could have the effect of *improving* the market mechanism rather than destroying it. Indeed, it could have the effect of making the market perform more in line with the competitive model than a completely unregulated market. If applied in a judicious and thoughtful manner, price and wage controls might well increase the efficiency of the market economy and, as a result, strengthen the market system rather than weaken it. This is not to say that such a wise policy is easy to formulate or to execute. Steering the right course between too much control and too little requires an acute balance of economic science and political art. But surely no one believes that it is easy to guide the path of an economy so diverse and complex as that of the United States, regardless of the tools used. It is important, though, to use tools adapted to economic realities, not ideological myths.

FURTHER QUESTIONS CONCERNING THE NATURE OF CONTROLS 9

> Altogether they puzzle me quite, They all seem wrong and they all seem right.
>
> Robert Buchanan

Controls and Productivity

There is a close relationship between the level of productivity increases in the economy and the inflationary impact of a given wage settlement. Specifically, the degree of wage-induced inflation is usually calculated as the difference between a wage increase and the increase in productivity (output per man-hour). In addition to highlighting the crucial role of productivity, this formula implies that any noninflationary guideline should be in line with the rate of increase in productivity. In the 1960s the guidepost was set at 3.2 percent and, since this was considered to be the trend increase in productivity, the result, if the guideposts had been followed, would have been stable price levels.

The Pay Board standard from 1971 to 1974 of 5.5 percent wage increases, along with an assumed trend rate increase of 3 percent in productivity, was, by the same reasoning, consistent with the stated goal of a 2.5-percent rise in the price index.

This arithmetic, which is deceptively simple, holds important implications. Of major concern is what measure of productivity to adopt in computing the limits of a noninflationary wage increase. Should each industry be considered in terms of *its own* productivity growth rate or in terms of the trend rate for the entirely economy?

Suppose, for example, that the trend rate of productivity for the entire economy is approximately 3 percent while that of industry X is 5 percent. Concerning union negotiations in this industry, is 3 percent or 5 percent the logical choice for the guideline? It can be argued with considerable merit that the wage rate could go up by 5 percent with no resulting inflationary pressures. Indeed, if wage increases of this amount were granted, prices could remain constant and so would the respective shares of income that would be allocated to labor and capital within the industry.

The problem is that many other industries experience productivity growth rates below the overall average of 3 percent. (Thus far, no one has discovered a method whereby part of a population can be above an average figure without the necessity for another part to be below it.) Suppose, then, that industry Y is experiencing a productivity growth rate of 1 percent. If the industry measure were adopted, employees of industry X would receive wage increases of 5 percent and those of industry Y would realize only a 1 percent gain. What would be the result?

Basically, the differential wage rates between the two industries would increase. This would soon become untenable for two reasons. First, if the industries are characterized by a fair degree of competition, it would be impossible for wage rates for similar work to spread too far apart. Given a competitive environment, workers from industry Y would soon move to industry X, where the pay is higher. In this case, the competitive solution is also the equitable one. It is difficult to justify differential wages for the same work just because the workers happen to be in industries that exhibit differing productivity growth rates. For example, consider a janitor in a manufacturing plant where productivity is increasing rapidly and another janitor in a department store where productivity is increasing more slowly. On grounds of equity, as well as efficiency, there is no reason why the first janitor should be receiving a larger paycheck than his counterpart.

Second, in the case where there is *little* competition, the spillover effects are likely to be substantial. Government employees, for example, are likely to demand (and receive) pay increases commensurate with those of private industry regardless of differences in the rate of productivity growth between the two sectors.

Indeed, a good part of the difficulties with rising prices and wages in the late 1960s and early 1970s resided in the fact that employees in all sectors of the economy were attempting to keep up with the wage increases in a few industries regardless of specific productivity increases. Since the target increases are invariably the high rather than the low increases, the results are inflationary. The clear implication is that wage increases must be tied in some manner to the *overall* level of productivity increases rather than to the productivity growth rates in a particular industry or sector of the economy.

Thus, in terms both of employee equity and price stabilization, it makes more sense to tie wages to the trend rate of productivity increases rather than to the increases in specific industries. This policy is also a sound one from the standpoint of consumer equity. If wages and prices increase by the amount of productivity increases in a given industry, the result is that the workers and the owners of that industry share in the productivity gains. But a part of this increase is undoubtedly due to factors outside their collective control. Therefore, society should reap some of the benefits of this growth in the form of lower prices. This can happen only if there are relative price declines in those areas where productivity growth is above average and, furthermore, if wages in this sector increase by less than the *industry* productivity increase.

This policy has a drawback, however, with respect to the incentive (or lack thereof) for increasing productivity on the industry level. There will be an added incentive for unions, workers, and managers to try to increase productivity if they will reap the rewards of these increases. And of course it is much easier for them to influence the productivity of their particular firm, or even their industry, than of the entire economy. Tying wages and price changes to the overall rate of productivity will dampen this incentive. Thus it is necessary to allow for productivity improvements at the local level. There is no neat solution to this dilemma; the best that can be hoped for is judicious decisions in specific cases.

A frequently cited objection to increasing wages in accord with productivity improvements is that this formula has the effect of holding constant the share of output to labor and capital. For example, if productivity and wages both increase by 5 percent, the return to capital will also increase by 5 percent. (Labor, in this case, does not get all the increase, as is frequently assumed.) Most labor leaders do not willingly accept the proposition that factor shares should remain constant. In particular, they would like to see labor's share increased at the expense of capital. Furthermore, many people say that increasing the share of output going to wages and salaries will promote equality in the distribution of income—a goal considered laudable. Industrialists, on the other hand, argue with convincing evidence that the share of output going to capital must increase if the nation's productive facilities are to be maintained and expanded.

These considerations, although sound, are outside the scope of wage and price controls. There are much more effective and appropriate policies than wage and price controls for dealing with questions of income distribution. Increasing or decreasing the relative share of income attributed to labor is a very blunt and somewhat misleading method for altering income distribution, a goal that can be handled much better through the use of tax policies. We will consider this point below.

Limited or Comprehensive Controls?

Considerations of simplicity argue for the use of limited controls whereas considerations of equity encourage the adoption of comprehensive controls so that everyone will be required to "sacrifice." The structure of the U.S. economy suggests that limited controls can be both effective in controlling aggregate price levels and acceptable from the standpoint of fairness. As discussed next, many people believe that the broad degree of coverage adopted in the last control program was a fundamental error. There are still many areas within the economy where competition remains effective as a controlling device and, consequently, where outside control is both unnecessary and unworkable. Moreover, as discussed in Chapter 6, there is evidence of substantial spillover effects from key wage settlements to agreements in other areas. The clear implication is that controls in these key sectors will mitigate the need for more extended controls.

Recognition that an incomes policy is only advisable during times of excess capacity and is not particularly useful for holding down an overheated economy also obviates extensive controls. In a wartime situation it may be impossible to hold down excessive demand pressures with anything other than comprehensive controls on the entire economy. At such times, the economy is overheated in the true sense of the word. Competitive elements must then be restricted along with the oligopolistic and monopolistic sectors.

A more moderate incomes policy, on the other hand, is not designed to deal with this type of situation. Its primary function is to mitigate inflationary processes that are reached *before* full employment is achieved. As a result, comprehensive controls are unnecessary.

Voluntary or Mandatory Controls?

Both the guidelines of the 1960s and the new economic policy of the 1970s sparked a controversy about whether the wage and price controls should be compulsory or voluntary. On purely economic grounds, it makes little difference which type of control is instituted so long as they are followed. From a policy standpoint, however, mandatory controls seem preferable. First, there is the simple matter of effectiveness. If the government is unable to persuade trade unions and business firms to follow voluntary restraints, the entire program will founder. Moreover, even if some companies and unions were willing to go along with informal guidelines, competitive reasons might make it impossible for them alone to do so.

A further justification for compulsory controls with built-in penalties is that they obviate the government's resorting to extra-legal means to enforce voluntary guidelines. Many people were concerned by the steps the government took during different episodes in the 1960s in attempting to force compliance with the wage-price guidelines. Without legal sanctions, the government had to resort to arm twisting of a very persuasive nature in order to get "cooperation" from some corporations.

This kind of activity is dangerous in that it allows—indeed, requires—the government to pry into the private aspects of individuals' and institutions' lives in order to force compliance with governmental regulations. If it is in the public interest to institute a given policy, formal sanctions should be available to use against individuals, corporations, or unions that are found to be in violation of these regulations. If it makes little difference whether a policy is followed, that policy should not be instituted in the first place.

A voluntary control program—if it is truly voluntary—also penalizes the firms and unions that attempt to follow the guidelines, whereas organizations that disregard the program gain at the expense of the public. Aside from the inequities of such an arrangement, it would not long last as companies and unions discovered that they were, in effect, being penalized for cooperating with the program. Phase III of the last control program effectively demonstrated the inequity and unworkability of a so-called self-administered program.

Controls and Equity

Organized labor has consistently said that it would support wage and price controls it considered to be equitable. At the same time, labor has consistently insisted that the last controls program was not equitable and, in particular, that it discriminated against the working man in favor of large business interests. The specific aspects of this charge are explored in the final chapter of this book. The more general question of whether or not wage and price controls are inequitable *per se* is considered next.

Equity, of course, means different things to different people. To some it means a more *equal* distribution of income; to others it implies the maintenance of historic differentials. In the following discussion, the impact of controls on equity is viewed in terms of likely *changes* in the distribution of income resulting from the imposition of controls. Such a method is highly imprecise and subjective. Much depends upon the type of economy that is compared to the "controlled economy."

As discussed below, there is considerable disagreement about what the state of the world would be if the Nixon Administration had not reversed its economic policy in 1971. Also, the impact of controls will vary considerably, depending on the administrative apparatus set up to run them. Even the most fair-minded set of rules will be quite unfair if the administrative machinery is inadequate to effectuate the regulations.

A. Controls and Labor's Share of Income

As noted above, a formula that ties the general wage level to the general productivity level has the effect of fixing the relative shares of national income attributed to labor and capital. Organized labor has traditionally and consistently argued that this is inequitable since, in effect, it prohibits labor from gaining at the expense of capital. As Walter Reuther used to observe, there is nothing sacred about the present distribution of income shares.

Such arguments are sound, but not overly convincing from the viewpoint of equity. The functional distribution of income—which is what "labor's share" and "capital's share" are all about—is, at most, a crude measure of equity or well-being. The real wages of working people are simply not closely tied to the *share* of total income they receive. More important, it is always possible for income distribution to be altered *after* the relative shares are parcelled out by the market mechanism. That is, if society does not like the functional distribution implied by the economic system, it can change it through the use of taxes and transfer payments. To a considerable extent, this method is already employed in an effort to benefit groups that are considered to be inadequately compensated by the unfettered distribution system of a mixed capitalistic economy. This has proven, in general, to be a much more effective method of providing a measure of equity than efforts to alter the functional distribution of income. As John Sheahan has argued in reference to the wage-price guideposts of the 1960s, "For questions concerning alleviation of poverty or achievement of more equal income distribution, the broad categories of profits and wages are not very meaningful" (96, p. 163).

In terms of the share of income going to labor versus that going to capital, there is little justification for assuming that wage and price controls are going to make the distribution either more or less "equitable." If followed, however, they do make it more difficult for labor to increase its share of income at the expense of capital. To argue that this is inequitable, one must assume that labor is, in fact, able to increase its relative share in the *absence* of controls. This has not occurred to any marked degree in the past several years.

B. Differential Incomes

Another major area of concern is the impact that limited wage and price controls are likely to have on differences in the levels of pay received by different groups—that is, the pay *differentials*. In particular, it is frequently asserted that controls imply a freezing of these differentials, and that, as a result, it becomes impossible to lessen the differences between the high- and the low-paid worker. Indeed, this is precisely the effect that rigid controls—such as a wage freeze—do have.

On the other hand, if the controls are not all-embracing and if, instead, they are aimed primarily at the large, powerful, and monopolistic sectors of the economy, there is no reason why this freezing of inequities would result. The large, powerful sectors of the work force are not those that exhibit poverty levels of pay. Poor workers consist largely of the unorganized, marginal, and part-time employees whose wages would not be restricted by limited controls. In this case, if market forces are working to improve the lot of the workers at the bottom of the income ladder, these forces will not be thwarted. Indeed, by holding down the rate of pay increase of those on the top, the relative differential between the two groups could be expected to diminish as a result of the imposition of controls.

In addition, as both the Construction Industry Stabilization Committee and the Pay Board demonstrated, it is possible to formulate a wage control program that considers historic differentials, catch-ups, and other institutional factors in wage determinations.

When discussing the relative impact of market controls, one must also keep in mind the dual evils of inflation and unemployment that these controls are meant to counteract. If an incomes policy is able to improve the trade-off between these social problems, there will be a differential impact on different groups since the brunt of unemployment and inflation is not shared equally by all groups within society. The poor, the disadvantaged, and the marginal worker suffer disproportionately. Thus, if the policy is effective, it will confer benefits disproportionately upon these groups.

All society would benefit from lowering the unemployment rate, but none would benefit so much as those who are out of work. By the same token, most people would benefit from a more stable price level, but none more so than the elderly poor living on fixed incomes. Thus, to the extent that market controls are able to reduce the economic dilemma of unemployment and inflation, the result will be a move toward increased equality in the sense that those at the bottom of the economic totem pole will be helped the most. Other features of controls, especially the manner in which they are instituted and carried out, may negate this movement toward equality. But there is nothing inherent in an incomes policy that makes it inequitable from this standpoint. If effective, controls can have the result of improving the equity of distribution of economic benefits among various groups within the society.

C. Equity and Comprehensiveness

Given the structure of the U.S. economy, limited controls are preferable to comprehensive controls. This would seem to imply inequity in the application of incomes policy since some groups would be subject to controls and others would not. It could be argued that the only hope for public acceptance of controls lies in a strictly equitable control system coupled with an equally fair enforcement mechanism. On the surface, then, it would appear that limited controls are in direct violation of the criterion of equity. It was largely this consideration that led to the comprehensive nature of the Nixon Administration controls.

It may be, in fact, the case that specific controls will, because of the choices made or the manner in which they are enforced, be inequitable. Such a result would be unfortunate because there is no basic conflict between the dual criteria of limited applicability and equitable treatment of all concerned parties. The misconception that there is once again comes from failing to realize that some areas of the economy are still controlled by market forces and that, in these cases—and they are substantial—it is unnecessary to impose additional *legal* controls. The true inequities arise from the fact that, in an economy free from any form of incomes policy, some groups within both labor and product markets *are* effectively controlled by market forces while others are not. The ideal purpose of controls is to impose restrictions on those groups that are not effectively controlled by market forces. To the extent that this can be done in a judicious manner, the result will be to promote equity rather than diminish it.

The structure of the American economy displays a highly diverse terrain, from almost complete monopoly to nearly perfect competition. It has been clearly recognized for some time that the most nearly monopolistic elements of the economy, the public utilities, must be controlled by public interests. It is obvious that without such controls the price of these goods and services would be higher than they are since utilities possess a considerable degree of market immunity.

Other areas of the economy, however, fall between the extremes of the utilities on the one hand and highly competitive sectors on the other. These middle areas (the oligopolies) possess differing degrees of market power, and thus call for differing degrees of external control. Considerations of equity, as well as those of economic efficiency, dictate the need to be selective in applying restraint.

Controls and Flexibility

A persistent fear concerning the implementation of market restraints is that the economy will become rigid and be unable to respond to changing market conditions. The virtue of a market system is the ability of prices to allocate resources efficiently and quickly in response to new conditions. If this feature is eroded, the cost of controls would be very high indeed.

There is no inherent reason why a moderate incomes policy should necessitate such a drastic occurrence. Limiting controls to the strategic sectors of the economy will not put the pricing system into a strait jacket, and the specter of an economy unable to move for lack of freedom need not become a reality. Part of the reason for this fear stems from the tendency to view the imposition of an incomes policy as a substitute for a perfectly competitive economy—a situation that is hardly descriptive of twentieth century realities.

A major function of price movements is to indicate areas of relative scarcities within the economy and to then channel existing resources into these areas. Where monopoly pricing occurs, however, prices do not reflect these relative scarcities; instead, they reflect the power of a business or labor union that sets the price. In such circumstances, it is not at all clear that restrictions on prices will have the effect of misallocating resources. In fact, quite the opposite may result.

Controls become dangerous when they become inflexible enough to preclude the price and wage changes that are the result of market forces (relative scarcities) and not the result of the exercise of market power. In such instances the function of the pricing system is thwarted and resources are directed out of their most productive pursuits and into less desirable channels. Evidence of this pattern resulting from controls during heavy demand pressures in 1973 began to appear during Phase IV of the Economic Stabilization Program. There are instances when higher than average wage increases are advisable for reasons of economic efficiency as well as equity, just as there are circumstances when higher than average price increases are justified. Market controls that are too rigid to allow such increases can have the effect of stifling the economy and decreasing efficiency. Controls, then—be they guidelines or yardsticks—should be flexible enough to allow the pricing system to breathe.

This flexibility, however, gives powerful interest groups room to search for all kinds of exceptions to the guidelines. Indeed, the very groups that possess the most political power also possess the most economic power, and therefore, they most require controlling. The Pay Board, for example, was immediately charged with favoring the powerful groups that came before it when, in the first days of its operation, it approved wage settlements well in excess of the stated wage goal of 5.5 percent.

There is no easy road out of this dilemma. The economist is prone to argue that such questions of political power are beyond his purview and that the economic implications of the situation are quite clear. In a sense, this is a reasonable position. Certainly, from an economic viewpoint it is necessary to control the wages and prices of the powerful groups in the economy and, at the same time, to have controls that are flexible enough to incorporate above average wage and price hikes in particular instances. The political aspects of the problem, however, cannot be ignored, and the economist who makes policy recommendations is of little value if he conveniently sidesteps such realities.

Unfortunately, saying that everyone should follow the same rules is neither equitable nor efficient. It is not equitable since there exist, at any time, many inequities in the economy. Forcing everyone to follow the same guideline would freeze these inequities. It is not efficient since relative prices must continually be changing in order to reflect changing consumption and investment patterns for the price system to work. Thus, the problem cannot be solved by legislating against flexibility.

The dilemma between the need for flexibility and the existence of market power poses one of the toughest jobs for any incomes policy. If policymakers err too much on one side, the program will become inequitable as well as ineffective. If they err on the other side, the program will lead to economic inefficiencies. The administration of such a judiciously responsive program is extremely difficult, *but it is not impossible.*

At the same time, it should be recognized that some inefficiencies and inequities are present at all times with all policies. To refrain from instituting a public policy on the grounds that some inefficiencies or inequities may occur is to benignly accept the alternative (and false) proposition that in the absence of the policy there are no inefficiencies or inequities. Such is hardly the case. Prices and wages that do not reflect relative scarcities already result in inefficiencies. The criterion of flexibility, if appropriately applied, is to lessen the likelihood of gross inefficiencies and inequities.

The problems inherent in determining the merits of a price or wage increase are formidable. Indeed, they constitute one of the most intractable and arduous difficulties associated with an incomes policy. Nevertheless, such problems cannot be neatly sidestepped by creating a formula to apply to all proposed wage and price increases. Formidable as it may be, individual cases and their merits must be considered and decisions rendered. This is always difficult. It is always easier to promulgate policies from behind the shelter of an "automatic system" or, if that is not possible, to formulate strict guidelines to apply in all circumstances. Succumbing to such tendencies does indeed make the administration of the policy much easier. Unfortunately, it also greatly increases the dangers of negative side-effects.

Price or Wage Controls?

Most forms of incomes policies attempt to restrain both price and wage increases. Price increases are, by definition, inflationary whereas wage increases in excess of productivity improvements will quickly become inflationary. Thus, there is sound logic supporting efforts to control both.

There is a secondary reason, however, why the control of prices is important. The reasoning for this rests not only on the obvious fact that rising prices are inflationary but also on the manner in which price and wage decisions are made. In the absence of governmental interference, prices are decided upon by business alone. There are, of course, market constraints, but no prior approval is required by another party if management decides to boost the price of its product.

Wages are another matter. Labor unions, even the most powerful, do not have the power to set their own pay rates without the consent of management. This consent, of course, may be very grudging and may be made under duress, but it is nevertheless necessary before the increase becomes effective. In other words, a union wage increase is the result of a collective agreement between labor and management, whereas a price increase is not subject to prior approval by a second party.

Since management consent is required for wage increases, policies that make this consent harder to come by can mitigate the level of wage increases. Price controls have the effect of stiffening management's resistance at the bargaining table since it, as well as the unions, knows that wage increases cannot automatically be passed forward in the form of higher prices.

Wage restraints, on the other hand, provide no immediate incentive to hold down prices where the power to increase them exists. And although it often appears as if prices rise only in response to wage boosts, this is often deceptive. Wage increases are frequently used to justify a price hike that was actually the result of an exercise of market power in an effort to increase profit margins. Timing a price increase to follow a wage settlement quickly may create the appearance of a wage-induced inflation when the actual reason for the increase is quite different.

In other situations, however, wage controls are of primary importance. The most obvious example is the situation where the union is very strong and the employer quite weak. The construction and trucking industries are good examples. Here, many of the inflationary pressures are wage push, with powerful unions necessitating continual price increases. Price controls alone would have the effect of putting smaller firms out of business while doing little to control the level of prices. Another area is that of governmental units. Here "prices" are set to cover costs with no market constraints.

The European experience discussed in the following chapter indicates that controlling both prices and wages may be essential to a successful incomes policy. Although scattered instances of success have occurred where this criterion was not met, in general it appears to be a necessary condition.

Permanent or Temporary Controls?

A stated objective of the last control program was to remove the controls as soon as possible. Indeed, the administration took unusual pains to display near-contempt for its own program. This was seen as economically desirable and politically necessary. The logic of this position was less clear. If market imperfections are increasing—and this likelihood seems highly plausible—the need for some type of incomes policy will exist far into the future. In the unlikely event that market power is broken up through the vigorous application of antitrust legislation, the need for controls would diminish. But this seems to be a very long-run solution at best.

This does not mean, however, that a comprehensive level of surveillance will always be necessary. If inflationary expectations are broken and price and wage demands subsequently lowered, most increases could be below a "guideline level" without any governmental prodding. In this manner, the controls would become ineffective as part of the decision-making (and allocating) process. Thus, they could remain on the books without necessarily prohibiting anyone's actions or restricting anyone's freedom. They would only become operational in instances in which wage and/or price settlements exceeded the flexible guidelines. To a large degree, the return to a noninflationary period would, by itself, result in the demise of bureaucratic interference in the marketplace.

The Limits of Controls

In spite of the apparent need for a limiting force to control excessive wage and price increases, the implementation of such controls will not be a panacea for the nation's economic ills. Controls can provide a useful function toward reducing the trade-off between inflation and unemployment, but they cannot, by any means, solve the entire problem. In particular, the existence of controls should not be allowed to create a smokescreen that will divert attention from the underlying problems and the policies they require. There are, in particular, three areas where increased attention is needed.

A. Productivity

It has become commonplace to assert that the key to increased wages without inflation lies in productivity improvements. This assertion is so commonplace, in fact, that its essential truth is often overlooked. Nonetheless, it is only by improving the nation's output per man-hour that everyone's well being can be improved simultaneously and, at the same time, the trade-off between inflation and unemployment can be improved.

This prescription may sound excessively "economic." Surely, one might say, in a developed society there are considerations of greater importance than increasing material output. Don't we have enough already? Such arguments have merit. Indeed, it may be unfortunate that there is a continual demand for "more" in a society already overrun with consumer goods.

Attractive as such arguments are, they cannot subvert the fact that most Americans *do* seem to want more economic goods. *Why* everyone wants more may be a question of concern and importance. But the fact remains that most groups are militant in their demands for a larger share of the economic pie and other groups are just as adamant in refusing to relinquish their share.

Furthermore, who is to say that these demands are not legitimate? Disadvantaged groups are certainly entitled to question a system that forces them into deprivation and then insists that, because of general affluence, they should no longer concern themselves with mundane economic affairs. The same argument applies to the bulk of middle-class Americans. For too many groups and individuals, such pronouncements constitute a cruel joke.

The only long-run way in which these, and legions of other, disparate demands can be met is through increases in material output. And this puts the burden squarely at the door of productivity improvements. The demand for higher incomes from all groups is unlikely to abate in the near, or foreseeable, future. At the same time, the equation implying that wage increases in excess of productivity improvements will result in inflation seems incontrovertible. Because of this, the need is great to develop methods by which productivity can be improved. And this is especially true with respect to the growing sectors of the economy that account for continually larger portions of total employment and that have traditionally displayed disappointingly slow rates of productive improvement.

B. Manpower Policies

Although controls can limit the exercise of arbitrary market power and thereby restrain inflationary pressures, they can do little by themselves to alleviate the structural bottlenecks and mismatches that further the worsening trade-off between unemployment and inflation. As the pace of technological change quickens and the composition of the labor force continues to change, the need for manpower programs to facilitate the adjustments of supply and demand becomes greater. While the United States has increased its efforts in these areas dramatically in the past ten years, the country remains well behind most Western European nations in terms of the percentage of total output committed to such programs.

There is one aspect to manpower training that is facilitated by the introduction of an incomes policy. With effective controls, it becomes increasingly difficult for firms to bid labor supplies away from other firms as the economy tightens in response to stimulative fiscal and monetary measures. The controls prohibit wages from jumping rapidly in response to competing firms, which would be the case in the absence of controls. As a result, firms will be forced to look to other sources for increased personnel, and a logical result will be increased efforts to train their own employees. This, in turn, will help to break the bottlenecks in the labor supply that originally contributed to the inflationary pressures that developed at less than full levels of employment.

In the final analysis, however, an incomes policy can only complement an active manpower policy. It cannot be a substitute for such a policy. And the deteriorating structural situation clearly necessitates an increasingly active and ambitious manpower policy. This should be kept clearly in mind as efforts are expended to reduce unemployment while attempts are made to mitigate the level of inflation.

C. Antitrust Policy

An alternative to controlling power is eliminating it. Advocates of increased antitrust efforts have long argued that movement along these lines would do much to promote price stability while eradicating many of the evils associated with private power groups. Although the extent of private power in the U.S. economy can be taken as an indication that these efforts have been none too successful, it does not follow that they should be abandoned. Indeed, many critics of incomes policies prescribe, instead, policies aimed at reducing market power in an effort to increase competitive pressures. Economist William Poole, in arguing against the present incomes policy, lists a number of structural changes that could, and should, be made in an effort to increase competition. These include ". . . antitrust action leading to dissolution of large firms in excessively concentrated industries" (87, p. 441).

No doubt, many proponents of wage and price controls would agree with policy prescriptions aimed at increasing the degree of competition in the economy. Where many would disagree is in the feasibility of such proposals, especially in the short run. If structural changes can be made that will increase competition without damaging efficiency, so much the better. But until such changes are made, it may be necessary to restrain existing market power.

An advantage of controls is that they can be effective in the absence of structural changes. When and if these changes are made, controls will be unnecessary. At that time (should it ever come) hardly anyone would favor continued market controls. However, the growth of market concentration along with continual calls for a more rigid application of antitrust statutes—two events that have been occurring simultaneously for the past seventy years—force us to question the speed with which these structural changes can be made.

In any case, antitrust efforts and market controls are complementary approaches to the same goal; namely, restricting the unbridled exercise of market power.

CAN CONTROLS WORK? EXAMINING THE EVIDENCE   10

> It is not best that we should all think alike; it is differences of opinion that makes horse-races.
>
> Mark Twain

Controls can be useful, but they are not a cure-all. Thus, as with any policy formulation, it is helpful—indeed necessary—to examine the successes and failures associated with the implementation of similar programs in the past. The past has provided us with three major examples, which help to delineate the strengths and weaknesses of controls. The first is a brief U.S. experience with extensive controls during World War II and Korea and the later program of limited restraints on wages and prices during the Kennedy-Johnson years. This latter attempt was the first peacetime effort in the U.S. to alleviate inflation by direct intervention into the marketplace. Thus, many arguments concerning controls at that time are applicable now. It must be recognized, however, that the economy is continually undergoing change and that what was true of the 1960s is not necessarily true of the 1970s. But this recent experience is by far the closest model available with which to view the market controls of the 1970s.

The second major source of experience is the attempt by Western European countries to limit inflationary pressures while moving toward full employment. Nearly all these mixed economies have had experiences with incomes policies. A look at their record can shed light on American efforts to achieve a lower trade-off between unemployment and inflation through the adoption of wage and price controls.

The third experience is the economic stabilization program of 1971–74. This important experience is considered separately in the following two chapters.

WORLD WAR II[1]

The relevance of America's war-time experience with wage and price controls to the situation of the 1970s is very limited. In the first place, public acceptance of controls was much greater during the second World War than during peacetime (although the degree of this acceptance and the voluntary compliance based upon it is frequently overstated). Also, the war-time controls were much more comprehensive and detailed than those provided by the moderate incomes policy formulated for the 1970s. Most important, the earlier controls were instituted in an attempt to control a severe case of demand-pull inflation, which had resulted from the massive war effort. In this respect, the problems associated with the policy as well as the economic conditions that immediately preceded it were quite different from those some thirty years later.

A freeze was first imposed on wages and prices in the United States in April 1942. This had been preceded by a period of moral suasion during which President Roosevelt had attempted to persuade business and labor to hold prices and wages down. Demand pressures had clearly necessitated strong action. From January 1941, to October 1942, hourly wages in manufacturing rose by 30.7 percent and the wholesale price index rose by 24 percent.

In spite of the many inequities that developed within the system, it was effective. From its inauguration in 1942 until its dissolution in August 1945, the Economic Stabilization Act helped to limit hourly manufacturing wages to an increase of 14.7 percent for the entire period and the wholesale price index to an overall increase of only 5.7 percent.

Such results, however, were obtained only at a high cost in terms of equity and efficiency. Under "general max" (the general maximum price regulation), which was instituted under the Emergency Price Control Act of 1941, prices were to be set at levels not exceeding those charged by the firm for the same or similar products in March 1942. In spite of the seeming simplicity of the control mechanism, it was quickly circumvented in practice. The problem of determining which class, and

---

[1] Only a very brief overview of the U.S. war-time experience with wage and price controls is considered here. For an excellent summary of this experience, see Colin D. Campbell (ed.), *Wage-Price Controls in World War II, United States and Germany* (American Enterprise Institute, 1971). Except where noted, the data in the present discussion are from this source.

hence which price ceiling, would apply to a given commodity proved formidable. Also, the problem of product quality, especially concerning agricultural products, proved to be sizable. A favorite method of getting around the letter of the law in this case was the continuous introduction of new brands of canned foodstuffs. Since the product was "new," it was hoped (and many times assumed) that the same price would not prevail as under the earlier label.

Such techniques were quickly adopted in other instances. Slight changes were often made in product quality that resulted in an effective price increase. At the same time, an alteration of the product with no corresponding change in quality might qualify the merchandise as a "new" product with a new price tag. And, inevitably, the inequities developed into black markets as the price system attempted to operate in the face of severe institutional restraints.

When the Office of Economic Stabilization came into effect by executive order on October 3, 1942, "general max" was replaced by more comprehensive and more specialized controls. Food items were henceforth regulated by the government, and wage increases were placed under the auspices of the National War Labor Board. But even these extended controls provided for exceptions. As the exceptions became increasingly widespread, President Roosevelt issued a hold-the-line order in 1943 that sharply decreased the number of justifications for price and wage increases.

By 1945 America's involvement with stringent wage and price controls ended along with the nation's participation in World War II. And the largely ineffective controls that still officially existed were lifted in November 1946.

The war-time experience with controls, although inadequate in many respects, did indicate one thing: serious inflation could be avoided by direct market intervention. In large part, both labor unions and business firms cooperated with the war-time effort. Workers were widely criticized for strikes, although those that occurred were mostly after the peak war effort had passed and were in sectors of the economy not directly related to this effort. And, to the slogan, "there are no strikes in foxholes," labor replied, with a good deal of justification, "there are no profits, either." Indeed, business receipts did soar during the war. After-tax corporate profits almost doubled from 1939 to 1944, going from $5 billion in the former year to $9.9 billion in the latter (46, p. 566).

War-time controls imposed at the height of a national emergency are one thing. Peace-time efforts to lower the trade-off between inflation and unemployment through direct intervention into the market are quite another. In an attempt to evaluate America's experience with this less pressured situation, it is necessary to examine the peace-time record of wage and price controls. To do so, we turn our attention to the 1960s.

THE GUIDEPOSTS

When John F. Kennedy assumed the presidency in 1961, he was determined to "get the country moving again." In economic terms, this meant stimulating aggregate demand in an effort to increase employment and thereby improve the rate of economic growth. It was, however, widely believed that such efforts would put increased pressure on price levels and that if new expansionary policies were to be successful, they would have to be matched by efforts to contain inflation.

The result was the formulation of the guidepost philosophy that was first introduced in the 1962 *Economic Report of the President*. Although there had been previous appeals for general price and wage restraints during the Eisenhower Administration, the guideposts represented the first formal policy in this direction and the first time that *specific* rules of acceptable behavior became official policy. However, by 1967 the Council of Economic Advisors was already retreating from stating numerical guideposts, and by 1968 most observers were ready to pronounce the concept dead. The general feeling was that the policy was a failure and that its early demise was a reward well-suited to its usefulness.

Certainly the guideposts were a failure if measured against a criterion of halting the inflationary pressures of the late 1960s. Critics point with glee to the fact that from mid-1965 prices began moving upward with increasing acceleration and that this, in turn, led to a complete breakdown of the guideposts shortly thereafter. The question, however, is not whether the guideposts were able to avert the powerful demand-pull pressures from boosting the price indexes but whether they were able to limit these increases to lower levels than if there had been no controls.

The effectiveness of the guideposts in this regard is, of course, impossible to prove or disprove. No one knows with certainty what would have happened in their absence. There is evidence, however, that the guideposts were able to moderate inflationary pressures, especially before the economy began operating at full blast. After briefly discussing the guidepost mechanics, this evidence will be examined.

The Logic of the Guideposts

The guideposts put down an explicit directive that in order for prices to remain stable, wages could increase by no more than the general rate of productivity improvements. Since this general trend rate of productivity growth (output per man-hour) was determined (somewhat arbitrarily) to be 3.2 percent per year, the guidepost stated that overall wages should increase by no more than this amount. At the same time, it was recognized that some industries enjoy productivity improvements of more than this whereas others fell short of the trend rate. In order to provide for guideline wage increases, then, the policy prescription was for prices to go up in industries that experienced less than average productivity gains and down in industries exhibiting greater than average gains. The result would be a stable overall price level with the division of income between labor and capital remaining constant. The 1968 *Economic Report of the President* succinctly summarized the philosophy of the guideposts:

> In general, the wage guidepost calls for increases in hourly compensation to be limited to the trend rate of productivity growth for the economy as a whole. The price guidepost calls for prices to remain stable in industries in which the trend gain in productivity approximates the average rate for the economy; it points to price declines where productivity gains exceed this average; and it recognizes the need for prices to be increased as required where the improvements are lower than average (20, pp. 120-121).

After establishing this guidepost and adopting the 3.2-percent productivity figure, the council further elaborated a number of exceptions to the formula that were intended to provide the necessary flexibility. It was recognized during the 1960s, as it was in the 1970s, that rigid adherence to any specific wage and price figure by all elements within the economy would seriously damage the allocative mechanism of the price system. It was further recognized that wage increases would have to be tied to the *overall* rate of productivity improvements, not to the productivity growth of a particular sector. This was meant to prevent serious disparities and inequities from developing in the wage structure.[2]

A glaring difference between the earlier guideposts and the stabilization program of the 1970s policy was in the area of enforcement. The guideposts were forced to rely upon moral suasion, arm twisting, jawboning, and the like to enforce wage-price decrees. In contrast, the later Phases I through IV included specific sanctions that could be applied to violators.

The guideposts promoted the belief that the consumer as well as business firms and labor unions should share in productivity increases. If an industry enjoyed greater than average productivity improvement, the savings should be passed on to the consumer in the form of lower prices.

---

[2] For a detailed presentation of the philosophy and mechanics of the guideposts see the *Economic Report of the President,* 1967, pp. 120-127. For a description, analysis, and evaluation of the guideposts, an excellent source is John Sheahan, *The Wage-Price Guideposts* (Brookings Institution, 1967).

Prices should not be maintained and the increased returns divided between wages and profits. Prices were allowed to increase in areas where productivity improvements were less than average, thereby implying that they must be decreasing in other sectors if the average were to remain stable.

The Effectiveness of the Guideposts

The objectives of the guideposts were clear, as was the rationale for their implementation. The question is, were the guideposts effective? Unfortunately, as with studies concerning the ability of unions to raise wages, it is impossible to measure precisely the impact of market controls. And the problem arises for the same reason: it is impossible to hold other things constant in order to examine the influence of the policy in isolation. It is one thing to say that prices and wages went up in the face of governmental pressure to hold them down, it is quite another to assert that the guideposts had no impact in holding these increases to levels lower than would have been achieved without the policy.

Ideally, in an effort to measure the impact of the guideposts, one would begin by determining what the behavior of wages and prices would have been during the 1960s had there been no official policy of restraint. This, of course, is impossible to determine. Several econometric models have been constructed, however, in an attempt to explain both price and wage behavior, and thus to predict what the levels of these variables would be under different circumstances. Many of these studies have been referred to earlier (see Chapter 5) and will not be reiterated here except where the results have a bearing on the effectiveness of the guideposts.

George Perry's model of wage changes (83), although inconclusive, lends support to the proposition that the guidelines were effective in mitigating wage increases during the early to mid-1960s. The model, when used as a predictive device, understates the degree of wage increases from 1960–62 but consistently overstates them from 1962 to 1965. Referring to Perry's model, Robert Solow states:

> Beginning with the third quarter of 1962, and without exception for the next fourteen quarters to the end of 1965, wages rose more slowly than the theory would expect. Runs in the residuals are not uncommon, but this run is uncommonly long. Moreover, although the overestimation of wage changes was initially small, it became substantial in 1964 and 1965. In 1965 the annual increase in wage rates was about 1.7 percent lower than the 1948–60 experience would lead one to expect (104, p. 46).

As Solow is quick to point out, it cannot be concluded that the guideposts were solely, or even primarily, responsible for this. But as he goes on to say, "The timing certainly suggests that the guideposts had something to do with it" (*ibid.*).

Explanations other than the guideposts were, however, put forth. Later in the decade, Norman Simler and Alfred Tella published their *labor reserves theory,* which shed light on what some of the "other things" were that could account for the overprediction of the original Perry model (100). They argue that reserves of secondary workers grow as unemployment increases since these secondary workers, by definition, drop out of the labor force as economic conditions worsen and unemployment rises. Then, as conditions improve and unemployment moves downward, wage increases are mitigated by the return of the secondary workers into the labor force. Furthermore, because of the substantial unemployment of the late 1950s and early 1960s, large numbers of labor reserves entered the labor force as employment expanded during the decade. These reserves held the level of wage increases below that which would be experienced with the same level of stated unemployment but with lower reserves. Later in the decade, there were fewer available reserves to mitigate the wage increases as markets tightened. And this phenomenon is quite independent of the existence of the guideposts.

John Sheahan has pointed out that while the Simler-Tella model appears to be valid, it does not negate the implication that the guideposts were a significant factor in holding down wage increases during this period (96, p. 88). If secondary workers were completely substitutable for primary workers, the labor reserves model would explain most of the discrepancy between actual and predicted behavior. However, the two groups are not perfectly interchangeable. The former consists mainly of women, students, and old people whereas the latter consists of prime-working-age males. For this latter group, the official unemployment rate continues to constitute a good measure of labor market tightness since people in this demographic category tend to remain in the labor force regardless of economic conditions.

The unfortunate implication of these results is that there are elements of truth in both explanations. But it is impossible to know how much weight should be applied to either of them. It is probable from these data that the guideposts had some effect on wage levels; just how much effect is impossible to say.

Data prepared by the Federal Reserve Bank of Cleveland and presented by Sheahan (96, p. 80) indicate that wholesale prices were more stable from 1961–65 than would have been expected on the basis of similar unemployment rates in the past. Sheahan adds that "more elaborate statistical tests by Frank Brechling and Robert Solow, using two different approaches, came to the same conclusion that the rate of price increase was reduced as compared to earlier relationships" (96, p. 81).

After discussing the details and differences of a number of statistical studies, Sheahan remarks, quite correctly, that "such comparisons can quickly generate headaches." He concludes, however, that although the studies differ in the techniques adopted as well as the numerical estimates they provide, "Those for industrial prices and wages support the idea of a downward deflection, holding the increase in prices from 1961 to 1965 to less than half of what could have been expected from earlier relationships" (96, p. 92).

More recent evidence supports the hypothesis that the guideposts were effective, although there are enough conflicting viewpoints to keep the issue open. Reporting on newer research, George Perry provides further evidence of the effectiveness of the policy (84, 85). He argues that the guideposts were applied selectively to certain "visible" (that is, large) industries and, furthermore, that they were effective in slowing down the rate of price increase in these areas.

The evidence presented by Perry has not gone unchallenged. Paul S. Anderson (4), Michael L. Wachter (121), and Adrian W. Throop (110), have carefully examined Perry's analysis and found it to be less than convincing. These critics take issue with the statistical techniques employed by Perry and argue that factors other than the guideposts can better explain the behavior of wages in the 1960s. In return, however, Perry has countered that these criticisms have failed to demonstrate serious deficiencies in his original analysis. Furthermore, he argues that when more recent data are included, the case in favor of the guideposts is even more convincing (85).

James Christian has analyzed similar data and concluded that the guidelines had no appreciable effect on wages (17). Christian builds upon the work of E. Kuh who has argued that productivity is a more appropriate variable than profits for the determination of wages (58). Perry, along with Eckstein and Wilson (31) considered profits to be an important determinant of wage rates, whereas Kuh argues that profits are, at best, only a proxy for productivity. Christian accepts this argument and uses it as a basis for testing the effectiveness of the guideposts in his model. After considering several statistical tests, he states, "Our findings, therefore, indicate that the guidepost was not successful while Perry's indicate, perhaps with equal force, that it was" (17, p. 62). The reason for this disagreement, argues Christian, lies in the use of profits as an explanatory variable in the Perry model and productivity in his.

The question of whether productivity is a better determinant of wage rates than profits is an open one. Eckstein and Wilson found productivity to be relatively unimportant, especially in the short run when there is almost no correlation between industry productivity increases and wage movements. This is in general agreement with William Bowen's findings (11).

Although one can find methodological shortcomings in virtually any type of statistical study, one aspect of the Christian study deserves special attention. Accepting the Perry assertion that the guideposts were aimed at visible industries rather than the smaller (invisible) ones, Christian attempts to measure the impact of the policy by observing whether there has been a significant difference in the wage behavior among these two rather arbitrarily defined groups. "If we find," he argues, "that the industries which appear to have been affected belong predominantly, or even in equal number, to the invisible or the unaffected group, we will be inclined to conclude that forces other than the guideposts were responsible" (17, p. 55).

Defining the test in such a manner, however, could result in negative findings, when in fact the guideposts may have been quite effective. If, as appears likely (see Chapter 6), there is a substantial spillover from wage settlements in key areas to those in more competitive sectors, mitigating the rate of increase in the former areas will also limit the size of settlements in the latter ones. In this very probable event, there would be no noticeable difference between the wage patterns of the controlled or affected industries and the uncontrolled or more competitive sectors. It is, therefore, difficult to draw any conclusions concerning the overall impact of the policy among various sectors of the economy.

The debate will undoubtedly continue. More sophisticated methods are continually being brought to bear upon the problems of factoring out the relative importance of different components in the determination of wage rates. But until a definitive method for evaluating influence of controls is discovered, the question will remain open.

The balance of the evidence supports the viewpoint that the wage-price guideposts did have some effect in placing downward pressure on wages and prices. It is significant that Christian, who presents one of the most persuasive arguments questioning the effectiveness of the guideposts, agrees with this general conclusion. Writing in 1970, he states, "Although the evidence against guidepost effectiveness is less persuasive, at the margin, than that in favor, the issue remains in doubt" (17, p. 51). Unfortunately, this is about as precise as one can get. Thomas Moore has recently concluded that "evidence on both sides can be presented. The impact of the guideposts, therefore, cannot be ascertained with any certainty" (70, p. 29).

Unresolved Questions

There is no doubt that, whatever the effects of the guideposts during the early to mid-1960s, the attempt at voluntary restraints began to break down after the middle of the decade and crumbled completely toward the end. As usual, proponents and critics of the policy alike can (and do) find support in this. The critics argue, quite correctly, that as economic conditions tightened, the guideposts quickly proved ineffective. Furthermore, they argue that the earlier appearance of success with the program was simply the result of loose market conditions and that it was the lack of inflationary expectations that provided for the lower than expected price and wage increases.

Supporters, on the other hand, argue that the guideposts were never intended to be effective in periods of excess aggregate demand. Therefore, it was no surprise that the policy lost its effectiveness when these conditions appeared after the middle of the decade.

Moreover, some supporters of market restraints—although by no means all of them—charge that much of the ineffectiveness of the guideposts during this period simply reflected the fact that they contained no enforcement provisions. When a few large unions and businesses could flaunt their disregard for the guideposts and then obtain government support for settlements well above the suggested level, other unions and companies quickly altered their stance toward the policy from one of grudging acceptance to one of active hostility.

Among the more visible violations of the guideposts was the airline machinists' strike of 1966. Here a 4.9 percent increase was finally settled upon after the union membership rejected an agreement of 4.3 percent—a figure already above the 3.2 percent guidepost. And when the president of the machinists' union publicly stated that the settlement "completely shatters" the guideposts, he was only observing what many others already believed and what the administration was soon forced to admit. In an interesting replay of the details of this settlement, Sheahan concludes that "the President, and his labor-management advisory committee, meeting shortly thereafter, concluded that some new approach to wage restraint had become necessary" (96, p. 60). Most observers agreed.

Nor were the only violations in the area of wages. Several industries, including the airlines, were enjoying substantial productivity increases during this period, which, according to the guidelines, should have induced price reductions. This did not happen and, instead, profits soared. High profits in turn provided further visibility to violations of the policy. In the face of this, labor unions were especially reluctant to hold down their demands.

In addition to questioning the effectiveness of the guideposts, these examples point to two important considerations for any incomes policy. The first is the matter of their voluntary nature. Where no clear-cut legal sanctions are available to enforce the policy, groups that are powerful enough to do so will quickly shed any spirit of cooperation when the opportunity for substantial gain presents itself.

Secondly, the matter of equity is extremely important. When parties on one side of the bargaining table see gross violations of the guidelines occurring on the other, a militant reaction invariably develops. The same applies to different sectors of the economy. If violations occur and the policy gains a reputation for being inequitable, feelings of hostility rapidly mount to the point where enforcement becomes virtually impossible. This undoubtedly had a pronounced effect on the early and rapid demise of the guideposts in the latter half of the 1960s.

EUROPEAN EXPERIENCE WITH INCOMES POLICIES

In other Western countries, incomes policies designed to mitigate inflation and promote full employment have exhibited mixed results. Certainly, one who attempts to find strong support for the effectiveness of wage and price restraints by looking abroad will be disappointed. Without exception, market controls have broken down at some time or another in all the free economies that have tried them.

At the same time, however, it is far from clear that the policies were totally ineffective or that they have failed to achieve at least a part of their stated goals. At any rate, the experience has not been so negative that other countries have stopped experimenting with direct market controls. Indeed, if anything, the search for a viable incomes policy has become more pronounced as Western Europe, Canada, and the United States find the dual goals of price stability and full employment ever more illusive.

It is important, in reviewing the results of other experiences, to keep in mind the myriad differences in background, culture, and institutional arrangements among the various countries. Such differences make meaningful comparisons difficult and generalizations dangerous since rarely, if ever, are "other things equal." Having stated this seemingly obvious fact, we will now examine the experiences of a number of other countries with incomes policies. We will then proceed to generalize from these experiences.[3]

The Netherlands

The Dutch experience with wage and price restraints has been more widespread than that of most other countries and the degree of success generally higher. This experience began immediately after World War

---

[3] A succinct discussion of the European experience with controls is contained in Sheahan (96). A more extended discussion that includes their relevance of Canada is provided by David Smith in a study prepared for the Economic Council of Canada (103). A more recent study of European experiences has been provided by Lloyd Ulman and Robert J. Flanagan (113). The present discussion relies heavily upon these sources.

II and only in recent years have controls broken down. As a result, there are currently fewer wage and price restraints in effect in the Netherlands than at any time since 1945.

The collective-bargaining structure in the Netherlands is fairly centralized—a situation that is generally considered a plus factor for the adoption of an incomes policy. Decisions concerning wages are made on a high level where national economic considerations can be taken into account, something that is impossible with a decentralized and fractionalized bargaining system.

Furthermore, there was generally a common desire on the part of all concerned parties to keep Dutch products competitive in international markets. Indeed, the balance of payments criterion has been the most important factor in promoting wage restraints in the Netherlands. This fact is hardly surprising when one considers that almost 50 percent of the nation's output is directed into exports.

The policy of restraints was quite effective during its early stages. During the entire period from 1947 to 1953, wages went up by only 1 percent. Prices during this stage were allowed to increase only by the amount of cost increases *exclusive* of wage hikes. By most reckoning, incomes policy in the immediate post-war Netherlands was a success. Indeed, an indication of this success can be seen in the fact that the unions, in 1951, agreed to take a 5-percent *decrease* in real wages in an effort to make exports more competitive.

This cooperation, however, began to wane by the late 1950s and throughout the 1960s. After a wage explosion in 1963, 1964, and 1965, support all but vanished. Until this time, unions and employers, working together through the jointly-created Foundation of Labor, had agreed upon guidelines to be followed in wage negotiations. These guidelines were based upon economic forecasts provided by the government's Central Planning Bureau. The bureau, along with the Foundation of Labor, provided the basis for Dutch wage policy. By 1968, the parties were no longer working together and formal guidelines were not being issued, let alone followed. To what can one attribute the early success and the later failure of incomes policy in the Netherlands? The reasons, of course, are many and complex but the following are among the more important.

First, with respect to the early success of the policy, it appears that one of the explanations lies in the common goal that existed for all elements of the economy; namely, that of a healthy position in international trade. Indeed, in almost all countries (including the U.S.), the foreign trade situation has triggered the adoption of wage and price restraints. With the extremely important role for foreign trade within the Dutch economy, there existed a common cause of obvious importance to everyone.

Another factor contributing to early success was the cooperation of the labor unions. This factor has usually proven to be critical to the success of market controls, and during the early years of the Dutch policy, the level of cooperation was high. When this support began to erode in the late 1950s and early 1960s, the chances for continued success diminished accordingly.

If it is clear that the Dutch incomes policy was able to restrain wages and prices in the early years of its adoption, it is equally clear that it was unable to do so during the later years. Why?

A part of the explanation must be found in the fact that the balance of payments situation improved during the 1950s, leading to substantial surpluses. Although the earlier success of the policy was in part responsible for this, the surplus trade accounts also lessened the need for continued restraints. Of possibly greater importance, it lessened the degree to which the different parties saw their interests tied to further controls. As a result, cooperation with the official policy began to diminish, in part because of the program's early success.

A further complication arose in 1963 when a form of productivity bargaining was replaced with a general wage guideline supplied by an econometric model devised by the Control Planning Bureau. This forecast turned out to be considerably less optimistic than the performance of the economy warranted, and when the results were in, organized labor became highly critical of the bureau on the grounds that it was excessively conservative in its estimates. The implication of this conservative bias was, of course, to issue a guideline for wage restraint below that which would have been consistent with stable prices. With increased skepticism, labor's confidence in, and cooperation with, the whole notion of wage controls rapidly diminished, thereby leading to the subsequent wage explosions.

Labor, it should be noted, was not alone in its disillusionment. Employers also began to resent wage controls as they found it increasingly difficult to recruit necessary labor supplies. Ways were found to circumvent the guidelines in order to bid labor away from competitors. The result was a tendency toward increased wage drift as the rate of promotions increased, job descriptions changed, and piecework earnings increased. Finally, outright defiance of the controls brought about "black" wages in excess of the official guidelines.

Of the many factors responsible for the decline in effectiveness of wage and price controls in the Netherlands, none was more important than the emergence of excess demand during the 1960s. This demand finally placed uncontrollable pressure on wage and price levels.

In most European countries, the unemployment rate, even when adjusted for differences in definition, is typically much lower than it is in the United States. From 1959 to 1964, the unemployment rate in the Netherlands averaged less than 1 percent of the labor force. In the U.S., where it is extremely difficult to achieve a 4-percent average, this seems incredible. Indeed, the highest unemployment rate for the entire post-World War II period in the Netherlands was reached during the recession of 1958 when the rate rose to an alarming 2.25 percent! One might wonder how a policy of wage restraints was able to have *any* affect under such labor market conditions.

During the late 1950s and throughout the 1960s, however, demand increased even further, thereby placing additional pressure on wages. In the face of this onslaught of aggregate demand, controls crumbled and became completely ineffective by 1968. In the process, the behavior of both unions and employers displayed symptoms associated with an overheated economy: labor would no longer abide by a guideline on wages, employers began disregarding the official target in an attempt to recruit increasingly scarce labor supplies, and the entire policy became ineffective.

The fact that controls become ineffective when faced with substantial excess demand should surprise no one. In the first place, the purpose of moderate wage and price restraints is not to control excessive demand inflation caused by "the furnace running at full blast."

In the second place, if controls *were* effective during periods of excessive aggregate demand, the result would be to stifle the allocative mechanism of the pricing system and thereby promote widespread inequities and inefficiencies within the economy. In this case, Professor Friedman is undoubtedly correct in asserting that "suppressed inflation is worse than open inflation" (33, p. 31).

As David Smith remarked concerning the Dutch experience, "Once the dam has begun to break, it is extraordinarily difficult to contain the pressures" (103, p. 41). Indeed, although there are considerable differences concerning the interpretation of post-war European experiences with income policies, the almost universally accepted conclusion is that the policies—whatever their specific nature—become ineffective when confronted with massive doses of excess aggregate demand.

Sweden

Almost at the opposite end of the policy spectrum from the Netherlands has been Sweden, which until quite recently had no formal incomes policy. In contrast to the Dutch situation, there has been a consistent bias on the part of the Swedish populace *against* governmental interference in the wage-setting process. Thus, throughout the post-World War II era there has been no official policy of wage or price restraint, although pressures began to develop for such a policy in the late 1960s and finally led to the imposition of a price freeze in 1970.

Structurally, the Swedish economy is characterized by even more centralization with respect to its collective-bargaining institutions than the Netherlands. Indeed, in terms of centralization of decision making, Sweden is unmatched in the free world. Making up this power are three major union federations of which the Swedish Confederation of Trade Unions (LO) is clearly the most influential. It represents approximately two-thirds of all organized employees (90 percent of the manual workers) and boasts a membership of forty-one national unions.

Offsetting this power on one side of the labor market is the Swedish Employers Federation (SAF), which represents the bulk of the nation's employers. Between them, these two organizations have been almost solely responsible for Sweden's post-war wage policy. Indeed, much of the reason for the lack of governmental policy in this area is to be found in the desire for both of these groups to act in such a manner as to negate the need for governmental interference. These two dominant and highly centralized organizations make their own forecasts of economic conditions and then decide upon acceptable wage levels in light of these broad considerations. The result, as Ulman and Flanagan point out, is that "centralized bargaining in the private sector has amounted to a privately operated income policy" (113, p. 93).

Coupled with this private determination of wage policy has been the widespread belief in Sweden in the effectiveness of an active manpower policy to ward off inflation pressures. This policy has resulted in a significant number of persons continually undertaking training and retraining programs in an attempt to halt the development of bottlenecks in labor markets. At the same time, there has been an equally strong commitment to the effective use of monetary and fiscal policies as a means of approaching wage and price stabilization. In contrast to the attitudes toward an income policy, the public has strongly supported these components of stabilization policy.

The results of this private incomes policy, coupled with an active manpower program, have been impressive. In terms of the inflation/unemployment trade-off, Sweden has fared better than the other European countries, the United States, and Canada. Throughout most of the 1960s unemployment averaged (in U.S. terms) less than 1.5 percent whereas productivity, during the first half of the decade, increased by an annual average of 4.3 percent. Annual inflation was held to 3.5 percent (103, p. 153). With such a record it is little wonder that interest did not develop in a governmental incomes policy. There was simply no need for it. At the same time, however, it is clear that an overall wage policy was operating during the post-war years. Given the highly centralized nature of the Swedish Industrial Relations System, this policy was quite effective.

By the mid to late 1960s, however, this enviable position began to show severe signs of strain. Wage drift—measured as the difference between bargained wages and the actual payments—began to increase considerably, thereby leading to increased unit labor costs, which, in turn, put pressure on the price level. Satisfaction with the wage-price policy began to decline.

Since much wage drift consists of piecework payments, such increases are not available to professional and salaried employees. As a result, this group began to see their compensation decline in relation to that of manual workers, and serious divisions began to appear within organized labor. In particular, the Swedish Confederation of Professional Association (SACO) began to make wage demands independent of those formulated by the LO and, as a result, the long-held dominance of the LO–SAF in determining wage policy was eroded.

Further signs of discontent also appeared during the late 1960s. As with many European labor movements, the militancy of the Swedish rank and file increased dramatically, with an unprecedented outbreak of strikes and related industrial unrest as a result. This finally culminated in February of 1971, in the passage of legislation outlawing strikes and lockouts.

In the meantime, because the LO and SAF are unable to formulate wage policy by themselves, interest is growing in the adoption of a public incomes policy. The SAF itself supported this concept in 1967 and has continued to advocate such a policy since then. It may well be, contrary to the accepted notion, that the diminished degree of centralization now surfacing in Swedish industrial affairs will *promote* the adoption of a public incomes policy. A private policy, such as that provided by unique Swedish experience since World War II, can only operate effectively if the powers at the top agree to the policy and can control their members. By the late 1960s it was becoming increasingly evident that both these conditions were waning in Sweden. Rivalries were developing among the labor federations. At the same time these organizations were increasingly being frustrated in attempts to dictate wage terms to their constituencies. With these developments, the probability is for increased governmental intervention in the industrial relations system and, in particular, for increased interest in the development of an official incomes policy. It will be interesting to see, should Sweden follow this course, whether she will be as successful in the formulation of a public policy as she has been in the execution of private policies.

The United Kingdom

If the degree of success with incomes policies, both public and private, is questionable in the Netherlands and Sweden, it is even more in doubt in the United Kingdom. There, the policy can be regarded as having been marginally useful in the immediate post-war years, but even limited success is questionable in later years.

The major thrust with the British experience, as with most countries, has been the attempt to improve the international trade situation by the adoption of wage and/or price controls. This was clearly the case as the English weathered one balance-of-payments crisis after another in the post-war years. This, in turn, is due in large part to the slow rate of productivity improvements within the United Kingdom, which have fostered unacceptable increases in the price level even without large wage increases. As a result, the British experience with incomes policy has consisted to a much larger extent than in the other countries of attempts to improve the rate of productivity growth.

The slow rate of productivity growth has been accompanied by low unemployment rates for the past 25 years. Unfortunately, efforts to stimulate demand in order to increase production were invariably felt in price and wage increases. Price increases would then make the trading situation worse as British goods became less competitive in foreign markets. This, in turn, would induce deflationary moves in order to dampen inflationary pressures. The result would be further declines in both investment and growth. The adoption of an incomes policy was seen as a means of escape from this dilemma.

The first attempts at wage and price restraints occurred when a wage freeze was imposed in 1948. This effort was fairly successful since it had the cooperation of the powerful Trades Union Congress (TUC). But when general support for the policy eroded in 1950, a wage explosion resulted. The TUC, faced with an increasingly militant and hostile membership, was unable to promote continued cooperation with the policy and, indeed, lost considerable influence with the membership for supporting the restraints as long as it did.

With the return of the Conservative Party to power in October 1951, union cooperation with any sort of an incomes policy declined even further. The Conservatives remained at the helm of the government until 1964 and, although attempts at restraint were frequently repeated during this period, there were virtually no signs of appreciable effect on wages or prices. The experience in the United Kingdom strongly suggests that cooperation between the governing party and the labor unions is vital to the adoption of effective wage and price controls.

Not that the Conservative government did not attempt to institute such a policy. As the balance-of-payments situation worsened during the 1950s, the government began to encourage unions to restrict their demands and employers to resist price increases. However, without support from the TUC or the public in general, such pleas had little effect.

As the international situation for Great Britain worsened, the government, under the leadership of the Chancellor of the Exchequer Selwyn Lloyd, attempted to institute a "pay pause" in 1961. In an effort to promote the idea, the government announced that there would be no pay increases for public employees in the near future. Contrary to official hopes, however, the private sector did not follow this attempt to restrain wages, nor did the TUC offer any cooperation. This, in turn, caused a great deal of turmoil and frustration among public-sector employees, but it had little impact on aggregate wage or price movements. Related measures, which were inaugurated at various times until the Labor government came into power in 1964, met a similar fate.

With a government more to the liking of organized labor, the chances for an effective incomes policy appeared to improve. Faced with a continuing deterioration in the balance of payments situation, the new government secured the cooperation of labor for a fresh attempt at controlling wages and prices. Finally, an incomes policy similar to the U.S. guidepost system was formulated, with a target rate for earnings increases set at 3 to 3.5 percent and a reliance upon voluntary compliance.

As it turned out, however, the intended cooperation of the TUC was not enough to ensure, or even to promote, success with the new policy. This is largely due to the decentralized nature of the British industrial-relations system in which the federation has little control over bargaining, even in the matter of wages. This is in sharp contrast to the Dutch and Swedish situation where, at least until recently, the labor federations had considerable control over local wage matters. In the United Kingdom, the TUC could agree with the Labor government's policy but could do little to ensure the cooperation of the bargaining units. And without this cooperation the policy had little effect.

With restraints having little impact, the balance-of-trade position continued to worsen, to the extent that fears of a devaluation of the pound became very real. In an effort to stave off this possibility, the government imposed a wage and price freeze from July 1966 until June 1967. This was followed by a period of "moderation" from 1967 to 1968 that was similar to the Nixon Administration's Phase II. During this period, advance notification was required for wage and price hikes, with the National Board for Prices and Incomes empowered to forbid any increases for a period of up to seven months.

While the freeze was fairly effective, the period of moderation was not. Hourly wages rose by 9.2 percent during this latter phase, although retail prices were held to an increase of only 2.8 percent (113, p. 19).

The attempts at wage and price restraint were unable to obviate a currency adjustment, and in 1967 the pound was devalued. Since a primary purpose of the incomes policy was to make this move unnecessary, support of the policy was even less evident after the readjustment.

Post-devaluation incomes policy has focused on attempts to institute productivity bargaining in an effort to improve Great Britain's traditionally poor record in this area. The essence of productivity bargaining is that wage increases above a certain guideline (4.5 percent in the United Kingdom) can be granted only in return for specific, detailed, local arrangements for increasing productivity. The purpose of the policy is to encourage labor unions to join in efforts to increase productivity by giving up restrictive work rules and habits in return for pay increases above the guideline figure. Such habits and rules are legion in the United Kingdom.

The results of productivity bargaining are not in yet, and a final evaluation must wait until more experience is gained. Ulman and Flanagan (113, p. 43) conclude that although the British policy had little apparent effect on prices, it may have been partially responsible for the recent increases in productivity. At the same time, efforts will almost certainly be made to find an acceptable and effective policy that can restrain wages and prices while fostering improvements in output. For without such a policy, there is little likelihood that the United Kingdom will be able to increase her growth rate and, hence, her position in international trading markets.

France

Government regulations and activities in the market were an established feature of the French economy long before Colbert began his famous reign as Chief Minister to Louis XIV in 1661. Indeed, the entire history of French economic development is one of active government involvement in economic matters to a considerably larger extent than is the case in either England or the United States. It is no surprise, then, that France has not hesitated to formulate an incomes policy that is, to a greater degree than most countries, an integral part of an overall economic plan.

In contrast to the Dutch experience, however, this integrated approach to wage and price controls was not characteristic of the immediate post-war period. The government had the authority to limit wages and prices during this time but this authority was used in a rather haphazard fashion. The result was a complete failure to restrain prices immediately after World War II. Again in the 1950s, efforts were made to mitigate the degree of inflation and, although there was some success from 1954 to 1956, excess demand eroded all efforts at stabilization in 1957. The Algerian War had an impact on the French economy similar to the impact of the Viet Nam War on the American economy. In both cases, war-time spending injected into an already tight economy made demand-pull inflation virtually inevitable.

In 1958 the French economy began what was to become a complete modernization. Following devaluation that year, the decision was made to abandon direct market restraints on prices and wages. This decision was shortlived. Unit labor costs began to escalate rapidly in the early 1960s and by September of 1963, the situation was serious enough to warrant the imposition of a general wage-price freeze. This policy was, at best, a stop-gap measure designed to deal with the immediate problems, and it had little regard for long-run consequences. Sheahan, in assessing the 1963 policy, has stated, "It proved unsatisfactory in practice by 1965, and unsatisfactory in principle from the beginning" (96, p. 13).

Following this disappointing application of restraints, a more elaborate system was adopted, which was to apply to the Fifth Economic Development Plan that ran from 1966 to 1970. Under this system, employers—in order to escape from the freeze on prices—could sign contracts with the government that included sectoral guidelines limiting price increases. A unique factor of the plan is that these guidelines are different depending upon the sector of the economy under consideration, as opposed to an overall, economy-wide guideline. Also, the controls rest exclusively on prices and do not cover wages. Indeed, France is the only country to have explicitly adopted an incomes policy that concentrates solely on price behavior.

French incomes policy also goes further than that of most other nations in that it consciously attempts to deal with the distribution pattern of productivity gains. The policy is integrated with the entire national economic planning scheme in an attempt to decide, through this comprehensive system of controls, just how much incremental income will go to labor, investment, dividends, and other areas.

Although there was a wage explosion in early 1968, the incomes policy appears to have been somewhat successful thereafter. Ulman and Flanagan (113, p. 157) report that prices and wages were held down during 1968 and 1969, with wages increasing much slower than in the immediately preceding years. At the same time, they argue that the traditional French policy of concentrating on price movements alone is undermining the success of the program since there appears to be considerable evidence of cost-push elements providing the impetus for inflationary pressures.

The policy is also showing signs of strain from other sources. When there exists several heterogeneous elements in a society that have sharply differing viewpoints as to what constitutes equity, it becomes exceedingly difficult to execute such a policy. French society, lacking the homogeneous interest groups that are more characteristic of the Dutch, is placed under strenuous pressures from such a goal.

The lack of a policy toward wages is the outgrowth of a general lack of collective-bargaining procedures in France, as opposed to the relatively smoothly operating systems of other Western European countries. The political emphasis of the labor movement is much stronger in France, where ideology holds sway over pragmatism. Furthermore, what the French labor movement lacks in collective-bargaining procedures it makes up for in its ability to create instant social turmoil. The government, being acutely aware of this power, has been reluctant to act in the face of such a possibility.

At the same time, there was evidence pointing to the fact that wages seemed to follow prices more than vice versa in France. Thus, it was felt that controls on wages were unnecessary. Recent experience indicates that this may not be strictly true, however. And the French appear to be in the process of reevaluating this long-held price policy.

West Germany

Following twelve years of rigid wage and price controls, which were finally terminated in 1948, West Germany was reluctant to experiment again with an incomes policy. The long period of controls before, during, and after World War II produced myriad inequities and inefficiencies in addition to sharply curtailing output and economic growth. The relaxation of controls, along with currency reform, was largely responsible for the amazing economic recovery experienced in West Germany during the fifties and sixties.

Inflationary pressures, however, began to induce renewed interest in a relatively modest incomes policy by the early 1960s, and this interest has continued to expand into the 1970s. In sharp contrast to the French experience, German flirtations with controls have been solely with respect to wages rather than prices. The reasoning behind this is that unions have traditionally been weak and relatively docile in Germany, whereas employers are strong and aggressive. Thus, it was thought that attempts to limit cost-push inflation could be handled easier by restricting union demands.

The first general wage guidepost of 4 percent was announced in 1961. This figure, however, was based upon official predictions of productivity improvements for the next year and, when these predictions proved to be low (actual productivity increased by 6.4 percent), labor lost faith in the government and interest in wage controls. Still, since 1965, the Council of Economic Experts has repeatedly advised the adoption of wage restraints to be based upon productivity, prices, and other factors that affect real income. The basic idea of the proposed plan is to set money wages at a level consistent with given improvements in real income when other variables (price changes and productivity improvements) are taken into account. Reinforcing the incomes policy would be monetary and fiscal measures geared to the expected wage increases. The idea is that these policies would not be used to bail out agreements that were higher than this.

Like France, which has relied solely on price behavior, West Germany's preoccupation with wages appears to be leading to difficulties. In the future, more attention may have to be given to prices. German workers, along with other segments of the population, have a strong fear of both unemployment and inflation. This attitude grew out of pre-World War II experiences with unemployment and post-war bouts with inflation. As a result, union leaders have been more cooperative than in most countries with attempts to promote price stability.

This traditional docility on the part of German unions, however, has recently been eroded as younger people whose pre-war memories are dim have become increasingly militant. Germany, in conjunction with most other European countries, felt the effects of this increased militancy in the late 1960s. Since labor's cooperation with controls will be more difficult to obtain, price restraints, along with those on wages, may have to be imposed as a matter of equity.

As Ulman and Flanagan point out (113, p. 198), this may be a matter of economic effectiveness as well. During the 1960s the West Germany economy increasingly exhibited signs of wage-push inflation in addition to the traditional excess demand variety.

Finally, this increased militancy can be expected to have two further significant effects. First, it will promote expanded wage demands, thereby adding to inflationary pressures from the cost side. This, in turn, will make the development of an effective incomes policy increasingly important. Second, this same militancy will make the adoption of such a policy difficult as the various segments of the economy more actively resist the imposition of controls on their behavior. This dilemma will not be easily resolved.

Italy

Italian interest in an incomes policy has also been of recent origin and, as yet, no official policy has evolved. Until the beginning of the 1960s, the dual nature of Italy's economy, in which the underdeveloped South was a ready source of labor for the rapidly industrializing North, had the effect of restricting labor costs even in conjunction with rapidly rising demand. By 1961, however, this system was no longer operating as effectively as before and a wage explosion occurred. The basic causes of this explosion are still the subject of arguments and studies, but the result was clearly a deflationary move on the part of the monetary authorities that increased unemployment and decreased economic growth. Italy was thus faced with the same economic dilemma of high employment versus stable prices that has continued to haunt the entire Western world since World War II, and particularly since the mid-sixties.

At the same time, the obstacles to a successful policy of wage and price controls are even more formidable in Italy than in many other

European nations. The ideological nature of the labor organizations is strong (as in France), which hinders agreement upon basic objectives. As always, pragmatic differences are much easier to bargain over and compromise on than are ideological differences. Ideological questions of principle will be defended to the death, and movements toward compromise are deemed evidence of moral bankruptcy.

There is also reluctance by the government to institute controls that may have the effect of restricting movements toward modernization with respect to personnel policies and employee relations. After recognizing this public-sector reluctance, Ulman and Flanagan conclude that ". . . the omission of a price guideline presumably would have resulted in the erosion of any wage policy, in the light of econometric evidence of the exceedingly strong role of price movements in aggregate wage determination. Finally, the wave of strikes, both wildcat and official, in 1969–1970 and the continuing political disequilibrium virtually precluded the introduction of incomes policy in Italy" (113, p. 215). As in Germany, the very conditions that make the introduction of such a policy desirable also make it very difficult to implement.

The Lessons of Experience

Generalizing from the experiences of other countries is difficult, not only because varied results have been encountered but also because many differing institutional characteristics exist among the countries. One of the most sound generalizations, however, is that the results of other countries as a whole do not give overwhelming support to the imposition of wage-price controls. On the contrary, the policies have, for the most part, been characterized by very limited degrees of success. One might wonder, in the face of this discouraging record with incomes policies, why interest in wage and price controls continues and, indeed, appears to be increasing both in Europe and the United States.

In the first place, the problem that gives rise to controls—namely, the unemployment/inflation dilemma—shows no signs of abating and, on the contrary, is increasing in intensity. With the traditional tools of macro-economic monetary and fiscal policy becoming increasingly unable to deal effectively with this situation, interest has grown in other policies. As in the United States, the imposition of wage and price controls looks attractive only in comparison with the alternatives.

Secondly, some failures with incomes policies do not lie in the inappropriateness of the policy *per se* but rather with incomplete design and implementation. That is, there are good and bad incomes policies just as there are good and bad policies in dealing with any other problem of public concern. Because ineffective programs have many times resulted from shortsightedness and administrative ineptitude, it does not follow that all policies of wage and price restraints must be doomed to failure. Thus, because of the problems themselves and the lack of success with other aggregate economic stabilization efforts, interest in incomes policies is likely to remain high. It is important, therefore, to look for relevant indications from the experience of other countries when evaluating attempts to achieve a noninflationary full employment in the United States.

The experience of European countries, as well as that of the U.S., indicates that almost any moderate system of controls will become ineffective in the face of massive increases in aggregate demand. Such a policy is inadequate and inefficient as a means of controlling inflation during such periods. Attempting to institute effective controls in the face of extremely high demand can have one of two undesirable results. First, it can mean that the controls will simply become ineffective as both price and wage guidelines are violated and evaded. This is the more favorable result. The second possibility is that the government will attempt to make the controls effective by widening their applicability. If such efforts become widespread and little is done to abate the demand pressures, the effect will be to destroy the allocative mechanism of the economy and thereby promote gross inefficiencies, wastes, and further inflation.

The fact that many European economies, which were operating in the post-war years at very low levels of unemployment, were unable to restrain prices and wages when demand increased does not prove the inapplicability of wage and price restraints in general. It is, rather, an indication that other policies, such as monetary and fiscal tools, must continually be used in conjunction with an incomes policy.

This latter consideration illuminates another important consideration with respect to the interdependence of these various policies. There is a continual danger in the implementation of wage and price controls that these controls will be considered a substitute for monetary and fiscal policies. If controls are in effect there will be, it is frequently argued, a decreased tendency to apply aggregate brakes as full employment is approached. This tendency is strong but unnecessary. It arises from attributing *too much* effectiveness to wage and price restraints. The result is then disillusionment when the policy is unable to perform up to expectations. This same result was evident in the United States in 1973 and 1974.

If an incomes policy is to be successful, it must have public support. This condition carries with it a number of implications. First, when the policy has enjoyed the most success, it has usually been preceded by a crisis of major proportions, usually with respect to the country's balance of payments. This is especially true in Europe, where a high proportion of output is associated with international trade. But this condition was also of paramount importance during the imposition of the wage-price freeze in the United States in 1971.

Second, in order to enjoy widespread support, the policy must be equitable—or at least appear to be equitable—to the parties involved. Usually this has meant that organized labor must find the controls palatable in order to actively cooperate with the policy. And this cooperation has invariably been crucial to the success of the program.

If wages are restricted more than prices during periods of increasing demand, the result will be an expansion in profit margins. Organized labor will view such an occurrence with justifiable resentment. Also, such a one-sided policy may also fail to achieve the primary goal of slowing down the rate of inflation as oligopolistic firms are able to push prices upward. The lesson appears to be that in the interest of equity, acceptability, and effectiveness, *both* wages and prices must be controlled. Relaxing the emphasis on prices implies rising profits in the face of controlled wages—a condition that organized labor soon finds intolerable. At the same time, limiting prices without restricting wages can lead to the development of serious cost-push pressures, which can result in decreased profits and investments thereby leading to a slower improvement in productivity and even more inflation.

Relevance for the U.S.

The economic conditions facing the United States in the 1970s are only partially similar to those of European countries. A major difference between the U.S. situation and that of the European countries in the 1960s is the relatively high unemployment in this country, which contrasts sharply with the low rates characteristic of other nations. Whereas there were few signs of excess demand in the United States in the early 1970s, there were virtually no signs of this condition by the middle of the decade.

When the policies of most European countries became ineffective, it was invariably in conjunction with low unemployment rates.

This same consideration applies to the experience in this country with guideposts in the last decade. This policy of voluntary wage and price restraint became largely ineffective when faced with massive increases in aggregate demand during the Viet Nam War buildup. As the French discovered in 1957, a moderate incomes policy will rapidly become ineffective under such conditions. The U.S. experience in 1974 again broke down, in part because of exceedingly strong demand pressures.

The Future

In response to a query concerning the probable outlook for the stock market, a leading authority recently replied, "In the past we have seen the market move up as well as down. I am sure that we will see similar movements in the future." Unfortunately, such a noncommittal outlook is about as certain as one can be concerning the future of incomes policies.

Such an outlook, however, is more revealing than if first appears. In particular, it implies that even though such policies have been designed, implemented, and scrapped repeatedly in the past, it is highly likely that fresh attempts will be made in the future. As long as other aggregate policies seeking to promote simultaneous price stabilization and full employment are unsuccessful, there will be continued and renewed interest in wage and price controls.

THE ECONOMIC STABILIZATION PROGRAM: PHASES I THROUGH IV

11

> The public . . . demands certainties; it must be told definitely and a bit raucously that this is true and that is false. But there *are* no certainties.
>
> H. L. Mencken

The new economic policy inaugurated in the fall of 1971 is now history. The much publicized Pay Board and Price Commission were abolished in January 1973 and the Cost of Living Council was terminated a little more than a year later. During its life span, the economic stabilization policy went from a high point of public approval during the first freeze and Phase II to an object of scorn and disgust at the time of its demise. By the time the program finally faded into oblivion, labor was convinced of its inherent unfairness, business of its inefficiency and counterproductiveness, and consumers of its ineffectiveness in restraining prices.

Unfortunately, the experiment did little to settle the debate concerning the general effectiveness of controls. Observers biased against controls call the experiment an unmitigated failure and calmly assert that, of course, it could never work and was doomed from the start. The experiences of Phases I through IV are cited as proof of this proposition. Supporters of controls, not unexpectedly, draw different conclusions from the same body of evidence. In an extreme form, their argument is that the controllers never really intended the program to be an effective anti-inflation tool and that it was purposely designed to "prove" that controls could only have counterproductive results. Between these extremes are those who believe that parts of the program were successful and other elements were not; that sweeping pronouncements about the entire program are generally oversimplifications; and that there are important lessons to be drawn from the stabilization experiences of the first half of the 1970s.

The thrust of this chapter is to discuss these lessons and their implications for future stabilization programs.[1] As argued elsewhere in this book, the prospects for renewed efforts at direct stabilization programs in the late 1970s and beyond are strong. It is highly unlikely that the public will long accept the burning inflation of 1973–75 or the unemployment of 1975–76 that resulted from the inflation and the policies implemented to stop it. Thus, it is likely that new wage and price control programs will be implemented in the future in an attempt to deal simultaneously with the twin evils of job losses and price increases. The prospects for success in such a program can be increased if we can learn from the experience of 1971–74.

THE INAUGURATION OF THE NEW ECONOMIC PROGRAM—AUGUST 1971

Judged by the standards of the mid-1970s, the rate of inflation in 1971 was low. The consumer price index averaged 4.2 percent above its level of 1970 and the wholesale index averaged only 3.2 percent above its 1970 level. However, the direction and tenacity of the price increases were worrisome, with the wholesale index seeming to gather steam throughout the year. At the same time, the unemployment rate was high by historical standards, averaging 5.9 percent for the year (1971). Adding to the domestic difficulties (or, perhaps, overshadowing them) was continuing pressure on the dollar in international markets and the perception both here and abroad that a strengthened international position could be gained only through a domestic display of decisive actions to combat inflation. Finally, the Nixon Administration feared that a perceived inability or unwillingness to take hold of economic events would seriously erode the chances for reelection in 1972.

These events led to the surprising institution of direct controls in the form of a freeze on wages and prices in August 1971. In addition to the economic impact of this move, it held two important implications for future stabilization efforts. First, it cast the control program in a political context. The nature of the policy made the administration of the program and its outcome a direct function and responsibility of the executive branch of government. Second, it showed that even a conservative administration, ideologically opposed to marketplace interference, would resort to controls.

Most observers considered the freeze, which was run and later described by Arnold Weber (124), a success. Inflation expectations, which were contributing to inflation, were stopped short. So were wage and

---

[1] For a more elaborate discussion of the many facets of the Economic Stabilization Program, see (19, 22, 41, 56, 58, 76, 124).

price movements themselves. In addition, because of the degree of slack in the economy, few serious market distortions were brought about by the freeze. The public overwhelmingly supported the program, and criticism from professional economists was muted as most adopted a cautious wait-and-see attitude.

In addition to the political benefits of the freeze and its impact on expectations, the three-month period also allowed for the development of Phase II compliance machinery, which subsequently formed the basis of the entire stabilization program. In addition, by imposing a surprise freeze, the administration was able to effectively eliminate the anticipatory price increases that might well have occurred had there been prior public discussion of a controls program (see 124).

Following the three-month wage-price freeze, Phase II was inaugurated amid a good deal of fanfare and public support. Immediately, a number of questions (discussed in earlier chapters) concerning the nature of a controls problem had to be resolved. A major question was the one of selective versus comprehensive controls. Economic logic, as discussed above, suggested a concentrated control program focusing on those areas of the economy characterized by a lack of competitive pressures. Political acceptance, on the other hand, argued for a comprehensive program designed for high public visibility. This was especially true given the seriousness with which the inflation in the food sector was perceived. After a series of arguments, the comprehensive view carried the day, and the coverage of the controls program was extended to services, rents, and wholesale and retail trade in addition to basic manufacturing.

Pay Board coverage was equally extensive, although the Cost of Living Council soon exempted several sectors of the economy from wage-price controls for both economic and political reasons. Thus, raw food products were exempted, as were small businesses and low-wage workers. In addition, the sale of homes and of other used products (for which price increases are not cost-justified) were soon exempted, as were products intended for export. A major on-going function of the Cost of Living Council was to determine those sectors of the economy that were to be exempt from controls. The Price Commission and Pay Board were charged with the immediate administration of price and pay regulations.

THE MECHANICS OF THE CONTROL SYSTEM

For the control of wage increases, a basic Pay Board standard—publicly adopted—became the 5.5-percent wage guideline in addition to 0.7 percent allowed for qualified fringe benefits. This standard applied to all covered employees with the exception of those increases resulting from contracts signed prior to November 14, 1971. In addition, a major function of the Pay Board was to analyze cases in order to determine the extent to which economic and institutional considerations warranted individual exceptions to these general rules. It was immediately (and rightly) recognized that the strict application of a simple formula for wage determination would seriously erode the nation's complex system of collective bargaining and industrial dispute settlement and would, in all likelihood, provoke significant increase in industrial conflict and strike activity.

The Price Commission adopted, at the outset of Phase II, a public goal of achieving a 2.5-percent rate of overall price inflation. Combined with the Pay Board guideline of 5.5 percent for wages, the macroeconomic logic of the 2.5 percent price goal was deceptively simple: The 5.5-percent wage standard, along with the trend productivity of 3 percent for the economy, made the 2.5-percent price goal a logical and reasonable one. At least it was logical in an era when unit labor costs were seen as the primary determinant of inflationary pressures. It became less appropriate as worldwide demand pressures and skyrocketing raw materials costs drastically changed the nature of the inflationary problem in 1973 and 1974.

A single standard, with a healthy exceptions procedure, makes sense from the wage side. There is little economic logic, and even less equity, in a wage standard that permits different levels of increase for different groups (unless, of course, the explicit purpose of the incomes policy is to effectuate a redistribution of income—a purpose that was not intended during the Economic Stabilization Program of the seventies).

Such logic, however, does not apply on the price side of the ledger. Because of different productivity movements, different cost pressures, and different market conditions, a single price standard would be hopelessly unworkable. Recognizing this, the Price Commission instituted instead a system of general price rules that focused on the nature and percent of the increases allowed, explicitly recognizing the multiplicity of cost structures and market conditions that characterize the economy. Thus, by its very nature price control is a more complex operation than wage control, a fact that was dramatically reflected in the increasing complexity of the price regulations.[2]

Classification Considerations

In addition to the degree of coverage discussed above, the Price Commission and Pay Board immediately faced other fundamental prob-

---

[2] This statement should not be taken to imply that wage control is a simple matter. The general Pay Board rules, along with the later executive compensation rulings, attest to the complexity of these controls as well.

lems. Given the broad level of coverage and the limited staff, it soon became necessary to implement rules designed to make the program administratively feasible. One of the first of these was the development of a classification scheme that segmented business firms into three groups, or tiers, according to size. Tier I firms had sales of $100 million or more for pricing purposes and collective-bargaining units of 5,000 or more employees for wage considerations. Tier II firms had sales of $50 to $100 million and collective-bargaining units of 1,000 to 5,000 employees. Tier III consisted of firms with sales of less than $50 million and bargaining unit with fewer than 1,000 workers.

Although the same price and pay regulations (discussed next) applied to all tiers, the reporting requirements were different. Tier I firms and bargaining units were required to obtain prior approval before implementing price and pay increases. Tier IIs were required to submit reports of price and wage increases. Tier III firms had no reporting requirements. These last firms and bargaining units were, however, subject to the same general rules and to spot enforcement procedures undertaken by the Internal Revenue Service.

Price Rules

The Price Commission adopted a firm-by-firm approach to controls rather than an industry-oriented approach. Basically, the same rules applied to all businesses. The major form of control was seen to be an allowable-cost rule whereby companies were allowed to increase prices only by the amount of allowable cost increases. In determining these costs, companies were allowed to reach back for cost justification to the date of the last price increase, but not earlier than January 1, 1971, even if the last price increase was prior to that.

As a second line of defense, a profit-margin rule was implemented that prohibited a company from realizing a gross profit margin greater than the firm experienced during its base period. In turn, the base period was defined as a company's best two fiscal years out of any three prior to August 14, 1971. Thus, even if a firm had allowable costs, it could not use them for price increases if the increases would cause it to exceed its base-period profit margin.[3]

A major exception was made to the profit-margin rule, namely, firms that had increased *no* prices were allowed to exceed their base-period margins. This was allowed on the grounds of providing an incentive for

---

[3] Early in the program, the commission faced the question of how to determine whether or not it was a given price increase that "caused" a base-period profit margin to be exceeded. It was decided that the *existence* of higher prices and profits in excess of the base period was prohibited, thereby removing from the commission the burden of demonstrating causality.

companies to absorb some costs and to refrain from exploiting their market possibilities fully in return for being allowed to reap higher-than-base-period profit margins. Later in the program, this policy was expanded to companies that had increased prices by allowing them to "repurify" themselves by reducing prices to base-period levels in return for freedom from the profit-margin constraint.[4]

Recognizing that the general allowable cost rules were inappropriate for wholesale and retail firms, the commission devised alternative rules for these sectors. These regulations prohibited trade firms from exceeding their "customary initial percentage markup" (CIPM) on classes of products. In addition to recognizing the normal method of doing business in these sectors, this form of control also avoided the mountains of paper work that would have been engendered by an item-by-item cost justification scheme. Wholesale and retail firms were still subject to the base-period profit-margin constraint.

The form of cost pass-through allowed for wholesale and retail firms was somewhat tighter than that designed for manufacturing and service organizations since the CIPM concept did *not* allow for pass-through of administrative and overhead costs. Manufacturing and service controls, on the other hand, allowed for a full cost pass-through.

Wholesale and retail controls were further complicated by the fact that the base period for determination of the CIPM was changed. Initially, it was the period from August 15, 1971 to November 13, 1971. This was then changed to the last CIPM of the company prior to November 14, 1971 *or* the CIPM of the company during its last fiscal year ending prior to August 15, 1971. The firm could choose between the two periods. In addition, firms were given the choice of using the CIPM method of control *or* an item-by-item approach. Different rules applied to each method, and the result was a rapid increase in both the complexity and the confusion of the program.

Health services were another area singled out for special treatment. Basically, the regulations provided for a maximum of 2.5-percent increase by doctors and dentists—if cost justified—with institutional providers of services allowed up to 6 percent with cost justification and excesses to that only on the basis of "exceptions and hardships." As expected, the exception requests in this area were voluminous.

Utilities too were treated separately. Control for rates was given to appropriate federal and state regulatory agencies, although Price Commission approval required at first. Finally, the extremely sensitive and complex area of rent controls was given separate treatment.

---

[4] Originally termed "revirginization," the concept was referred to as "repurification" by the time it became public.

As a further means of easing the administrative burden of controls, the Price Commission formulated its *term limit pricing* (TLP) agreements with several large firms. While easing the administrative load for itself and the companies involved, the commission also thought that such agreements would allow a greater degree of pricing freedom without abandoning the concept of controls entirely. These agreements allowed the participating companies to increase their prices by an agreed-upon, weighted average (2 percent at first) in return for freedom from cost-justifying each increase and for the further freedom to increase individual prices by more than the weighted average. As discussed next, these agreements led to considerable controversy.

Even the multiplicity of regulations could not accomodate the large number of special circumstances that would arise during the control program to make the regulations sometimes inequitable, unworkable, or both. As a result, an exceptions procedure was adopted to deal with specific circumstances and to provide relief in individual cases.

This overview of the basic price and wage regulations is very broad and does not do justice to the complex nature of the regulations nor to the economic and political considerations that went into their formulation and evolution. There were many such factors,[5] and the regulations became increasingly complex as the program continued. Nonetheless, we have the essentials necessary to discuss the logic of the program and its implications for future efforts.

EXAMINING THE RULES

One method of examining the effectiveness of a controls program is to look at the evidence in terms of aggregate price and output measures, usually with the aid of econometric models. This we have done in Chapter 10, and the results are discussed in Chapter 12. The question that concerns us now is, could the regulations, by their very nature, be expected to have an impact on inflation? In other words, did the various regulations we have just outlined make sense? It is often assumed that controls are controls are controls, with the implication that all controls programs are the same. That is hardly the reality. As with other public policies, there can be good, or appropriate, incomes policies as well as bad and inappropriate ones. The same considerations, of course, apply to the administration of the controls system, a subject discussed next. It is time now to take a look at the implications of the control mechanism of the Economic Stabilization Program.

---

[5] See footnote 1 for the sources of comprehensive reviews of the regulations, their formulation, and evolution.

The Degree of Coverage

The economic analysis developed in the earlier chapters suggests that comprehensive coverage for a controls program is unnecessary and unworkable. Although many people recognized this at the outset of Phase II, political considerations overrode the economic implications of policy, and broad coverage was opted for. This, however, undoubtedly diffused the effectiveness of the program by thinly spreading the available staff and interfering in markets where competition was providing effective regulation. In addition (from the advantageous viewpoint of hindsight), the decision for broad coverage may have proven to be a political mistake. Certainly it led the public to expect results that the economic realities and the nature of the stabilization program did not warrant. When these expectations were not realized, disillusionment set in leading to near-total rejection of the program during its final phases.

An example was the posting requirement for retailers. Stores were required to display their base prices for all nonexempt food items and for the forty items in each department having the highest dollar sales volume (or those items accounting for over 50 percent of sales if fewer than forty items). This requirement was designed to lend public visibility to the program—which it did—and to facilitate detection of violations—which it did not.

During the freeze, it was easy to detect a violation by comparing the price of an item to its posted price. During Phase II, however, this was impossible because by then it was necessary to know the CIPM (customary initial percentage markup) for the item in question. Thus, the requirement did little to help the public monitor price increases, and there was no other sensible reason for requiring posting. Predictably, the results were confusion, disgust, and a feeling that the entire program was just another public relations fraud designed to hoodwink a gullible public. Then, too, the IRS spent valuable man-hours following up complaints of violations that, in most cases, were not violations.

Given the competitive nature of most retail markets and a situation of confusing rules dealt with by insufficient staff, it was probably a mistake to implement controls on this sector. For this reason, experience with controls in this sector should not be used to indict the efficacy of all incomes policies.

Allowable Costs

The allowable-cost concept adopted by the Price Commission provided for a full pass-through of cost increases *along with* profit-margin maintenance. That is, price increases were allowed to reflect increased costs *plus* a customary profit margin on these new costs. The result was to preserve *percentage* profit margins by allowing dollar profits to increase with increases in costs.

A number of observers believed that a dollar-for-dollar or other fractional, cost pass-through system would have had more impact in mitigating price increases. A dollar-for-dollar system would have meant that margins would have been squeezed as costs increased, thereby placing more pressure on firms to resist cost increases. Indeed, some observers argued that full cost pass-through resulted in the "institutionalization of cost-push inflation" (5). Such arguments have a good deal of merit. The control system was ostensibly designed to resist cost-push inflation. Yet, by allowing a full cost-pass-through along with margins, there was no mechanism to prevent *or even slow down* cost-push pressures.

The only method by which cost pressures on prices can be curtailed is by forcing some cost absorption throughout the production and distribution lines. Given this consideration, an incomes policy should promote an equitable system of absorption so that the various parties will absorb the same proportion of costs. The allowable-cost system, as promulgated by the Price Commission during Phase II, did not force this kind of absorption.

Going a step further, it can be argued that the allowable-cost system of Phase II was more appropriate in dealing with a demand-pull inflation (setting aside, for the moment the question of whether any control system can deal with demand pressures). Excess demand will pull prices up (see the discussion in Chapter 5) *without* the existence of cost pressures. This will result in an *expansion* of profit margins, which would, in turn, be prevented by the rigid application of Phase II allowable-cost rules. Cost-push inflation, on the other hand, requires an *absorption* of costs. Cost absorption, however, is not a feature of a profit-margin maintenance, allowable-cost system.

An important exception to the full cost pass-through feature of the ESP was developed toward the beginning of Phase II. This involved Price Commission policy toward the pass-through of a large coal industry wage settlement early in the program. The Cost of Living Council strongly urged the Price Commission to accept the total settlement that the Pay Board had approved as allowable costs for purposes of price increases. The argument was that since the Pay Board deemed the settlement reasonable, the Price Commission should not try to second-guess such a wage decision by refusing to allow the costs to be passed on. Instead, the Price Commission determined that only the 5.5 percent of the wage hike plus 0.7 percent of the fringe benefits could be used as cost justification, thereby setting a precedent that was maintained throughout the control program.

From an economic standpoint, the Price Commission made the right decision. The essence of wage-push inflation in oligopolistic sectors of the economy is that unions are able to obtain large settlements, which corporations, because of their market power, are able to pass on promptly in the form of price increases. By not allowing large increases to be passed on, the control agency—in this case the Price Commission—was able to exert pressure on collective-bargaining agreements by negating the expectation that all wage increases can automatically be passed on to consumers.

Did the Price Commission's position interfere with the collective-bargaining process? Actually, competitive sectors of the economy face similar pressure because firms in these areas are unable to pass along all wage increases since, for them, short-term price determination is more a matter of demand than of cost. This hardly negates the role of collective bargaining in these sectors, but it does help to explain why collective-bargaining agreements are typically smaller here than in the oligopolistic sectors of the economy. Thus, in this instance, the Price Commission was fulfilling a legitimate role of forcing cost absorption and resisting the market power of large corporations and unions acting in unison.

Profit Margins

Originally intended as a backup to the major control mechanism of allowable costs, profit-margin limitations became the most effective form of control toward the end of Phase II as economic conditions improved and profits correspondingly increased. (Many would add to the description, as the ineffectiveness of the allowable-cost formulas became increasingly apparent.) In addition, profit-margin controls are intrinsically easier to administer than allowable-cost rules since they are a more readily understood part of generally accepted accounting procedures. Thus, in terms of effectiveness, comprehension, and administrative ease, profit controls appear preferable to other forms of price controls.

At the same time, the control of prices through the control of profits is intrinsically dissatisfying. Profits serve the extremely useful functions of rewarding productive effort, directing production, and allowing for the accumulation of capital for expanded future output. Given the administrative problems inherent in any attempt to directly control prices, however, the profit-margin test becomes more attractive. In addition, profit-margin control is undoubtedly preferable to a return-on-equity form of control, which plunges the program much deeper into the area of income distribution and, implicitly, redistribution.[6]

Furthermore, it should be noted that profit-margin controls do not

---

[6] Income redistribution may be considered a worthy social goal, but it is better approached directly through tax and transfer systems than through the comparatively inefficient method of an incomes policy. Throughout this discussion, incomes policy is seen as a possible tool for economic stabiliza-

limit the *amount* of profits; instead, they limit the *manner* in which profits can be increased. Specifically, profits can be increased through an increased volume of sales but not through increased profit per unit of sale. Such a system is not incompatible with the goals of a free enterprise economy. It may even promote increased production as a means of increasing profits in a manner analogous to that of a competitive market.

By imposing a firm-by-firm profit-margin constraint on companies, the Price Commission was forced to develop several exceptions to the general rules. Several companies were incurring losses during their base periods, and to force them to continue in such a position would, of course, have been thoroughly unfair. Thus, "loss and low profit rules" were promulgated whereby firms were, in effect, allowed a 10-percent return on equity regardless of their base-period performance (in effect, introducing return-on-equity controls through the back door). Other firms that had abnormal base periods were able to gain relief through the exceptions procedures of the program.

The development of the TLP (term limit pricing) concept during Phase II is of particular interest. As noted, the concept was designed to allow a degree of pricing freedom to multiple product line companies while easing the administrative burdens imposed on the commission by individual product line pricing requests. (The agreements were limited to Tier I firms since others were not required to file for pricing authority in advance.)

During Phase II, a total of 187 TLP agreements were entered into, with mixed results. There is little doubt that the first TLPs were too loose in the sense that they provided the firms with more pricing authority than the market would allow, thereby providing no control. In fact, one study has estimated that only about half the TLP firms were ever able to implement the magnitude of the price increases granted them by the commission (58).

The logic of the agreements is also open to question. Economist Willard F. Mueller argues, "The Price Commission's so-called 'term limit pricing' thus does not come to grips with the problem of seller inflation. It ignores precisely the products on which it should be focusing its attention, granting a broad license to exercise monopoly power wherever it is the greatest . . ." (71). No doubt this was exactly the case in several instances where firms that obtained a TLP had several product lines, including some in which prices were declining.

---

tion, not income redistribution *except* to the extent that the latter is a by-product of the former and to the extent that reduced unemployment and inflation have important welfare and income distribution effects and implications.

An alternative would be an application of the TLP concept on an industry and product line basis rather than a company basis. A firm might then be subject to several TLP price maximums, which would be set according to the economics of the particular industry rather than in accord with administrative ease. Such a system could retain some of the benefits of the TLP concept while circumventing the shortcomings of a company-implemented agreement. The development of such a control system would require a marked departure from the firm-by-firm controls characteristic of Phases II, III, and most of IV.

Further Difficulties

Additional problems resulted from the control mechanism here. The fears often expressed by Price Commission Chairman C. Jackson Grayson and others that controls would breed ever more complicated procedures were rapidly becoming a truism by the end of 1972. For example, in order to have an allowable-cost or profit-control system, it is necessary to define an arbitrary base period from which to work. However, the further one moves from the base period, the less relevant it becomes to current operations. One answer would be to implement a rolling base period, but such a system was never considered seriously during the life of the Economic Stabilization Program. In addition, the program's internal inconsistencies led to increasing frustration on the part of business, labor, and consumer groups, and to increasingly complex formulations and reformulations of the regulations. Inconsistencies and inequities can be tolerated, but not for very long.

The firm-by-firm controls led to a special problem in the case of conglomerates with their multiple product lines. Conglomerates were often prevented from raising prices because of profit-margin limitations. As a result, several smaller, single-product-line competitors were brought close to bankruptcy because they could not afford to sell products (at a loss) at prices equal to those the conglomerate was forced to charge. Thus companies that had broken no control rules were faced with the awful dilemma of losing money by selling at a loss or of facing the shrinkage of their markets if they did not stay price-competitive.

Another example of market distortions caused by the price rulings involved the treatment of interest costs. Interest payments on short-term debts were considered allowable costs whereas those on long-term debt were not. The result was an economically inefficient move toward short-term financing until the Price Commission changed its ruling so that *all* interest costs could be treated as allowable cost increase for pricing purposes.

Such examples abound, but there is a single lesson: controlling prices is a complex process. Anyone who advocates using a form of direct market intervention as a tool of economic stabilization policy should be prepared to deal with the complexities with well thought-out regulations tailored to meet the specific needs of different industries and continually changing economic conditions.

PHASES III AND IV

In January 1973, Phase II was abruptly scrapped by the Nixon Administration and Phase III was initiated. There is considerable uncertainty about the precise reasons for the abrupt shift from Phase II. A number of factors, however, seemed to influence the move. First, you will remember that the administrative burdens and the inconsistencies and inequities of Phase II were becoming more pronounced. Economic conditions too were changing in a manner that made the regulations and rationale of Phase II less meaningful. At the same time, however, the program remained popular among most segments of the economy, and it seemed to be having an impact on the level of inflation. Furthermore, the developing problems were not beyond resolution if the Price Commission had been given a mandate to revise the program.

A less charitable view is that the administration, which had never approved of its own program (especially the independent spirit of the Price Commission), felt it could safely scrap the Price Commission and Pay Board now that the 1972 elections had successfully been passed.

At any rate, regardless of the reasons, Phase III was inaugurated in January 1973 as a program of self-administered controls and a stick in the closet to be taken to firms and unions that failed to heed the guidelines. It was never clear just what the administration had in mind for Phase III. Supposedly, it was to be a period of some controls while the Cost of Living Council worked to deregulate the economy and return to a state of no controls. But the entire program was characterized by considerable confusion, on the part of business firms who did not know what was legal and what was not, and on the part of consumers who wondered what it all meant.

Whatever it meant, it did not seem to mean a control of inflation. The consumer index shot up at an annual rate of 8.3 percent, led by skyrocketing food prices. Even nonfood prices soared at nearly double the rate of Phases I and II. (See Table 11–1.) In the face of this price onslaught, the public increasingly wondered when, and if, the administration was going to take its much-publicized stick out of the closet. Businessmen, wary that the administration might soon take action, pushed prices up ever more rapidly in fear of being caught with their prices down if the action happened to be another freeze.

Table 11–1. Measures of price and wage change during and after the Economic Stabilization Program
[Percent of change; seasonally adjusted annual rate]

Price or wage measure	Freeze and Phase II Aug. 1971 to Jan. 1973	Phase III Jan. 1973 to June 1973	Second freeze and Phase IV June 1973 to Apr. 1974	Phase IV Dec. 1973 to Apr. 1974	1974 Apr. to Aug.	Aug. to Dec.
PRICES						
Consumer price index:						
All items	3.4	8.3	10.7	12.2	12.7	11.8
Food	5.9	20.2	16.2	12.8	7.0	17.0
All items less food	2.7	5.0	8.7	11.8	15.3	9.7
Commodities less food	2.2	4.8	9.2	14.9	16.4	8.6
Services	3.5	4.3	8.6	8.8	13.3	11.7
Personal consumption expenditures deflator	2.8	6.7	10.8	13.9	11.8	11.4
Wholesale price index:						
All commodities	5.9	22.2	15.2	12.9	31.8	10.2
Farm products and processed foods and feeds	13.4	48.9	6.3	.4	24.5	9.5
Industrial commodities	2.9	12.3	19.6	33.9	35.5	9.4
Finished goods, consumer and producer	1.9	7.2	13.4	23.4	25.8	14.6
Crude and intermediate materials	3.6	15.1	23.3	39.1	40.9	7.1
WAGES						
Average hourly earnings, private nonfarm economy:						
Monthly series	6.2	6.3	6.9	6.5	11.9	9.3
Quarterly series	6.4	5.9	7.0	6.3	10.3	9.7
Average hourly compensation:						
Total private economy	5.8	8.9	7.0	7.0	11.2	9.0
Nonfarm	5.9	8.8	7.5	7.9	10.7	9.3

Source: Economic Report of the President, 1975, p. 227.

Partly in response to such self-fulfilling expectations, the administration junked its ill-fated Phase III in June 1973, and put prices and wages into another freeze—this one destined to be much less successful than the first.

The second freeze was more a response to political pressures from an embattled president struggling for public support than a response to economic conditions. To be sure, inflation was even more virulent than in the summer of 1971, but otherwise the situations were sharply different. Price increases in 1973 were the result of strong demand pressures resulting from the worldwide stimulative policies undertaken in 1972. Thus, the results of the freeze were as ineffective as they were predictable. Shortages were exacerbated, allocative distortions were widespread, and all the evils associated with a control program during a period of intense demand pressure were realized. As a result, the freeze was cut short, and the stabilization program moved into Phase IV and, shortly thereafter, phaseout.

The final phase of the Economic Stabilization Program was begun in August 1973, two years after the initial freeze. The regulations were similar to those of Phase II, although allowable costs were limited to a dollar-for-dollar pass-through. Thus, the program was somewhat tighter than Phase II; at the same time, it was designed to be more flexible by considering industrywide problems with the emphasis on industry exemptions (decontrol) tied to agreements to prevent a sharp price bulge at the end. In addition, the degree of coverage was considerably reduced; controls covered less than half the items in the consumer price index. As Table 11–2 illustrates, the degree of coverage rapidly dimin-

Table 11–2. Selected exemptions of industrial sectors from wage and price controls, 1974

Date		Exemption
January:	4	Nonferrous alloys
	14	Ferronickel (prices only)
	21	Mobile homes and recreational vehicles
		Semiconductors
	23	Miscellaneous health service providers
	25	Nonprofit tax exempt organizations
		Selected steel products
	30	Rubber tires and tubes
		Most basic petrochemical feedstocks
February:	1	Retail trade except: food; petroleum products; motor vehicles, parts, and equipment; large eating and drinking facilities
	11	Checker Motors Corporation
		Steel drum reconditioners
		Stevedoring and marine terminal services (prices only)

	12	Rendering industry
	15	Ferrous and ferroalloy scrap metal
		Nonrubber shoes
	19	Postcards
	20	Iron and steel foundries
	22	Furniture
	26	Valves
		Mining and oilfield machinery
March:	1	Toys
	5	Opthalmic goods: scientific, mechanical and optical instruments
		Jewelry and silverware
	6	Fabricated lumber and wood products
	7	Engineered fastener products
	8	Paper and allied products
	13	Fabricated rubber products
		Petrochemicals (medium- and small-sized firms)
	15	Printing, publishing, broadcasting, advertising, and other communications media
	18	Canned fruits and vegetables
	20	Selected machinery
	21	Ferroalloy metals (prices only)
	26	Cordage and twine
	27	Coal
	28	Aluminum
		Musical instruments
	29	Aerospace and general aviation
April:	15	Food retailing and wholesaling

Source: Cost of Living Council; Economic Report of the President, 1975, p. 225.

ished (as the number of exemptions increased) during 1974 until the program was finally terminated on April 30, 1974.

If the impact of Phase II on the price indexes is difficult to assess, that of Phase IV is virtually impossible. The roughest estimate, illustrated in Table 11–3, is that the program had very little, if any, effect on prices. Prices not only continued to increase but did so at an increasing rate. Furthermore, several political and economic forces were at work in the economy at the same time, thereby making it even more difficult to attempt to assess what would have been the state of affairs in the absence of controls. As the Council of Economic Advisors pointed out, "The special inflationary impact of the oil price increase and its effect on aggregate output during the first half of 1974 make it unrealistic to attempt an assessment of the Stabilization Program in the final months" (23, p. 226).

By the time the controls expired in April 1974, they had outlived their usefulness. Public support, evident throughout Phases I and II, had evaporated. The business community had turned against the program and its voluntary support of the policy disappeared. Congressional critics

Table 11–3. Coverage of price and wage controls under the Economic Stabilization Program, selected dates during Phase IV

	Percent covered		
Date during Phase IV	Consumer price index (CPI)	Wholesale price index (WPI)	Civilian labor force[1]
1973: September 10	42.6	69.4	44.1
1974: March 1	28.0	54.2	37.4
April 1	24.2	37.4	26.8
30	8.6[2]	27.6[2]	24.1

[1] Percent of the civilian labor force whose wages and salaries were covered.
[2] An additional 3.5 percent of the CPI and 4.0 percent of the WPI were under price controls of the Federal Energy Office, which remained in effect after April 30.

Source: Cost of Living Council; Economic Report of the President, 1975, p. 226.

and consumer groups alike were disillusioned, and the White House had made clear its intention to demolish the program as early as January 1973, when it ushered in the voluntary controls of Phase III.

Thus ended the nation's first peacetime experiment with an incomes policy. In the beginning the public strongly supported both the concept and the results of the program. At the end these early successes had largely been dissipated by bitterness, resentment, and disillusionment. Peacetime controls were, most observers concluded, an idea whose time had come—and gone.

FURTHER ASSESSMENTS, FURTHER CONSIDERATIONS   12

> We have always known that heedless self-interest was bad morals; we know now that it is bad economics.
>
> Franklin D. Roosevelt

The surging inflation of 1973 and 1974 makes it easy to conclude that the controls program had no impact on inflation. Such an assessment, however, is more the result of price movements subsequent to the controls program than to an objective analysis of the stabilization program itself. Of course, it is impossible to measure precisely the impact of the program and to determine without ambiguity the effect it had on wages and prices. As the Council of Economic Advisors succinctly states, "The final judgment on the effects of price and wage controls imposed under authority of the Economic Stabilization Act beginning in August, 1971 and continuing for more than 32 months will be long debated and may never be resolved." Furthermore, the council has accurately summed up the source of this ambiguity: "The primary reason for an inconclusive judgment is that there is no way of accurately simulating the course of events which would have evolved in the absence of control" (23, p. 228).

This chapter summarizes some major studies that have been undertaken in an attempt to isolate the impact of the controls program. The interested reader is encouraged to consult the original sources for complete discussions of methodology and results.

The simplest method for assessing the results of the program is to compare price and wage movements before, during, and after the controls program. Table 11–1 illustrates several of these wage and price measures. Clearly, inflation moderated during Phase II of the control program and then accelerated again during Phases III and IV.

Such comparisons, however, are less than convincing. This is because myriad forces are at work at any given time; it is difficult to isolate causal factors and, therefore, to judge accurately the specific impact of the controls on price and wage movements.

As a result, most studies of the impact of the controls program have adopted methodologies such as those discussed in Chapter 10. These studies use econometric models to project the probable course of prices and wages in the absence of controls—what *would* have happened—and then compare these simulations with the actual behavior of prices and wages during the periods under question.

The studies discussed here refer primarily to Phase II of the stabilization program. This is the period of the most formal controls, and there were fewer major outside shocks to the system—such as the oil embargo—than occurred during the later phases.

Most of the econometric analyses of Phase II suggest that the controls program reduced both the rate of price increase and the rate of wage increase from the levels they would have attained in the absence of the program. However, the results are ambiguous and the studies differ in their interpretation. Robert Gordon, after doing extensive analysis of wage determination, concluded in 1972 that Phases I and II of the stabilization program had slightly reduced the rate of increase in wages and prices (40).

In a follow-up analysis (39), Gordon reaffirms these conclusions, estimating that nonfarm prices rose at an anual rate of approximately 2.3 percent less during Phases I and II than they would have in the absence of controls. In addition, and in contrast to what might have been expected from the price explosions of Phases III and IV, Gordon argues on the basis of his model that none of the mitigation in price activity was made up for during these later phases. That is, external events—such as worldwide demand pressures and the like—completely explain the rapid price increases of 1973 and 1974 and these increases were not the result of a catch-up psychology after Phase II.

Concerning wages, Gordon estimates that they rose at a rate of about 0.6 percent less during Phases I and II than they would have in the absence of controls, and at a rate of approximately 1.1 percent less in 1973. Significantly, he attributes this slowdown in wage rates to the reduced pressure on wages from slower price increases, not to the direct effect of wage controls. That is, although the wage controls were seen to have no direct effect, price controls did slow inflation and this, in turn, reduced labor demand for wage hikes (39).

Other researchers agree with the conclusion that wage controls had little direct impact. Lanzillotti, Roberts, and Hamilton use variations of three major price-wage models to develop various measures of the effectiveness of price and wage controls (58). The models they constructed are variations of the Eckstein-Brinner model (30), the Gordon model (40), and a third model developed by Seibert and Zaidi (98). Each model uses different estimating procedures by the inclusion of alternative independent variables and, as a result, provides somewhat different estimates of what prices and wages would have been in the absence of the control system. Using these models, they estimate that the increase in prices was approximately 2.3 to 1.7 percent less during Phase II than it would have been without controls. Wages, on the other hand, slowed −1.3 to +0.4 percent, again implying that the program had little direct impact on wage rates. For a discussion on the modifications made to these models, see (58). These figures, Lanzillotti, Roberts, and Hamilton conclude, suggest ". . . a significant reduction in the rate of increase in the private nonfarm deflator but an ambiguous effect on private nonfarm wage rates" (58, p. 21).

In their extensive research into the impact of price and wage controls, Bosworth and Vroman are somewhat more impressed with the effect of direct wage controls than are the other researchers. Their methodology is disaggregated to a greater extent than that of the other studies cited, thereby allowing for an assessment of *union* wage rates instead of looking only at the broad measure of average hourly earnings. They estimate that the reduction in union wages attributable to Phases I and II controls was in the range of 1.5 to 3.0 percent. This is a significant finding since, as discussed in Chapter 6, there are significant spillover effects from union to nonunion wages. Furthermore, Bosworth and Vroman believe that the impact of the lower wage increases is felt beyond the initial period of measurement instead of being lost in a post-controls bulge. They write that ". . . because the controls program focused on union settlements and in the short run on newly negotiated contracts, equations based on hourly earnings data may understate the long-run impact of the controls program. If the unusually large union wage adjustments of 1970–71 had been permitted to continue into 1972 and 1973 their impact on average hourly earnings would have been larger than in the earlier historic periods simply because these adjustments were becoming so large . . . thus, the full impact of controls on hourly earnings would extend beyond the initial periods with a cumulative effect" (10, p. 21).

Bosworth and Vroman also apply their disaggregate approach to an examination of the price side of the picture in an attempt to determine the sectoral impact of these controls. They conclude that retail price controls had little, if any, effect and argue with many others that controls should not have been placed on this competitive sector of the economy.

Services, on the other hand, showed a significant slowing of price movement, especially in the area of medical care. Within manufacturing there is some evidence of restraint, but much of this has to do with the delayed impact on auto price increases rather than with a permanent lowering of inflation. Nondurable goods, they contend, display the greatest restraint in price movements due to the controls program. In the critical area of food prices, these researchers find little evidence of impact from controls, nor do they believe that it was reasonable to expect moderation in this area. In sum, Bosworth and Vroman tend to find a greater impact on wages from the control program than do other researchers, while seeing a somewhat smaller direct price effect.

In one critical area, the findings of Gordon are in sharp conflict with those of Bosworth and Vroman. Gordon, concluding that the controls did have a restraining influence on prices and wages, argues that this was done by squeezing profit margins. When these margins are later regained, he argues, the inflation will be just that much greater, thus implying that the control program was a failure in spite of its apparent short-term success. Bosworth and Vroman dispute this thesis and contend that there is little evidence that the controls program significantly squeezed profit margins. They also cite the evidence gathered by William Nordhaus that a squeeze in margins was under way prior to the imposition of controls and that the controls did not alter this movement one way or another (74).

An important element in the econometric analysis of wage and price controls is that nearly all models underpredicted the rate of change both in prices and wages in the period immediately prior to the imposition of controls. This makes it difficult to assess the true impact of the controls since, as Bosworth and Vroman observe, one's conclusions depend significantly upon whether one believes these larger-than-average, rapid movements in prices and wages were a one-time affair that would slow by themselves or whether they represented a continuing acceleration in price and wage movements. If the latter is the case, then the controls program can be credited with breaking the cycle. If the former is the case, then the controls program only had the appearance of success. In spite of this latter possibility, however, Bosworth and Vroman conclude that by compressing wage differentials that were widening between union settlements and nonunion settlements prior to the controls program, the program helped to stabilize wages to a greater degree than aggregate data would suggest.

Daniel J. B. Mitchell, UCLA economist and chief Pay Board economist during Phase II, agrees essentially with this view. Mitchell argues that it is difficult to gauge accurately the program's impact on wages through traditional econometric analysis since its goal was to *stabilize* wages, not lower them. The collective-bargaining environment was unstable going into controls, he believes, since there was a lot of catching up to be done among various groups. The major goal of the Pay Board, then, was to augment the movement back toward a more stable collective-bargaining environment—a goal that would be difficult to measure through econometric techniques even if achieved. "The economic stabilization program, in short," writes Mitchell, "was not intended to alter the essential structure of wage and price determination at the economy-wide level. . . . most of the program was an insurance policy against a deviation from normality" (68).

Given this assessment, along with the likely view that the volatility apparent in wage settlements prior to the controls was not a one-shot affair, it appears quite likely that the controls program did play a significant role in calming wage-push inflation. The Council of Economic Advisors, a group not noted for its sympathy for the controls program, argues essentially this same point: ". . . the controls were intended to deal with the *risk* that inflation would again accelerate. To reduce that risk substantially, as we believe the controls did, was a very significant contribution, but one that would not necessarily show up in a reduction of the inflation rate below what would most probably have occurred without the controls" (22, p. 60). In addition, the council is in substantial agreement with the proposition that the controls did have a significant impact on the largest of the wage increases, thereby narrowing wage differentials and mitigating the demands for catch-ups (22, p. 60).

In spite of the wave of dissatisfaction with the controls experiment resulting from the high-speed inflation of 1973 and 1974, the evidence suggests that the program, especially through Phase II, was successful in mitigating both price and wage increases and in helping to stabilize collective-bargaining conditions. It should also be remembered that the purpose of the program was not to stop inflation but rather to lower it slightly. Also, the fact that inflation broke out even more severely after the removal of the program is no proof, nor even evidence, of the ineffectiveness of controls. The economic environment had changed considerably by 1973. Inflation was rapidly becoming a demand-pull phenomenon due to a worldwide boom among industrialized countries. As discussed above, it is doubtful that any control program short of one run by the army could control wages and prices in the face of such severe pressures. At the same time, the experience of 1971–74 also illustrates the marginal nature of an incomes policy and the fact that any such program should not be expected to produce spectacular results.[1]

---

[1] For further and more detailed discussions concerning various aspects of controls and their pros and cons, see (10, 22, 23, 24, 41, 42, 43, 52, 56, 58, 66, 76, 124, 125).

COSTS AND BENEFITS

It is difficult, if not impossible, to measure accurately the costs and benefits associated with an incomes policy. There are monetary costs imposed upon the government and taxpayers as well as the direct costs of business groups forced to comply with the regulations. In addition, there are the real, although unquantifiable, social costs imposed by governmental regulation and interference in the marketplace. These take the form of dislocations and inefficiencies brought about by the controls, as well as the diminution of the freedom of economic agents to strike a mutually agreed upon bargain (see Chapter 10).

In terms of direct costs, Lanzillotti, Roberts, and Hamilton have estimated that the program cost approximately $125 million in governmental outlays for Phase I and II. This is in substantial agreement with government calculations (23). In addition, they estimate the program cost business approximately $0.5 billion annually in terms of direct compliance, and they roughly calculate another $0.5 billion in indirect costs. Using these admittedly rough calculations, the total cost of Phases I and II comes to approximately $1.2 billion.

Using the modified Gordon, Siebert and Zaidi, and Eckstein-Brinner econometric models, Lanzillotti, Roberts, and Hamilton then estimated the economic benefits to the economy. This was done by assuming that the decrease in inflation attributable to controls resulted in increased output; that is, nominal GNP would be the same with or without the controls. This implies that real GNP and, consequently, employment, would be higher due to the fact that less of the stimulation is being burned up in price increases. Based upon these calculations, the Phase I and II controls led to approximately $14 to $21 billion in increased gross national product over a six-quarter period, which translates into 140,000 to 220,000 jobs. Thus, comparing costs to benefits, they arrive at a cost-benefit ratio of 11.7 to 17.5 to 1 (58, p. 193). Even allowing for a sufficient degree of possible error in these figures, it seems clear that the economic benefits of the program greatly outweighed the costs.

Of course, as noted, not all the costs of the program are economic. To the extent that controls breed unwanted social and economic side effects—such as a diminution of individual freedom, the encouragement of a new and expanding bureaucracy, and the increased possibility of a misuse of government power down the road—the social costs are increased. There is little evidence that these harmful side effects developed during the economic stabilization program of the early and mid 1970s. There is, however, no guarantee that such side effects would not have developed had the program continued.

AN ONGOING ASSESSMENT: LESSONS FROM THE SEVENTIES

The studies cited above, which are representative of the serious analyses which have been undertaken to determine the impact of the controls program, clearly suggest that the program had a mitigating influence on wage and price determination. However, it would be of little benefit if the controls merely suppressed inflation and resulted in even more rapid price increases after their removal. Few researchers found evidence that this was, in fact, the case. There is little solid evidence that the suppression of prices and wages in Phases I and II helped lead to a price bulge in Phases III and IV. The price increases in Phases III and IV were the result of demand pressures, not cost-push or catch-up wage and price movements.

An argument concerning the pricing behavior of firms in response to the anticipation of a controls program should be noted. First, it is often said that companies will increase their price in anticipation of a controls program in order to have higher base-period prices. Thus, the Administration often argued during Phase III, that Congressional talk about reimposing more formal controls was furthering inflation. It was also said that there was a good deal of anticipatory price increasing during Phase III, which, in fact, led to the imposition of the second price freeze. By arguing that firms engage in anticipatory price increases, one must accept the proposition that firms have considerable pricing freedom and that prices are at least partially administered rather than solely reactive to market forces. Only if there is some discretionary pricing ability—that is, market power—are firms in a position to engage in anticipatory price increases. Thus, to the extent that these phenomena do take place, it would seem to follow that a necessary ingredient for a controls program—market power—must also exist. It cannot go both ways. It simply cannot be that all prices are the result of market forces and at the same time business firms have the discretionary power needed to allow anticipatory price increases.

Why the Disillusionment?

In spite of the evidence that the controls had a mitigating influence on prices and wages and a positive influence on employment and output, by the middle of the decade they were held in universally low esteem. Why?

First, the rapidly accelerating inflation during the latter phases of the stabilization program was taken by many persons as proof of the unworkability of direct wage and price controls. The implication is partially correct; direct controls are largely ineffective, or counterproductive, or both, during a period of intense demand-fueled inflation. The controls were never designed to deal with this pressure. The public, unfortunately, was justifiably ill-prepared to make such distinctions. Economists, on the other hand, had far less reason for disillusionment.

The manner in which the administration sold the economic stabilization program to the public also contributed to the later disillusionment. Price and wage controls were hailed as *the* means by which the war on inflation would be won. Less promise at the outset may well have fostered less disillusionment at the end. The social theory of unfulfilled expectations goes far toward explaining public disillusionment with the economic stabilization program. In addition, public understanding and acceptance of the policy was hardly furthered by the administration when it continually undercut its own program during the latter stages. The administration's public stance and the fact that the economy was rapidly approaching its capacity limitations made inevitable the lack of effectiveness and support for the program by mid-1973. By the middle of Phase III, the program was largely an exercise in futility. No one quite knew what Phase III was all about; and the second freeze in June 1973 was greeted with dismay by nearly everyone. Economic conditions were simply not amenable to such actions, and public response was less than enthusiastic. By the time of Phase IV, the game was nearly over; the only thing left was to attempt an orderly exit. Pressures were building, cooperation was rapidly evaporating, and it was clear that the earlier effectiveness of the program was gone. Few mourned its official death on April 30, 1974.

Was Anything Learned?

Perhaps the most important lesson to be drawn from this recent controls experience is that controls can have a useful but limited effectiveness in *certain* areas and in *certain* stages of the business cycle. Controls can help to lower the trade-off between inflation and unemployment within that band of possibilities between very high unemployment (where controls are not needed) and very low unemployment (where controls cannot work). Moreover, they can be effective only in those segments of the economy characterized by lack of effective price competition. Comprehensive controls may seem to be politically attractive, but economically they make little sense.

Wage controls (as the Pay Board and, even more dramatically, the Construction Industry Stabilization Board made evident) can play an active role in mitigating large collective-bargaining agreements and their concomitant spillover effects. In addition, properly handled, such a program can assist in stabilizing collective-bargaining arrangements that have been destabilized through external shocks to the economic system.

Such possibilities for a well thought out economic stabilization program are by no means insignificant. The fact that an incomes policy cannot stop inflation should not detract from the useful role that it can provide. Furthermore, the fact that controls are inappropriate under some circumstances should not be taken to mean that they are unwarranted in all circumstances. An appropriate monetary and fiscal policy surely must recognize the economic context in which it is operating. Different policies are mandated by different circumstances, and so it is with an incomes policy. Economic conditions must be considered in the application, administration, and timing of such a policy.

The experience of the early 1970s also dramatically points to the necessity for voluntary cooperation with the program, even though mandatory controls are necessary to insure cooperation. This cooperation was forthcoming through the early stages of the program and, as a result, the program had substantial benefits while imposing few real costs upon society. Cooperation with the program, however, evaporated rapidly later on as business became confused about what the government was trying to do, dismayed at the manner in which it was being done, and utterly frustrated in attempting to deal with the issue. The interminable delays in responding to legitimate pressures, the visible lack of concern for the effects of its program, and the general low esteem in which the administration held its own policy contributed greatly to the rapid decline in voluntary support. Given the small size of the staff, it was impossible to expect success from the program once this voluntary cooperation evaporated.

The rules of the Price Commission during Phase II, seemingly objective in applying the same standards to all sectors, were in fact quite discriminatory. The U.S. economy is an incredibly complex system of interrelationships and differing business practices. By treating the economy as a homogeneous unit, the effect is to impact different sectors quite differently. Indeed, given the nature of the Phase II regulations, it is likely that the controls had as much effect simply by "being there" and influencing business decisions as through the real bite of the rules themselves. A less comprehensive program could better focus its limited resources upon generating truly effective and equitable regulations.

Finally, to be successful, a future incomes policy must devote considerable energy toward improving the workings of the competitive system. The program must, as the indefatigable John Dunlop attempted to do during Phase IV, come to grips with structural bottlenecks and imbalances. As the pace of economic and societal changes continues to accelerate, increasing pressures are placed upon the adjustment processes of institutions. Focusing on structural bottlenecks has the effect of oiling the competitive mechanism and making it respond in a more satisfactory manner to these changes. Furthermore, the importance of this lubrication increases in direct proportion to the acceleration of the rate of change. Only by focusing on this immensely important and extremely complicated process while applying selective pressure through controls applied at appropriate points and times can an incomes policy become an important component of an overall stabilization policy.

The Future of Controls

The first half of the 1970s witnessed the most extreme inflation and unemployment of the post-war years. The business cycle, once thought to be manageable, if not a thing of the past, has seemingly been revived in full force. The severe social distortions and inequities wrought by raging inflation and massive unemployment have been exacerbated rather than relieved. The experience of the early 1970s has taught us that there are no easy answers. Those who look for an explanation of inflation from one single cause will continue to be as disappointed as those who advocate one particular policy as its remedy. Inflation results from extremely complex interactions of economic forces of differing importance at different times. As a consequence, it can only be approached through alternative policy mixes at various stages of the business cycle and at different times. But the severity of both inflation and the unemployment problems leaves little doubt that new policies, including new incomes policies, will be tried. Thus, we are likely to witness periods of no controls, periods of reimposition of controls, and possibly several combinations in between. Few people will ever again believe that the government, regardless of the party in power, will not under any circumstances reimpose and implement an active incomes policy. Instead, we are likely to see different forms of controls adopted from time to time as the search in this country and elsewhere continues for a viable incomes policy that will allow us to reach a higher level of noninflationary employment while preserving private institutions in the wage and price sphere.

The evolving nature of stabilization policies will necessitate changes in long-held beliefs concerning the nature of the mixed capitalist system. In particular, economic realities dictate that alterations be made in the traditional belief concerning the separation of private and state power. It is no longer possible, if indeed it ever was, to speak of the "private" sector if by "private" one means a sector of the economy where decisions (including those of wage and price matters) are made without regard to their larger implications.

This is not to say that the market system is dead, that there is no such thing as competition, or that we must allow the government somehow to pervade every facet of our lives. Such scare talk prevents too many people from discovering that the economy—and the society in which it operates—have changed in fundamental ways. There is a need to recognize that different sectors of the economy possess different characteristics and, therefore, require different public attitudes and policies.

During the 1930s economists and politicians had to be convinced of what the public knew all too well—the economy was sick and needed help. Finally, catching up with public opinion, policymakers and economists alike recognized that the system was not automatically self-regulating and could not always be counted upon to correct its own deficiencies. In the last quarter of the twentieth century, public policy is again striving to catch up with public awareness. Certainly, the attempts to formulate an incomes policy in the 1970s, like earlier attempts, have been neither faultless nor unblemished. Just as it is likely that there will be few clear-cut victories, it is equally likely that the search for new and more effective stabilization policies will continue in response to the exceedingly severe social problems at which they are directed.

BIBLIOGRAPHY

1. Adams, Walter, "Competition, Monopoly, and Planning." In Maurice Zeitlin (ed.), *American Society, Inc.* Chicago: Markham Publishing Co., 1970.
2. Adelman, M. A., "The Two Faces of Economic Concentration." *The Public Interest,* No. 21, Fall 1970.
3. Allen, Bruce T., "Market Concentration and Wage Increases: U.S. Manufacturing, 1947–1964." *Industrial and Labor Relations Review,* April 1958.
4. Anderson, Paul S., "Wages and the Guideposts: Comment." *American Economic Review,* June 1969.
5. Askin, A. Bradley, "Wage-Price Controls in Administrative and Political Perspective: The Case of the Price Commission During Phase 2." In Kraft and Roberts (57).
6. Barth, Peter S., "Unemployment and Labor Force Participation." *Southern Economic Journal,* January 1968.
7. Bhatia, R. J., "Unemployment and the Rate of Change of Money Earnings in the U.S., 1900–1958." *Economica,* August 1961.
8. Blair, John M., *Economic Concentration: Structure Behavior and Public Policy.* New York: Harcourt-Brace, Jovanovich, Inc., 1972.

9. Bosworth, Barry, "The Inflation Problem During Phase 3." *American Economic Review,* May 1974.
10. Bosworth, Barry and Vroman, Wayne, "An Appraisal of the Wage-Price Control Program." *National Bureau of Economic Research, Conference for Research on Income and Wealth.* New York: November 1974.
11. Bowen, William G., *Wage Behavior in the Postwar Period.* Princeton: Princeton University Industrial Relations Section, Department of Economics, 1960.
12. Bowen, William G. and Finegan, T. A., "Labor Force Participation and Unemployment." In Arthur M. Ross (ed.), *Employment Policy and the Labor Market.* Berkeley: University of California Press, 1965.
13. Boye, Stanley E., "The Average Concentration Ratio: An Inappropriate Measure of Industry Structure." *Journal of Political Economy,* 81, Part 1, No. 2, March-April 1973.
14. Brechling, Frank, "The Trade-Off Between Inflation and Unemployment." *Journal of Political Economy,* July/August 1968, II.
15. *Brookings Papers on Economic Activity* (2:1971). Washington, D.C.: The Brookings Institution.
16. *Brookings Papers on Economic Activity* (3:1973). Washington, D.C.: The Brookings Institution.
17. Christian, James W., "Bargaining Functions and the Effectiveness of the Wage-Price Guideposts." *Southern Economic Journal,* July 1970.
18. Cohany, Harry P. and Dewey, Lucretia M., "Union Membership Among Government Employees." *Monthly Labor Review,* July 1970.
19. Economic Stabilization Program Quarterly Reports. Washington, D.C.: U.S.G.P.O., 1971–74.
20. Council of Economic Advisors, *Economic Report of the President.* Washington, D.C.: U.S.G.P.O., 1968.
21. Council of Economic Advisors, *Economic Report of the President.* Washington, D.C.: U.S.G.P.O., 1971.
22. Council of Economic Advisors, *Economic Report of the President.* Washington, D.C.: U.S.G.P.O., January 1973.
23. Council of Economic Advisors, *Economic Report of the President.* Washington, D.C.: U.S.G.P.O, February 1975.
24. Day, Virgil B., "A Year of Controls: A View from Business." *Business Economics,* 8, No. 1, January 1973.

25. Delehanty, John A. (ed.), *Manpower Problems and Policies.* Scranton, Pa.: International Textbook Co., 1969.
26. Dunlop, John T., "Towards a Less Inflationary Economy." *Sloan Management Review,* Fall 1974.
27. Earl, Paul H., "An Analysis of the Economic Stabilization Program Through Stages of Processing." In Kraft and Roberts (57).
28. Eckstein, Otto, "Guideposts and the Prosperity of Our Day." *Proceedings for a Symposium on Business-Government Relations,* April 1966. Reprinted in Samuelson, Coleman, and Skidmore, *Readings in Economics.* 5th ed. New York: McGraw Hill.
29. ———, "Money Wake Determination Revisited. *Review of Economic Studies,* April 1968.
30. ——— and Roger Brinner, "The Inflation Process in the United States." U.S. Joint Economic Committee, 92nd Congress, 2nd Session. Washington, D.C.: U.S.G.P.O., 1972.
31. ——— and Thomas Wilson, "The Determination of Money Wages in American Industry." *Quarterly Journal of Economics,* August 1962.
32. Friedman, Milton, *Capitalism and Freedom.* Chicago: University of Chicago Press, 1962.
33. ———, "What Price Guideposts?" In George P. Schultz and Robert Z. Aliber, *Guidelines: Informal Controls and the Market Place.* Chicago: University of Chicago Press, 1966.
34. Galbraith, J. K., *The New Industrial State.* Boston: Houghton Mifflin Co., 1967.
35. Gallaway, Lowell E., "Labor Mobility, Resource Allocation, and Structural Unemployment." *American Economic Review,* September 1963.
36. Gallaway, Lowell E., *Manpower Economics.* Homewood, Ill.: Richard D. Irwin, Inc., 1971.
37. Gitlow, Abraham L., *Labor and Manpower Economics.* Homewood, Ill.: Richard D. Irwin, Inc., 1971.
38. Goldfinger, Nat, "A Labor View of One Year of the New Economic Policy." *Business Economics,* 8, No. 1, January 1973.
39. Gordon, Robert J. "Response of Wages and Prices to the First Two Years of Controls," *Brookings Papers on Economic Activity* (3:1973). Washington, D.C.: The Brookings Institution.
40. Gordon, Robert J., "Wage-Price Controls and the Shifting Phillips Curve," *Brookings Papers on Economic Activity* (2:1972). Washington, D.C.: The Brookings Institution.

41. Grayson, C. Jackson, *Confessions of a Price Controller.* Homewood, Ill.: Dow Jones-Irwin, Inc., 1974.
42. ———, "Ten Months of Stabilization: An Insider's Evaluation." *Business Economics,* January 1973.
43. Haberler, Gottfried, "Incomes Policy and Inflation: Some Further Reflections." *American Economic Review,* 72, No. 2, May 1972.
44. Hamermesh, Daniel S., "Market Power and Wage Inflation." Princeton University Dept. of Economics, Working Paper #22, May, 1971.
45. Hildebrand, George H., "Structural Unemployment and Cost-Push Inflation in the United States." In George Horwick (ed.), *Monetary Process and Policy: A Symposium.* Homewood, Ill.: Richard D. Irwin, Inc., 1967.
46. Hofstadter, Richard, William Miller, and David Aaron, *The American Republic,* II. Englewood Cliffs, N.J.: Prentice-Hall, Inc., 1959.
47. Holt, C. C., D. MacRae, S. Schweitzer, and R. E. Smith, "A Manpower Approach to the Unemployment-Inflation Dilemma." *Monthly Labor Review,* May 1971.
48. Jones, Sidney L., "The Lessons of Wage and Price Controls." *The Canadian Business Review,* Summer 1974.
49. Keynes, John M., *The General Theory of Employment, Interest, and Money.* London: Macmillan & Co., 1936.
50. Killingsworth, Charles C., "Rising Unemployment: A 'Transitional' Problem?" *Hearings, Subcommittee on Employment, Manpower, and Poverty,* 91st Congress, March 25, 1970.
51. ———, "The Continuing Labor Market Twist." *Monthly Labor Review,* September 1968.
52. Kosters, Marvin H., "Controls and Inflation: An Overview." *National Bureau of Economic Research.* November 1974.
53. ———, K. Fedor, and A. Eckstein, "Collective Bargaining Settlements and the Wage Structure." *Labor Law Journal,* August 1973.
54. Kraft, John and A. Bradley Askin, "Econometric Wage-Price Models and Their Imbedded Phillips Curves." (*Working paper.*)
55. ——— and Arthur Kraft, "A Phillips Curve for the United States Segmented by Population Subgroups." (*Working paper.*)
56. Kraft, J., and Roberts, B. (eds.), *Wage-Price Controls: Essays on the U.S. Experiment.* New York: Praeger Publishers, Inc., 1975.
57. Kuh, E., "A Productivity Theory of Wage Levels—An Alternative

to the Phillips Curve." *Review of Economic Studies,* October 1967.
58. Lanzillotti, Robert, Blaine Roberts, and Mary Hamilton, "Phase II in Review: The Price Commission Experience." Washington, D.C.: The Brookings Institution, 1975.
59. Levinson, Harold M., "Unionism, Concentration, and Wage Changes: Toward a Unified Theory." *Industrial and Labor Relations Review,* January 1967.
60. Lewis, H. Gregg, *Unionism and Relative Wages in the United States.* Chicago: University of Chicago Press, 1963.
61. Liebling, H. I. and A. T. Cluff, "U.S. Postwar Inflation and the Phillips Curve." *Kyklos,* 22, No. 2, 1969.
62. Mansfield, Harvey C., "Control of Prices by the OPA." In Colin D. Campbell (ed.), *Wage Price Controls in World War II, United States and Germany.* Washington, D.C.: American Enterprise Institute, 1971.
63. Means, Gardner C., "How to Control Inflation in the United States: An Alternative to 'Planned Stagnation.' " *Wage-Price Law and Economics Review,* 1, No. 1, 1975.
64. ———, *Pricing Power and the Public Interest.* New York: Harper & Brothers, 1962.
65. ———, "The Administered Price Thesis Reconfirmed." *American Economic Review,* 62, No. 3, June 1971.
66. Mills, D. Quinn, "Recent Experience with Wage and Price Controls." *Sloan Management Review,* Fall 1974.
67. Mincer, Jacob, "The Short-Run Elasticity of Labor Supply," *Industrial Relations Research Association Proceedings.* Madison, Wisc.: 1966.
68. Mitchell, Daniel J. B., "The Impact and Administration of Wage Controls." In Kraft and Roberts (57).
69. ——— and Arnold R. Webber, "Wages and the Pay Board." *American Economic Review,* May 1974.
70. Moore, Thomas Gale, *U.S. Incomes Policy, Its Rationale and Development.* Washington, D.C.: American Enterprise Institute, 1971.
71. Mueller, Willard F., "Trustbusting Versus Administrative Controls." *Antitrust Law and Economics Review,* Summer 1972.
72. ———, *Monopoly and Competition.* New York: Random House, Inc., 1970.
73. National Bureau of Economic Research, "Explorations in Economic Research." 2, No. 1, Winter 1975.

74. Nordhaus, William, "The Falling Share of Profits." *Brookings Papers on Economic Activity* (1:1974). Washington, D.C.: The Brookings Institution.
75. ——— and John Shoven, "Inflation 1973: The Year of Infamy." *Challenge.* May/June 1974.
76. Office of Economic Stabilization, Department of the Treasury, *Historical Working Papers on the Economic Stabilization Program.* Washington, D.C.: U.S.G.P.O., 1974.
77. Okun, Arthur M., "The Gap Between Actual and Potential Output," in Arthur M. Okun (ed.), *The Battle Against Unemployment.* New York: W. W. Norton & Co., 1965.
78. ———, "Inflation: The Problems and Prospects Before Us." In Okun, Fowler, and Gilbert (eds.), *Inflation.* New York: New York University Press, 1970.
79. Patman Committee Staff Report for the Domestic Subcommittee of the House Committee on Banking and Currency, 90th Congress, 2nd Session, *Commercial Banks and Their Trust Activities: Emerging Influence on the American Economy.* Washington, D.C.: U.S.G.P.O., July, 1968.
80. Perry, George L., "After the Freeze." *Brookings Papers on Economic Activity* (2:1971). Washington, D.C.: The Brookings Institution.
81. ———, "Changing Labor Markets and Inflation." *Brookings Papers on Economic Activity* (3:1970). Washington, D.C.: The Brookings Institution.
82. ———, "Inflation Versus Unemployment: The Worsening Trade-Off." *Monthly Labor Review,* February 1971.
83. ———, *Unemployment, Money Wage Rates, and Inflation.* Cambridge, Mass.: The M.I.T. Press, 1966.
84. ———, "Wages and the Guideposts." *American Economic Review,* September 1967.
85. ———, "Wages and the Guideposts: Reply." *American Economic Review,* June 1969.
86. Phillips, A. W., "The Relation Between Unemployment and the Rate of Change in Money Wage Rates in the United Kingdom, 1862–1957." *Economica,* November 1958.
87. Poole, William, "Thoughts on the Wage-Price Freeze." *Brookings Papers on Economic Activity* (2:1971). Washington, D.C.: The Brookings Institution.
88. Preston, Lee E., *The Industry and Enterprise Structure of the U.S. Economy.* New York: General Learning Press, 1971.

89. Rees, Albert, *The Economics of Trade Unions.* Chicago: University of Chicago Press, 1962.
90. ———— and Mary T. Hamilton, "The Wage-Price Productivity Perplex." *Journal of Political Economy,* February 1967.
91. Ryscavage, Paul M. and Hazel M. Willary, "Employment of the Nation's Urban Poor." *Monthly Labor Review,* August 1968.
92. Samuelson, Paul A. and Robert M. Solow, "The Analytics of Anti-Inflation Policy." *American Economic Review,* May 1960.
93. ————, "Stabilization Policies in the Contemporary U.S. Economy." In George Horwich (ed.), *Monetary Process and Policy: A Symposium.* Homewood, Ill.: Richard D. Irwin, Inc., 1967.
94. Schultze, Charles L., "Demand-Pull Versus Cost-Push Inflation." *Recent Inflation in the United States,* Study Paper No. 1, Joint Economic Committee. Washington, D.C.: U.S.G.P.O., 1959.
95. ————, "Has the Phillips Curve Shifted? Some Additional Evidence." *Brookings Papers on Economic Activity* (2:1971). Washington, D.C.: The Brookings Institution.
96. Sheahan, John, *The Wage-Price Guideposts.* Washington, D.C.: The Brookings Institution, 1967.
97. Sheehan, Robert, "Proprietors in the World of Big Business." *Fortune,* June 15, 1967.
98. Siebert, Calvin and Mahood Zaidi, "The Short Run Wage-Price Mechanism in U.S. Manufacturing." *Western Economic Journal,* 9, September 1971.
99. Simler, N. J., "Long Term Unemployment, the Structural Hypothesis, and Public Policy." *American Economic Review,* December 1964.
100. ———— and Alfred Tella, "Labor Reserves and the Phillips Curve." *Review of Economics and Statistics,* February 1968.
101. Smith, Adam, "Essay of Philosophical Subjects: History of Astronomy." In *The Whole Works of Adam Smith.* Alexander Murray & Son, 1969.
102. ————, *Wealth of Nations,* Cannon edition. New York: Modern Library, 1936.
103. Smith, David C., *Incomes Policies: Some Foreign Experiences and their Relevance for Canada.* Ottawa: Queen's Printer, Special Study No. 4, 1966.
104. Solow, Robert M., "The Case Against the Case Against Guidelines." In George Schultz and Robert Aliber, *Guidelines: Informal Controls and the Market Place.* Chicago: University of Chicago Press, 1966.

105. Sorrentino, Constance, "Comparing Employment Shifts in Ten Industrialized Countries." *Monthly Labor Review*, October 1971.
106. Stein, Herbert and John Dunlop, Testimony Before a Joint Economic Committee. Washington, D.C.: U.S.G.P.O., May 23, 1973.
107. Stoikov, Vladimir, "Increasing Structural Unemployment Re-Examined." *Industrial and Labor Relations Review*, April 1966.
108. Studies by the Staff of the Cabinet Committee on Price Stability. Washington, D.C.: U.S.G.P.O., January 1969.
109. Tella, Alfred, "The Relationship of Labor Force to Employment." *Industrial and Labor Relations Review*, April 1964.
110. Throop, Adrian W., "The Union-Nonunion Wage Differential and Cost-Push Inflation." *American Economic Review*, March 1968.
111. ———, "Wages and the Guideposts: Comment." *American Economic Review*, June 1969.
112. Ulman, Lloyd, "Cost-Push and Some Policy Alternatives." *American Economic Review*, 72, No. 2, May 1972.
113. ——— and Robert J. Flanagan, *Wage Restraint: A Study of Incomes Policies in Western Europe*. Berkeley: University of California Press, 1971.
114. U.S. Department of Labor, Bureau of Labor Statistics, *Employment in Perspective: Discouraged Workers and Recent Changes in Labor Force Growth*. Report 396, August 1971.
115. ———, Bureau of Labor Statistics, *The Labor Market 'Twist,' 1964–69*. Special Labor Force Report 133, 1971.
116. ———, Bureau of Labor Statistics, *Municipal Public Employee Associations*, Bulletin 1702. Washington, D.C.: U.S.G.P.O., 1971.
117. ———, Bureau of Labor Statistics, *Productivity and the Economy*, Bulletin 1710. Washington, D.C.: U.S.G.P.O., 1971.
118. ———, *Manpower Report of the President*. Washington, D.C.: U.S.G.P.O., 1971.
119. ———, *Monthly Labor Review*, June 1971.
120. ———, *Monthly Labor Review*, November 1971.
121. Wachter, Michael L., "Wages and the Guideposts: Comment." *American Economic Review*, June 1969.
122. *Wage-Price Law and Economics Review*, 1, No. 1, 1975 (Washington, D.C.).
123. Wallack, Stanley S., "Inflation Versus Unemployment: Another View of the Trade-Off." *Monthly Labor Review*, November 1971.

124. Weber, Arnold, *In Pursuit of Price Stability: The Wage-Price Freeze of 1971.* Washington, D.C.: The Brookings Institution, 1973.
125. ———, "Issues in Incomes Policy." *Proceedings, Industrial Relations Research Associations,* 1971 annual meetings, Spring 1972.
126. Weiss, Leonard W., "Concentration and Labor Earnings." *American Economic Review,* March 1966.

INDEX

Aged 7
Allocation 117, 149-50
   of resources 17-18
American Dream 41
Antitrust policy 174-75
Automation 20-22
   unemployment 76-77

Berle 28
Benefits 226
Business firms, market power of 102-9

Collective bargaining 88-89, 126-27
Consumer spending 3
Controls 145-75, 177-202
   market 8, 10
Corporate planning 105-6
Corporations 9, 10
Cost of Living Council 203
Cost-push inflation 53-55, 55-56, 115-17, 118-19
Costs 210-12, 226
Cross-section analysis 111

Deficient demand unemployment 45-46
Demand curve, kinked 134
Demand-pull inflation 52-53
Demand-shift inflation 55
Depression 4, 68, 76, 123

Economic Advisors, President's Council of 5
Economic Concentration 108
Economic growth 3
Economic Stabilization Program 203-20
Economy changes 135-43
Economy, problems in 26-28

Employment 81-99, 122-24
Employment Act of 1946 .... 4, 69
Equity 165-68
Exploitation 18-19

Federal Reserve System 69
Free markets 13-33
Freeze (on wages and prices) 2
Frictional unemployment 44-45

Galbraith, John K. 29, 105-107
Government's role 68-69

Horatio Alger Myth 14

Incomes policy 9
  European 87-99
Inflation 22, 47-56
Interest rates 3
Investment 63-65

Jefferson, Thomas 14

Keynes, John Maynard 4, 7, 13, 62, 63, 66-67,
.... 69, 70, 81, 82
Killingsworth, Charles 72, 73, 75

Labor market 86-87
Locke, John 14

Manpower policies 173-74
Market controls 8, 10
Market, labor 86-87
Market power 28-29, 101-29, 140-43
Markets, free 13-33
Means 28
Modern Corporation and Private Property, The 28-29
Momentum inflation 133-35
Money supply 119-20

New Deal 2, 69
New Economic Policy 2
New Industrial State 29, 105, 107-8
Nietzsche 14

Occupations 43-44
Oligopoly theory 133-35

244   INDEX

Pay Board 4, 5, 98, 203, 207, 229
Prices 216, 219
Phillips curve 90, 91-95, 99
Poverty 8, 38, 56-60
President's Council of Economic Advisors 5
Price Commission 4, 5, 98, 203, 207, 229
Price competition 104-5
Price controls 170-72
Price freeze 2
Price movements 108-9
Price setting 9
Prices 122-24, 207-9
Production 17
Productivity 89, 137-40, 161-63, 172-73
Profit margins 212-14
Purchasing power 63

Saving 63-65
Say's Law 19, 20, 22, 63
Seasonal unemployment 45
Sector shifts 113-14
Sharpies 48
Skill levels 41
Smith, Adam 14, 16
Socialism 158-60
Spending 3, 17
Stabilization, Economic, Program 203-20
Steel industry 106-8
Structural thesis 70-79
Structural unemployment 46-47
Suckers 48

Teenage situation 76
Time-series analyses 111
Trade-off ....:.................... 48, 131-44

Unemployment 8, 11, 19-20, 35-79
    insurance 37
    security amendments to the Social Security Act ... 37
    teenage rates 40
Unions 9, 10, 109-29

Wage controls 170-72
Wage differentials 111-12, 125-26, 127-28
Wage freeze 2
Wages 122-24, 216, 219
Welfare 56-60
World War II 178-79